BLACK DIVINITY

The Institutes of the Black Theocracy

SHAHIDI COLLECTION VOL I

SHAHIDI ISLAM

ISBN: 978-1-64669-655-0   (Paperback Edition)
ISBN: 978-1-64669-656-7   (Hardcover Edition)
ISBN: 978-1-64669-654-3   (E-book Edition)

Some characters and events in this book are fictitious. Any similarity to real persons, living or dead, is coincidental and not intended by the author.

Illustrations:

Front Cover – (c. 950–700 BCE); "Ancient Egyptian wooden stela depicting Lady Djedkhonsuiwesankh re-enacting the strip-tease of Hethor before Re-Horakhty." In N. Gibson (Ed), *Cover of KMT: A Modern Journal of Ancient Egypt, Vol. 4, No. 2, Summer 1993*; Photograph by Oriental Institute, the University of Chicago.

Book Ordering Information

Phone Number: 347-901-4929 or 347-901-4920
Email: info@globalsummithouse.com
Global Summit House
www.globalsummithouse.com

Printed in the United States of America

CONTENTS

*This book is dedicated to Albert
Johnson aka Prodigy from
Mobb Deep,
who passed away two years
ago after representing that true
New York City street life.
Peace to you Almighty*

GLOSSARY

All words names and definitions in this glossary are provided by Merriam Webster's Dictionary and Thesaurus and The Encyclopaedia Britannica Standard Edition unless the word is accompanied by an *.

Absolutize: to make absolute: convert into an absolute.

Abstract: 1 a: disassociated from any specific instance ‹an ~ entity› b: difficult to understand: abstruse ‹~ problems› c: insufficiently factual: formal ‹possessed only an ~ right›; 2: expressing a quality apart from an object ‹the word poem is concrete, poetry is ~›; 3 a: dealing with a subject in its abstract aspects: theoretical ‹~ science› b: impersonal detached ‹the ~ compassion of a surgeon —Time›; 4: having only intrinsic form with little or no attempt at pictorial representation or narrative content ‹~ painting›.

Abstract: 1: a summary of points (as of a writing) usu. presented in skeletal form; also: something that summarizes or concentrates the essentials of a larger thing or several things, 2: an abstract thing or state, 3: abstraction.

Abstract: 1: remove separate, 2: to consider apart from application to or association with a particular instance, 3: to make an abstract of: summarize, 4: to draw away the attention of, 5: steal purloin, vi: to make an abstraction.

Absurdity: 1: the quality or state of being absurd: absurdness; 2: something that is absurd.

Acquiesce: to be quiet — more at quiescent] (1651): to accept, comply, or submit tacitly or passively — often used with in and sometimes with to assent.

Actuality: 1: the quality or state of being actual, 2: something that is actual: fact reality ‹possible risks which have been seized upon as actualities —T. S. Eliot› — in actuality: in actual fact.

Albumen: 1: the white of an egg see egg illustration; 2: albumin.

Albumin: any of numerous simple heat-coagulable water-soluble proteins that occur in blood plasma or serum, muscle, the whites of eggs, milk, and other animal substances and in many plant tissues and fluids.

Ali, Noble Drew: *original name **Timothy Drew**, he was believe by his followers to have been called by Allah to be a prophet. He also founded the Moorish Science Temple and wrote his own version of the Holy Koran.

Allah/God: GOD 1a — used in Islam.

Allah 13X: *original name **Clarence Edward Smith**, Allah joined the Nation of Islam in 1960 and was given the name Clarence 13X. After leaving the Nation in 1964 Clarence took the name Allah and is forever called that by his followers in the 5 Percent Nation he founded.

Allusion: 1: an implied or indirect reference esp. in literature; also: the use of such references; 2: the act of alluding to or hinting at something.

Alt Right: *Founded by American white nationalist Richard B. Spencer based on his webzine The Alternative Right in which he unified anti-immigrationists, white nationalists, and Far Rightist all over the United States; his views were launched to prominence during Donald Trump's successful Presidential campaign.

Amplitudes: 1: extent of dignity, excellence, or splendour, 2: the quality or state of being ample: fullness abundance, 3: the extent or range of a quality, property, process, or phenomenon: as a: the extent of a vibratory movement (as of a pendulum) measured from the mean position to an extreme b: the maximum departure of the value of an alternating current or wave from the average value, 4: the angle assigned to a complex number when it is plotted in a complex plane using polar coordinates called also argument compare absolute value 2.

Analogy: 1: inference that if two or more things agree with one another in some respects they will prob. agree in others; 2 a: resemblance in some particulars between things otherwise unlike: similarity b: comparison based on such resemblance; 3: correspondence between the members of pairs or sets of linguistic forms that serves as a basis for the creation of another form; 4: correspondence in function between anatomical parts of different structure and origin compare homology likeness.

Anti-Christ: 1: one who denies or opposes Christ; specif: a great antagonist expected to fill the world with wickedness but to be conquered forever by Christ at his second coming; 2: a false Christ.

Anti-Establishment: *Views or beliefs that stand counter to the views and beliefs of conventional society.

Anti-Modernism: opposed to the values of modernism or modernity.

Antinomian: 1: one who holds that under the gospel dispensation of grace the moral law is of no use or obligation because faith alone is necessary to salvation, 2: one who rejects a socially established morality.

Antipathetic: 1: having a natural aversion; also: not sympathetic: hostile ‹a government ~ to democracy›; 2: arousing antipathy ‹an ~ experience with an insurance company —G. F. McCann›.

Aphid: very small soft-bodied homopterous insects (superfamily Aphidoidea) that suck the juices of plants.

Arian: Arius or his doctrines esp. that the Son is not of the same substance as the Father but was created as an agent for creating the world.

Aristotle: Greek *Aristoteles* ancient Greek philosopher and scientist, one of the greatest intellectual figures of Western history. He was the author of a philosophical and scientific system that became the framework and vehicle for both Christian Scholasticism and medieval Islamic philosophy. Even after the intellectual revolutions of the Renaissance, the Reformation, and the Enlightenment, Aristotelian concepts remained embedded in Western thinking.

Ashkenazi: (1839): a member of one of the two great divisions of Jews comprising the eastern European Yiddish-speaking Jews compare Sephardi.

Audubon, John James: *original name Fougère Rabin*, or *Jean Rabin*, baptismal name *Jean-jacques Fougère Audubon* ornithologist, artist, and naturalist who became particularly well known for his drawings and paintings of North American birds.

Bourgeois: 1: of, relating to, or characteristic of the townsman or of the social middle class, 2: marked by a concern for material interests and respectability and a tendency toward mediocrity, 3: dominated by commercial and industrial interests: capitalistic.

Bourgeois: 1 a: burgher b: a middle-class person, 2: a person with social behavior and political views held to be influenced by private-property interest: capitalist, 3 pl: bourgeoisie.

Bureaucracy: 1 a: a body of nonelective government officials b: an administrative policy-making group; 2: government characterized by specialization of functions, adherence to fixed rules, and a hierarchy of authority; 3: a system of administration marked by officialism, red tape, and proliferation.

Bush, George: *in full George Herbert Walker Bush* politician and businessman who was vice president of the United States (1981–89) and the 41st president of the United States (1989–93). As president, Bush assembled a multinational force to compel the withdrawal of Iraq from Kuwait in the Persian Gulf War. (For a discussion of the history and nature of the presidency, see presidency of the United States of America. See also Cabinet of President George Bush.)

Byzantium: later *Constantinople*, modern *Istanbul* ancient Greek city on the shore of the Bosporus; also, an alternative name for the Byzantine Empire, which had its capital at Constantinople.

Caricature: (1712) 1: exaggeration by means of often ludicrous distortion of parts or characteristics, 2: a representation esp. in literature or art that has the qualities of caricature, 3: a distortion so gross as to seem like caricature.

Caricature: (ca. 1771)**:** to make or draw a caricature of**:** represent in caricature ‹the portrait *caricatured* its subject›.

Caricature of Science: *turning science into a joke or an over-the-top cartoon.

Celestial: 1: of, relating to, or suggesting heaven or divinity ‹~ beings›; 2: of or relating to the sky or visible heavens ‹the sun, moon, and stars are ~ bodies›; 3 a: ethereal otherworldly ‹~ music› b: olympian supreme.
4 cap [Celestial Empire, old name for China]: of or relating to China or the Chinese

Charisma: 1: a personal magic of leadership arousing special popular loyalty or enthusiasm for a public figure (as a political leader), 2: a special magnetic charm or appeal ‹the ~ of a popular actor›.

Charismata: (ca. 1641): an extraordinary power (as of healing) given a Christian by the Holy Spirit for the good of the church.

Charlemagne: As king of the Franks, Charlemagne conquered the Lombard kingdom in Italy, subdued the Saxons, annexed Bavaria to his kingdom, fought campaigns in Spain and Hungary, and, with the exception of the Kingdom of Asturias in Spain, southern Italy, and the British Isles, united in one superstate practically all the Christian lands of western Europe.

Christology: (1673): theological interpretation of the person and work of Christ.

Clairalience: *Extrasensory Perception through scent, clear smelling.

Clairaudience: *Extrasensory Perception through hearing, clear hearing.

Clairgustance: *Extrasensory Perception through taste, clear tasting.

Clairsentience: *Extrasensory Perception through touch, clear touching or clear feeling.

Clairvoyance: *Extrasensory Perception through sight, clear vision.

Classification: 1: the act or process of classifying; 2 a: systematic arrangement in groups or categories according to established criteria; specif: taxonomy b: class category.

Cognitive: 1: of, relating to, being, or involving conscious intellectual activity (as thinking, reasoning, or remembering) ‹~ impairment›; 2: based on or capable of being reduced to empirical factual knowledge.

Cold War: the open yet restricted rivalry that developed after World War II between the United States and the Soviet Union and their respective allies. The Cold War was waged on political, economic, and propaganda fronts and had only limited recourse to weapons.

Contradiction: 1: act or an instance of contradicting; 2 a: a proposition, statement, or phrase that asserts or implies both the truth and falsity of something b: a statement or phrase whose parts contradict each other ‹a round square is a ~ in terms›; 3 a: logical incongruity b: a situation in which inherent factors, actions, or propositions are inconsistent or contrary to one another.

Contradistinction: (1647): distinction by means of contrast ‹painting in ~ to sculpture›

Conspicuous: 1: obvious to the eye or mind ‹~ changes›, 2: attracting attention: striking ‹a ~ success›, 3: marked by a noticeable violation of good taste noticeable.

Conundrum: 1: a riddle whose answer is or involves a pun; 2 a: a question or problem having only a conjectural answer b: an intricate and difficult problem

Converge: (1691) 1: to tend or move toward one point or one another: come together: meet ‹converging paths›; 2: to come together and unite in a common interest or focus; 3: to approach a limit as the number of terms increases without limit ‹the series ~s›.

Cosmogony: 1: a theory of the origin of the universe, 2: the creation or origin of the world or universe.

Darwin, Charles: *in full* ***Charles Robert Darwin*** English naturalist whose theory of evolution by natural selection became the foundation of modern evolutionary studies.

Darwin, Dr. Erasmus: prominent English physician, grandfather of the naturalist Charles Darwin and the biologist Francis Galton.

Darwinian: 1: of or relating to Charles Darwin, his theories esp. of evolution, or his followers; 2: of, relating to, or being a competitive environment or situation in which only the fittest persons or organizations prosper.

Dehumanize: (1818): to deprive of human qualities, personality, or spirit.

Deism: (1682): a movement or system of thought advocating natural religion, emphasizing morality, and in the 18th century denying the interference of the Creator with the laws of the universe.

Deist: (1682): a movement or system of thought advocating natural religion, emphasizing morality, and in the 18th century denying the interference of the Creator with the laws of the universe.

Demodernization: *the state of removing modern elements and entities from.

Depersonalize: 1: to deprive of the sense of personal identity ‹schools that ~ students›, 2: to make impersonal ‹depersonalizing medical care›.

Dialectic: 1: logic; 2 a: discussion and reasoning by dialogue as a method of intellectual investigation; specif: the Socratic techniques of exposing false beliefs and eliciting truth b: the Platonic investigation of the eternal ideas; 3: the logic of fallacy; 4 a: the Hegelian process of change in which a concept or its realization passes over into and is preserved and fulfilled by its opposite; also: the critical investigation of this process b (1)usu pl but sing or pl in constr: development through the stages of thesis, antithesis, and synthesis in accordance with the laws of dialectical materialism (2): the investigation of this process (3): the theoretical application of this process esp. in the social sciences; 5 usu pl but sing or pl in constra: any systematic reasoning, exposition, or argument that juxtaposes opposed or contradictory ideas and usu. seeks to resolve their conflict b: an intellectual exchange of ideas; 6: the dialectical tension or opposition between two interacting forces or elements.

Diop, Cheikh Anta: *Senegalese anthropologist, historian, politician, and physicist who studied pre-colonial African history and culture as well as humanity's African origins.

Disclose: 1 obs: to open up; 2 a: to expose to view b : hatch c: to make known or public ‹demands that politicians ~ the sources of their income› reveal.

Discourse: 1 : the capacity of orderly thought or procedure: rationality; 2: verbal interchange of ideas; esp: conversation; 3 a: formal and orderly and usu. extended expression of thought on a subject b: connected speech or writing c: a linguistic unit (as a conversation or a story) larger than a sentence; 4 obs: social familiarity; 5 : a mode of organizing knowledge, ideas, or experience that is rooted in language and its concrete contexts (as history or institutions) ‹critical ~›.

Discourse: (1559) 1: to express oneself esp. in oral discourse, 2: talk converse: : to give forth: utter.

Disillusion: condition of being disenchanted.

Disillusion: (1855): to free from illusion; also: to cause to lose naive faith and trust

Dissimulate: to hide under a false appearance ‹smiled to ~ her urgency —Alice Glenday›.

Dixon, Roland: *Professor Dixon was a student of Franz Boas at Harvard University and became a contributor to both anthropological and ethnological journals.

Dühring, Eugen: *German economist, philosopher, positivist, and socialist who heavily critiqued Marxism.

Durkheim, Emile: French social scientist who developed a vigorous methodology combining empirical research with sociological theory. He is widely regarded as the founder of the French school of sociology.

Effectuate: effect.

Efficacious: (1528): having the power to produce a desired effect ‹an ~ remedy› effective.

Egalitarianism: 1: a belief in human equality esp. with respect to social, political, and economic rights and privileges; 2: a social philosophy advocating the removal of inequalities among people.

Elephantine: *Arabic Jazīrat Aswān,* island in the Nile opposite Aswān city in Aswān *muḥāfaẓah* (governorate), Upper Egypt. Elephantine is the Greek name for pharaonic Abu.

Endemic: 1 a: belonging or native to a particular people or country b: characteristic of or prevalent in a particular field, area, or environment ‹problems ~ to translation› ‹the self-indulgence ~ in the film industry›; 2: restricted or peculiar to a locality or region ‹~ diseases› ‹an ~ species› native.

Endocrine: 1: secreting internally; specif: producing secretions that are distributed in the body by way of the bloodstream ⟨hormones produced by the ~ system⟩; 2: of, relating to, affecting, or resembling an endocrine gland or secretion ⟨~ tumors⟩.

Engels, Friedrich: German Socialist philosopher, the closest collaborator of Karl Marx in the foundation of modern Communism. They co-authored the Communist Manifesto (1848), and Engels edited the second and third volumes of Das Kapital after Marx's death.

Enrapturement: *state of being filled with bliss, the statement also has eschatological overtones.

Epistemology: (ca. 1856): the study or a theory of the nature and grounds of knowledge esp. with reference to its limits and validity.

Equivocal: 1 a: subject to two or more interpretations and usu. used to mislead or confuse ⟨an ~ statement⟩ b: uncertain as an indication or sign ⟨~ evidence⟩; 2 a: of uncertain nature or classification ⟨~ shapes⟩ b: of uncertain disposition toward a person or thing: undecided ⟨an ~ attitude⟩ c: of doubtful advantage, genuineness, or moral rectitude ⟨~ behavior⟩ obscure.

Erotogenic: erogenous.

Erogenous: 1: producing sexual excitement or libidinal gratification when stimulated: sexually sensitive; 2: of, relating to, or arousing sexual feelings.

Eschatology: (1844) 1: a branch of theology concerned with the final events in the history of the world or of humankind; 2: a belief concerning death, the end of the world, or the ultimate destiny of humankind; specif: any of various Christian doctrines concerning the Second Coming, the resurrection of the dead, or the Last Judgment.

Etymology: 1: the history of a linguistic form (as a word) shown by tracing its development since its earliest recorded occurrence in the language where it is found, by tracing its transmission from one language to another, by analyzing it into its component parts, by identifying its cognates in other languages, or by tracing it and its cognates to a common ancestral form in an ancestral language; 2: a branch of linguistics concerned with etymologies.

Exacerbate: (1660): to make more violent, bitter, or severe ‹the proposed shutdown…would ~ unemployment problems —Science›.

Exhibitionism: 1 a: a perversion in which sexual gratification is obtained from the indecent exposure of one's genitals (as to a stranger) b: an act of such exposure, 2: the act or practice of behaving so as to attract attention to oneself.

Feudum: *also known as a fief, a territory owned by a lord in which a vassal is allowed to live upon the payment of taxes to said lord.

Figurative: 1 a: representing by a figure or resemblance: emblematic b: of or relating to representation of form or figure in art ‹~ sculpture›, 2 a: expressing one thing in terms normally denoting another with which it may be regarded as analogous: metaphorical ‹~ language› b: characterized by figures of speech ‹a ~ description›.

Forage: 1: food for animals esp. when taken by browsing or grazing, 2: the act of foraging: search for provisions.

Forage: 1: to strip of provisions: collect forage from, 2: to secure by foraging ‹foraged a chicken for the feast›; 1: to wander in search of forage or food; 2: to secure forage (as for horses) by stripping the country; 3: ravage raid; 4: to make a search: rummage.

Forel, François-Alphonse: Swiss physician, scientist, and founder of limnology, the study of lakes.

Fourier, Charles: French social theorist who advocated a reconstruction of society based on communal associations of producers known as phalanges (phalanxes). His system came to be known as Fourierism.

Frequency: 1: the fact or condition of occurring frequently; 2 a: the number of times that a periodic function repeats the same sequence of values during a unit variation of the independent variable b: the number, proportion, or percentage of items in a particular category in a set of data; 3: the number of repetitions of a periodic process in a unit of time: as a: the number of complete alternations per second of an alternating current b: the number of complete oscillations per second of energy (as sound or electromagnetic radiation) in the form of waves.

Godbody: *the militant, street section of the 5 Percent Nation.

Grand Narratives: *any religious, institutional or ideological knowledge system.

Hegemony: (1567) 1: preponderant influence or authority over others: domination ‹battled for ~ in Asia›; 2: the social, cultural, ideological, or economic influence exerted by a dominant group ‹extend their own ~ over American culture as a whole.

Heliopolis: (Greek), *Egyptian **Iunu**, or **Onu ("Pillar City")* , *biblical **On*** one of the most ancient Egyptian cities, and the seat of worship of the sun god, <u>Re</u>.

Hermopolis: *modern **al-Ashmūnayn*** ancient town of Upper Egypt, located on the Nile River south of al-Minyā in al-Minyā *muḥāfaẓah* (governorate). It was known as Khmunu ("City of the Eight") and was the capital of the Hare nome (province), the 15th nome of Upper Egypt.

Hobbs, Thomas: English philosopher and political theorist, best known for his publications on individual security and the social contract, which are important statements of both the nascent ideas of liberalism and the long-standing assumptions of political absolutism characteristic of the times.

Holy Roman Empire: *German* ***Heiliges Römisches Reich*** , *Latin* ***Sacrum Romanum Imperium*** the varying complex of lands in western and central Europe ruled over first by <u>Frankish</u> and then by German kings for 10 centuries, from Charlemagne's coronation in 800 until the renunciation of the imperial title in 1806.

Hypothalamus: (1896): a basal part of the diencephalon that lies beneath the thalamus on each side, forms the floor of the third ventricle, and includes vital autonomic regulatory centers.

Idealism: (1796) 1 a (1): a theory that ultimate reality lies in a realm transcending phenomena (2): a theory that the essential nature of reality lies in consciousness or reason b (1): a theory that only the perceptible is real (2): a theory that only mental states or entities are knowable; 2 a: the practice of forming ideals or living under their influence b: something that is idealized; 3: literary or artistic theory or practice that affirms the preeminent value of imagination as compared with faithful copying of nature compare realism.

Imaginal: (1647): of or relating to imagination, images, or imagery.

Imperative: 1 a: of, relating to, or constituting the grammatical mood that expresses the will to influence the behavior of another b: expressive of a command, entreaty, or exhortation c: having power to restrain, control, and direct; 2: not to be avoided or evaded: necessary ‹an ~ duty› masterful.

Imperative: (1530) 1: the imperative mood or a verb form or verbal phrase expressing it; 2: something that is imperative: as a: command order b: rule guide c: an obligatory act or duty d: an imperative judgment or proposition.

Implacable: not placable: not capable of being appeased, significantly changed, or mitigated ‹an ~ enemy›.

Importunity: 1: the quality or state of being importunate, 2: an importunate request or demand.

Incarnation: 1 a (1): the embodiment of a deity or spirit in some earthly form (2)cap: the union of divinity with humanity in Jesus Christ b: a concrete or actual form of a quality or concept; esp: a person showing a trait or typical character to a marked degree ‹she is the ~ of goodness›; 2: the act of incarnating : the state of being incarnate; 3: a particular physical form or state: version ‹in another ~ he might be a first vice-president.

Inexorable: (1542): not to be persuaded, moved, or stopped : relentless ‹~ progress›.

Inhibition: 1 a: the act of inhibiting: the state of being inhibited b: something that forbids, debars, or restricts; 2: an inner impediment to free activity, expression, or functioning: as a: a mental process imposing restraint upon behavior or another mental process (as a desire) b: a restraining of the function of a bodily organ or an agent (as an enzyme).

Institution: 1: an act of instituting: establishment; 2 a: a significant practice, relationship, or organization in a society or culture ‹the ~ of marriage›; also: something or someone firmly associated with a place or thing ‹she has become an ~ in the theater› b: an established organization or corporation (as a bank or university) esp. of a public character; also: asylum.

Interrogate: 1: to question formally and systematically, 2: to give or send out a signal to (as a transponder) for triggering an appropriate response ask.

Intersubjective: 1: involving or occurring between separate conscious minds ‹~ communication›, 2: accessible to or capable of being established for two or more subjects: objective ‹~ reality of the physical world›.

Invective: of, relating to, or characterized by insult or abuse.

Invective: (1523) 1: an abusive expression or speech, 2: insulting or abusive language: vituperation abuse.

Irony of Truth: *all irony is a form of distorting the truth, however, in this case it is used to the effect of diminishing the value of truth.

Jesus Christ: *also called **Jesus of Galilee** or **Jesus of Nazareth*** founder of Christianity, one of the world's largest religions, and the incarnation of God according to most Christians. His teachings and deeds are recorded in the New Testament, which is essentially a theological document that makes discovery of the "historical Jesus" difficult. The basic outlines of his career and message, however, can be characterized when considered in the context of 1st-century Judaism and, especially, Jewish eschatology.

John the Apostle: *also called **Saint John The Evangelist**, or **Saint John The Divine*** in Christian tradition, the author of three letters, the Fourth Gospel, and the Revelation to John in the New Testament. He played a leading role in the early church at Jerusalem.

John the Baptist: Jewish prophet of priestly origin who preached the imminence of God's Final Judgment and baptized those who repented in self-preparation for it; he is revered in the Christian Church as the forerunner of Jesus Christ.

Judean: *a Jew in the proper sense of the term, however, in this case it is used to distinguish the black Jews from the white Jews.

Kemet: *derived from Khem Ta, an ancient name for Egypt which meant "the black land."

King, Dr. Martin Luther, Jr.: *original name Michael Luther King, Jr.* Baptist minister and social activist who led the civil rights movement in the United States from the mid-1950s until his death by assassination in 1968. His leadership was fundamental to that movement's success in ending the legal segregation of African Americans in the South and other parts of the United States. King rose to national prominence through the organization of the Southern Christian Leadership Conference, promoting nonviolent tactics such as the massive March on Washington (1963) to achieve civil rights. He was awarded the Nobel Prize for Peace in 1964.

Knox, John: foremost leader of the Scottish Reformation, who set the austere moral tone of the Church of Scotland and shaped the democratic form of government it adopted. He was influenced by George Wishart, who was burned for heresy in 1546, and the following year Knox became the spokesman for the Reformation in Scotland. After a period of intermittent imprisonment and exile in England and on the European continent, in 1559 he returned to Scotland, where he supervised the preparation of the constitution and liturgy of the Reformed Church. His most important literary work was his History of the Reformation in Scotland.

Kropotkin, Peter: Russian revolutionary and geographer, the foremost theorist of the anarchist movement. Although he achieved renown in a number of different fields, ranging from geography and zoology to sociology and history, he shunned material success for the life of a revolutionist.

Laissez Faire: (1825) 1: a doctrine opposing governmental interference in economic affairs beyond the minimum necessary for the maintenance of peace and property rights, 2: a philosophy or practice characterized by a usu. deliberate abstention from direction or interference esp. with individual freedom of choice and action

Landed Aristocracy: *a section of the nobility whose primary privilege was ownership of land.

Legitimate: (1531): to make legitimate: a (1): to give legal status or authorization to (2): to show or affirm to be justified (3): to lend authority or respectability to b : to put (a bastard) in the state of a legitimate child before the law by legal means.

Libido: (1909) 1: instinctual psychic energy that in psychoanalytic theory is derived from primitive biological urges (as for sexual pleasure or self-preservation) and that is expressed in conscious activity, 2: sexual drive.

Libidinal: (1922): of or relating to the libido ‹~ impulses›.

Luther, Martin: German priest and scholar whose questioning of certain church practices led to the Protestant Reformation. He is one of the pivotal figures of Western civilization, as well as of Christianity. By his actions and writings he precipitated a movement that was to yield not only one of the three major theological units of Christianity (along with Roman Catholicism and Eastern Orthodoxy) but was to be a seedbed for social, economic, and political thought.

For further treatment of the historical context and consequences of Luther's work, see Protestantism.

Machineism: *the mechanicalizing of vivified or organic matter.

Mahogany: 1: the wood of any of various chiefly tropical trees (family Meliaceae, the mahogany family): a (1): the durable yellowish-brown to reddish-brown usu. moderately hard and heavy wood of a West Indian tree (Swietenia mahagoni) that is widely used for cabinetwork and fine finish work (2): a wood similar to mahogany from a congeneric tropical American tree (esp. S. macrophylla) b (1): the rather hard heavy usu. odorless wood of any of several African trees (genus Khaya) (2): the rather lightweight cedar-scented wood of any of several African trees (genus Entandrophragma) that varies in color from pinkish to deep reddish brown; 2: any of various woods resembling or substituted for mahogany obtained from trees of the mahogany family; 3: a tree that yields mahogany; 4: a moderate reddish brown.

Make Poverty History: *a coalition in mid-2000s Britain based around the issues of poverty, international trade, aid and economic justice.

Malaise: 1: an indefinite feeling of debility or lack of health often indicative of or accompanying the onset of an illness, 2: a vague sense of mental or moral ill-being ‹a ~ of cynicism and despair —Malcolm Boyd›.

Malcolm X: *original name* **Malcolm Little**, *Muslim name* **el-Hajj Malik el-Shabazz** black militant leader who articulated concepts of race pride and black nationalism in the early 1960s. After his assassination, the widespread distribution of his life story—*The Autobiography of Malcolm X* (1965)—made him an ideological hero, especially among black youth.

Malthus, Thomas Robert: English economist and demographer who is best known for his theory that population growth will always tend to outrun the food supply and that betterment of humankind is impossible without stern limits on reproduction. This thinking is commonly referred to as Malthusianism.

Manichaeism: dualistic religious movement founded in Persia in the 3rd century AD by Mani (q.v.), who was known as the "Apostle of Light" and supreme "Illuminator." Although Manichaeism was long considered a Christian heresy, it was a religion in its own right that, because of the coherence of its doctrines and the rigidness of its structure and institutions, preserved throughout its history a unity and unique character.

Mantra: (1795): a mystical formula of invocation or incantation (as in Hinduism); also: watchword.

Marx, Karl: *in full **Karl Heinrich Marx*** revolutionary, sociologist, historian, and economist. He published (with Friedrich Engels) *Manifest der Kommunistischen Partei* (1848), commonly known as *The Communist Manifesto*, the most celebrated pamphlet in the history of the socialist movement. He also was the author of the movement's most important book, *Das Kapital*. These writings and others by Marx and Engels form the basis of the body of thought and belief known as Marxism.

Marxism: a body of doctrine developed by Karl Marx and, to a lesser extent, by Friedrich Engels in the mid-19th century. It originally consisted of three related ideas: a philosophical view of man, a theory of history, and an economic and political program.

Mary I: *also called **Mary Tudor**, byname **Bloody Mary*** the first queen to rule England (1553–58) in her own right. She was known as Bloody Mary for her persecution of Protestants in a vain attempt to restore Roman Catholicism in England.

Materialism: 1 a: a theory that physical matter is the only or fundamental reality and that all being and processes and phenomena can be explained as manifestations or results of matter b: a doctrine that the only or the highest values or objectives lie in material well-being and in the furtherance of material progress c: a doctrine that economic or social change is materially caused compare historical materialism, 2: a preoccupation with or stress upon material rather than intellectual or spiritual things.

McLennan, John: Scottish lawyer and ethnologist whose ideas on cultural evolution, kinship, and the origins of religion stimulated anthropological research.

Melanin: a dark biological pigment (biochrome) found in skin, hair, feathers, scales, eyes, and some internal membranes ... Formed as an end product during metabolism of the amino acid tyrosine, melanins are conspicuous in dark skin moles of humans; in the black dermal melanocytes (pigment cells) of most dark-skinned peoples; and as brown, diffuse spots in the epidermis.

Melatonin: hormone secreted by the pineal gland, a tiny endocrine gland situated at the centre of the brain....In humans, melatonin seems to play an important role in the regulation of sleep cycles. The pineal gland's production of melatonin varies both with the time of day and with age; production of melatonin is dramatically increased during the nighttime hours and falls off during the day, and melatonin levels at night are higher in children than in adults. It is thought that the increased production of melatonin coincident with nightfall acts as a fundamental mechanism for making people sleepy. With dawn the pineal gland stops producing melatonin, resulting in wakefulness and alertness. The high level of melatonin production in young children may explain their tendency to sleep longer than adults.

Memphis: city and capital of ancient Egypt during the Old Kingdom (c. 2575–c. 2130 BC), located south of the Nile River delta, on the west bank of the river, and about 15 miles (25 km) south of modern Cairo.

Mészáros, István: *philosopher and Western Marxist who specialized in working out ways for society to transition from capitalism to socialism.

Millenarianism: 1: belief in the millennium of Christian prophecy, 2: belief in a coming ideal society and esp. one created by revolutionary action.

Modernism: 1: a practice, usage, or expression peculiar to modern times; 2: often cap: a tendency in theology to accommodate traditional religious teaching to contemporary thought and esp. to devalue supernatural elements; 3: modern artistic or literary philosophy and practice; esp: a self-conscious break with the past and a search for new forms of expression.

Modernization: (1770) 1: the act of modernizing: the state of being modernized; 2: something modernized: a modernized version.

Moneran: (1876): prokaryote.

Morgan, Lewis: American ethnologist and a principal founder of scientific anthropology, known especially for establishing the study of kinship systems and for his comprehensive theory of social evolution.

Muhammad, Elijah: *original name* ***Elijah Poole*** leader of the black separatist religious movement known as the Nation of Islam (sometimes called Black Muslims) in the United States.

Mahammad, Master Fard: *founder of the Nation of Islam.

Nebula: 1: any of numerous clouds of gas or dust in interstellar space; 2: galaxy 1b; esp: a galaxy other than the Milky Way galaxy — not used technically.

Neoliberalism: (1945): a liberal who de-emphasizes traditional liberal doctrines in order to seek progress by more pragmatic methods.

Nepotism: (1670): favoritism (as in appointment to a job) based on kinship.

New Right: *a sociological and ideological perspective begun in the 1970s based on radical conservative views and ideas.

Newton, Huey P: *in full **Huey Percy Newton** American political activist, cofounder (with Bobby Seale) of the Black Panther Party (originally called Black Panther Party for Self-Defense).

Newton, Isaac: English physicist and mathematician, who was the culminating figure of the scientific revolution of the 17th century. In optics, his discovery of the composition of white light integrated the phenomena of colours into the science of light and laid the foundation for modern physical optics. In mechanics, his three laws of motion, the basic principles of modern physics, resulted in the formulation of the law of universal gravitation. In mathematics, he was the original discoverer of the infinitesimal calculus. Newton's *Philosophiae Naturalis Principia Mathematica* (*Mathematical Principles of Natural Philosophy*), 1687, was one of the most important single works in the history of modern science.

Nihilism: (ca. 1817) 1 a: a viewpoint that traditional values and beliefs are unfounded and that existence is senseless and useless b: a doctrine that denies any objective ground of truth and esp. of moral truths; 2 a: a doctrine or belief that conditions in the social organization are so bad as to make destruction desirable for its own sake independent of any constructive program or possibility b cap: the program of a 19th century Russian party advocating revolutionary reform and using terrorism and assassination.

North Atlantic Treaty Organization (NATO): military alliance established by the North Atlantic Treaty (also called the Washington Treaty) of April 4, 1949, which sought to create a counterweight to Soviet armies stationed in central and eastern Europe after World War II. Its original members were Belgium, Canada, Denmark, France, Iceland, Italy, Luxembourg, The Netherlands, Norway, Portugal, the United Kingdom, and the United States. Joining the original signatories were Greece and Turkey (1952); West Germany (1955; from 1990 as Germany); Spain (1982); the Czech Republic, Hungary, and Poland (1999); and Bulgaria, Estonia, Latvia, Lithuania, Romania, Slovakia, and Slovenia (2004). France withdrew from the integrated military command of NATO in 1966, but it remained a member of the organization.

Nova: (1927): a star that suddenly increases its light output tremendously and then fades away to its former obscurity in a few months or years.

Objectify: (ca. 1837) 1: to treat as an object or cause to have objective reality, 2: to give expression to (as an abstract notion, feeling, or ideal) in a form that can be experienced by others ‹it is the essence of the fairy tale to ~ differing facets of the child's emotional experience.

Objective: 1 a: relating to or existing as an object of thought without consideration of independent existence — used chiefly in medieval philosophy b: of, relating to, or being an object, phenomenon, or condition in the realm of sensible experience independent of individual thought and perceptible by all observers: having reality independent of the mind ‹~ reality› ‹our reveries…are significantly and repeatedly shaped by our transactions with the ~ world —Marvin Reznikoff› compare subjective 3a c of a symptom of disease: perceptible to persons other than the affected individual compare subjective 4c d: involving or deriving from sense perception or experience with actual objects, conditions, or phenomena ‹~ awareness› ‹~ data›; 2: relating to, characteristic of, or constituting the case of words that follow prepositions or transitive verbs; 3 a: expressing or dealing with facts or conditions as perceived without distortion by personal feelings, prejudices, or interpretations ‹~ art› ‹an ~ history of the war› ‹an ~ judgment› b of a test: limited to choices of fixed alternatives and reducing subjective factors to a minimum material, fair.

Obsolete: 1 a: no longer in use or no longer useful ‹an ~ word› b: of a kind or style no longer current: old-fashioned ‹an ~ technology›, 2: of a plant or animal part: indistinct or imperfect as compared with a corresponding part in related organisms: vestigial old.

Obsolescence: (ca. 1828): the process of becoming obsolete or the condition of being nearly obsolete ‹the gradual ~ of machinery› ‹reduced to ~›.

Oedipus: (1557): the son of Laius and Jocasta who in fulfillment of an oracle unknowingly kills his father and marries his mother.

Oedipal: (1939): of, relating to, or resulting from the Oedipus complex.

Oedipus Complex: (1910): the positive libidinal feelings of a child toward the parent of the opposite sex and hostile or jealous feelings toward the parent of the same sex that may be a source of adult personality disorder when unresolved.

Omnibenevolence: *unlimited or infinite in goodness usu regarded as unconditional love.

Owen, Robert: Welsh manufacturer turned reformer, one of the most influential early 19th-century advocates of utopian socialism. His New Lanark mills in Lanarkshire, Scotland, with their social and industrial welfare programs, became a place of pilgrimage for statesmen and social reformers. He also sponsored or encouraged many experimental "utopian" communities, including one in New Harmony, Indiana, U.S.

Pandemic: (1666): occurring over a wide geographic area and affecting an exceptionally high proportion of the population ‹~ malaria›.

Pandemic: (ca. 1853): a pandemic outbreak of a disease.

Parapsychology: (1925): a field of study concerned with the investigation of evidence for paranormal psychological phenomena (as telepathy, clairvoyance, and psychokinesis).

Paul the Apostle: *original name* **Saul of Tarsus** 1st-century Jew who, after first being a bitter enemy of Christianity, later became an important figure in its history.

Pentecostal: (ca. 1663) 1: of, relating to, or suggesting Pentecost; 2: of, relating to, or constituting any of various Christian religious bodies that emphasize individual experiences of grace, spiritual gifts (as glossolalia and faith healing), expressive worship, and evangelism.

Pentecostal n (1904): a member of a Pentecostal religious body.

Pernicious: 1: highly injurious or destructive: deadly, 2: wicked.

Phalange: phalanx.

Phalanx: 1: a body of heavily armed infantry in ancient Greece formed in close deep ranks and files; broadly: a body of troops in close array; 2 pl phalanges: one of the digital bones of the hand or foot of a vertebrate; 3 pl usu phalanxesa: a massed arrangement of persons, animals, or things ‹a ~ of armed guards› b: an organized body of persons ‹a ~ of lawyers›.

Phantasm: 1: a product of fantasy: as a: delusive appearance: illusion b: ghost specter c: a figment of the imagination; 2: a mental representation of a real object.

Phase-Space: *multidimensional space in which phase transitions are represented for the purpose of measuring possibilities.

Pineal Gland: *also called* **Pineal Body**, or **Epiphysis Cerebri**, an endocrine gland found in vertebrates that regulates the production of the hormone melatonin. Though it is not part of the brain, the pineal gland develops from the roof of the diencephalon, a section of the brain. In some lower vertebrates the gland has a well-developed eyelike structure; in others, though not organized as an eye, it functions as a light receptor. Studies that were carried out in the 1980s suggested that the pineal gland was the evolutionary forerunner of the modern eye.

Pituitary Gland: (1825 : a small oval endocrine organ that is attached to the infundibulum of the brain, consists of an epithelial anterior lobe joined by an intermediate part to a posterior lobe of nervous origin, and produces various internal secretions directly or indirectly impinging on most basic body functions called also hypophysis pituitary body see brain illustration.

Plato: ancient Greek philosopher, the second of the great trio of ancient Greeks—Socrates, Plato, and Aristotle—who between them laid the philosophical foundations of Western culture. Building on the life and thought of Socrates, Plato developed a profound and wide-ranging system of philosophy. His thought has logical, epistemological, and metaphysical aspects; but its underlying motivation is ethical. It sometimes relies upon conjectures and myth, and it is occasionally mystical in tone; but fundamentally Plato is a rationalist, devoted to the proposition that reason must be followed wherever it leads. Thus the core of Plato's philosophy is a rationalistic ethics.

Pneumatology: (1678): the study of spiritual beings or phenomena.

Postmodern: 1: of, relating to, or being an era after a modern one ‹~ times› ‹a ~ metropolis›; 2 a: of, relating to, or being any of various movements in reaction to modernism that are typically characterized by a return to traditional materials and forms (as in architecture) or by ironic self-reference and absurdity (as in literature) b: of, relating to, or being a theory that involves a radical reappraisal of modern assumptions about culture, identity, history, or language ‹~ feminism›.

Potentiality: 1: the ability to develop or come into existence, 2: potential.

Predecessor: 1: one that precedes; esp: a person who has previously occupied a position or office to which another has succeeded; 2: ancestor.

Predilection: (1742): an established preference for something.

Prescribe: 1: to lay down a rule: dictate; 2: to claim a title to something by right of prescription; 3: to write or give medical prescriptions; 4: to become by prescription invalid or unenforceable.

Prescribe: 1 a: to lay down as a guide, direction, or rule of action: ordain b: to specify with authority; 2: to designate or order the use of as a remedy ‹prescribed a painkiller› ‹a prescribed burn to restore natural forest conditions›.

Prokaryote: (1963): any of the typically unicellular microorganisms that lack a distinct nucleus and membrane-bound organelles and that are classified as a kingdom (Prokaryotae syn. Monera) or into two domains (Bacteria and Archaea) compare archaea bacterium eukaryote.

Progeny: 1 a: descendants children b: offspring of animals or plants; 2: outcome product; 3: a body of followers, disciples, or successors.

Proletariat: 1: the laboring class; esp: the class of industrial workers who lack their own means of production and hence sell their labor to live; 2: the lowest social or economic class of a community.

Propaganda: 1 cap: a congregation of the Roman curia having jurisdiction over missionary territories and related institutions; 2: the spreading of ideas, information, or rumor for the purpose of helping or injuring an institution, a cause, or a person; 3: ideas, facts, or allegations spread deliberately to further one's cause or to damage an opposing cause; also: a public action having such an effect.

Propagation: the act or action of propagating: as a: increase (as of a kind of organism) in numbers b: the spreading of something (as a belief) abroad or into new regions c: enlargement or extension (as of a crack) in a solid body.

Proprietor: 1: one granted ownership of a colony (as one of the original American colonies) and full prerogatives of establishing a government and distributing land; 2 a: a person who has the legal right or exclusive title to something: owner b: one having an interest (as control or present use) less than absolute and exclusive right.

Propriety: 1 obs: true nature; 2 obs: a special characteristic: peculiarity; 3: the quality or state of being proper: appropriateness; 4 a: conformity to what is socially acceptable in conduct or speech b: fear of offending against conventional rules of behavior esp. between the sexes c pl: the customs and manners of polite society.

Proscribe: (1560) 1: to publish the name of as condemned to death with the property of the condemned forfeited to the state, 2: to condemn or forbid as harmful or unlawful: prohibit.

Protamoeba: *a type of amoeba.

Protestant: (1539) 1 capa: any of a group of German princes and cities presenting a defense of freedom of conscience against an edict of the Diet of Spires in 1529 intended to suppress the Lutheran movement b: a member of any of several church denominations denying the universal authority of the Pope and affirming the Reformation principles of justification by faith alone, the priesthood of all believers, and the primacy of the Bible as the only source of revealed truth; broadly: a Christian not of a Catholic or Eastern church; 2: one who makes or enters a protest.

Protestant adj (1539) 1 cap: of or relating to Protestants, their churches, or their religion; 2: making or sounding a protest ‹the two ~ ladies up and marched out —Time›.

Protist: (1889): any of a diverse taxonomic group and esp. a kingdom (Protista syn. Protoctista) of eukaryotic organisms that are unicellular and sometimes colonial or less often multicellular and that typically include the protozoans, most algae, and often some fungi (as slime molds).

Protocols: 1: an original draft, minute, or record of a document or transaction; 2 a: a preliminary memorandum often formulated and signed by diplomatic negotiators as a basis for a final convention or treaty b : the records or minutes of a diplomatic conference or congress that show officially the agreements arrived at by the negotiators; 3 a: a code prescribing strict adherence to correct etiquette and precedence (as in diplomatic exchange and in the military services) ‹a breach of ~› b: a set of conventions governing the treatment and esp. the formatting of data in an electronic communications system ‹network ~s› c: convention; 4: a detailed plan of a scientific or medical experiment, treatment, or procedure.

Prussia: *German **Preussen** Polish **Prusy*** in European history, any of certain areas of eastern and central Europe, respectively (1) the land of the Prussians on the southeastern coast of the Baltic Sea, which came under Polish and German rule in the Middle Ages; (2) the kingdom ruled from 1701 by the German Hohenzollern dynasty, including Prussia and Brandenburg, with Berlin as its capital, which seized much of northern Germany and western Poland in the 18th and 19th centuries and united Germany under its leadership in 1871; and (3) the Land (state) created after the fall of the Hohenzollerns in 1918, which included most of their former kingdom and which was abolished by the Allies in 1947 as part of the political reorganization of Germany after its defeat in World War II.

Psychokinesis: (1914): movement of physical objects by the mind without use of physical means compare precognition telekinesis.

Puritan: (ca. 1567) 1 cap: a member of a 16th and 17th century Protestant group in England and New England opposing as unscriptural the ceremonial worship and the prelacy of the Church of England; 2: one who practices or preaches a more rigorous or professedly purer moral code than that which prevails

Puritan adj, often cap, (1581): of or relating to puritans, the Puritans, or puritanism

Reactionary: (1840): relating to, marked by, or favoring reaction; esp: ultraconservative in politics.

Rousseau, Jean-Jacques: French philosopher, writer, and political theorist whose treatises and novels inspired the leaders of the French Revolution and the Romantic generation.

Saint-Simon, Henri de: *in full **Claude-Henri de Rouvroy, Comte (count) de Saint-Simon*** French social theorist and one of the chief founders of Christian socialism. In his major work, *Nouveau*

Christianisme (1825), he proclaimed a brotherhood of man that must accompany the scientific organization of industry and society.

Seductionist: *anyone who receives pleasure from driving others mad with sexual lust.

Self-Disclosure: *the process of revealing the full details of one-self.

Serotonin: *also called **5-hydroxytryptamine,** a chemical substance that is derived from the amino acid <u>tryptophan</u>. It occurs in the brain, intestinal tissue, blood platelets, and mast cells and is a constituent of many venoms, including wasp venom and toad venom. Serotonin is a potent vasoconstrictor and functions as a neurotransmitter. It is concentrated in certain areas of the brain, especially the midbrain and the hypothalamus, and changes in its concentration are associated with several mood disorders.

Simulation: 1: the act or process of simulating; 2: a sham object: counterfeit; 3 a: the imitative representation of the functioning of one system or process by means of the functioning of another ‹a computer ~ of an industrial process› b: examination of a problem often not subject to direct experimentation by means of a simulating device.

Socrates: Greek philosopher whose way of life, character, and thought exerted a profound influence on ancient and modern philosophy.

Soteriology: (ca. 1774): theology dealing with salvation esp. as effected by Jesus Christ.

Spookish: *a term used to express the non-existent nature of a being or object.

Strabo: Greek geographer and historian whose Geography is the only extant work covering the whole range of peoples and countries known to both Greeks and Romans during the reign of Augustus

(27 BC–AD 14). Its numerous quotations from technical literature, moreover, provide a remarkable account of the state of Greek geographical science, as well as of the history of the countries it surveys.

Supra-Religious: *transcending religion.

Systemic Indoctrination: *a form of indoctrination that exists within systems.

Telekinesis: (1890): the production of motion in objects (as by a spiritualistic medium) without contact or other physical means.

Tentative: (1626) 1: not fully worked out or developed ‹~ plans›, 2: hesitant uncertain ‹a ~ smile›.

The Anti-Capitalist Movement: *movement started in the late-twentieth century and early-twenty first century to fight against neoliberalism, corporate globalization, environmental damage, wage-slavery and ownership of private property.

The Enlightenment: *French Siècle De Lumières ("Age of the Enlightened"), German Aufklärung*, a European intellectual movement of the 17th and 18th centuries in which ideas concerning God, reason, nature, and man were synthesized into a worldview that gained wide assent and that instigated revolutionary developments in art, philosophy, and politics. Central to Enlightenment thought were the use and the celebration of reason, the power by which man understands the universe and improves his own condition. The goals of rational man were considered to be knowledge, freedom, and happiness.

The People's Charter of England: *the outline of an Act allowing for the just representation of the people of Great Britain and Ireland in the House of Commons; encompassing many progressive ideas such as: annual parliaments, equal representation, payment of members, qualification without property, universal suffrage and vote by ballot.

The Prophet Muhammad: *in full Abū al-Qāsim Muḥammad ibn ʿAbd Allāh ibn ʿAbd al-Muṭṭalib ibn Hāshim* founder of the religion of <u>Islam</u>, accepted by Muslims throughout the world as the last of the prophets of God.

The Reformation: the religious revolution that took place in the Western church in the 16th century; its greatest leaders undoubtedly were Martin Luther and John Calvin. Having far-reaching political, economic, and social effects, the Reformation became the basis for the founding of Protestantism, one of the three major branches of Christianity.

The Renaissance: literally "rebirth," the period in European civilization immediately following the Middle Ages, conventionally held to have been characterized by a surge of interest in classical learning and values. The Renaissance also witnessed the discovery and exploration of new continents, the substitution of the Copernican for the Ptolemaic system of astronomy, the decline of the feudal system and the growth of commerce, and the invention or application of such potentially powerful innovations as paper, printing, the mariner's compass, and gunpowder. To the scholars and thinkers of the day, however, it was primarily a time of the revival of classical learning and wisdom after a long period of cultural decline and stagnation.

The Restoration: Restoration of the monarchy in England in 1660. It marked the return of Charles II as king (1660–85) following the period of Oliver Cromwell's Commonwealth. The bishops were restored to Parliament, which established a strict Anglican orthodoxy. The period, which also included the reign of James II (1685–88), was marked by an expansion in colonial trade, the Anglo-Dutch Wars, and a revival of drama and literature (see Restoration literature).

Thebes: *ancient Egyptian **Wase**, or **Wo'se**, or (from c. 21st century BC) **Nowe**, or **Nuwe***, one of the famed cities of antiquity, the capital of the ancient Egyptian empire at its heyday.

Theocentric: (1886): having God as the central interest and ultimate concern ‹a ~ culture›.

Theocracy: 1: government of a state by immediate divine guidance or by officials who are regarded as divinely guided, 2: a state governed by a theocracy.

Theocratic: (1690): of, relating to, or being a theocracy.

Theodicy: (1797): defense of God's goodness and omnipotence in view of the existence of evil.

Timaeus: *a dialogue of Timaeus of Locri which includes Socrates, Hermocrates, and Critias and was written by Plato.

Torah: in Judaism, in the broadest sense the substance of divine revelation to Israel, the Jewish people: God's revealed teaching or guidance for mankind. The meaning of "Torah" is often restricted to signify the first five books of the Old Testament, also called the Law or the Pentateuch. These are the books traditionally ascribed to Moses, the recipient of the original revelation from God on Mount Sinai.

Traumata: 1 a: an injury (as a wound) to living tissue caused by an extrinsic agent b: a disordered psychic or behavioral state resulting from severe mental or emotional stress or physical injury c: an emotional upset ‹the personal ~ of an executive who is not living up to his own expectations —Karen W. Arenson›; 2: an agent, force, or mechanism that causes trauma.

True Postmodernism: *due to the theoretical, philosophical and cultural nature of current postmodern trends it is understood that we have not transcended modernity. For this cause, true postmodernism believes that modernity will only be superseded when the anti-modern struggle is victorious and the main institutions that make up modernity are overcome such as: the national-state, liberal democracy and capitalism.

Tryptophan: (1890): a crystalline essential amino acid $C_{11}H_{12}N_2O_2$ that is widely distributed in proteins.

Ubiquity: (1579): presence everywhere or in many places esp. simultaneously: omnipresence.

Unequivocal: (1784) 1: leaving no doubt: clear unambiguous; 2: unquestionable ‹production of ~ masterpieces —Carole Cook›.

Uninhibited: (1880): free from inhibition ‹~ exuberance›; also: boisterously informal ‹a festive ~ party›.

Univocal: (1599) 1: having one meaning only, 2: unambiguous ‹in search of a morally ~ answer›.

Velocity: 1 a: quickness of motion: speed ‹the ~ of sound› b: rapidity of movement ‹[my horse's] strong suit is grace & personal comeliness, rather than ~ —Mark Twain› c: speed imparted to something ‹the power pitcher relies on ~ —Tony Scherman›; 2: the rate of change of position along a straight line with respect to time : the derivative of position with respect to time; 3 a: rate of occurrence or action: rapidity ‹the ~ of historical change —R. J. Lifton› b: rate of turnover ‹the ~ of money›.

Venerable: 1: deserving to be venerated — used as a title for an Anglican archdeacon or for a Roman Catholic who has been accorded the lowest of three degrees of recognition for sanctity; 2: made sacred esp. by religious or historical association; 3 a: calling forth respect through age, character, and attainments ‹a ~ jazz musician› ; broadly: conveying an impression of aged goodness and benevolence ‹encouraged by the ~ doctor's head-nodding› b: impressive by reason of age ‹under ~ pines› old.

Wavelength: (1850) 1: the distance in the line of advance of a wave from any one point to the next point of corresponding phase; 2: a particular course or line of thought esp. as related to mutual understanding ‹two people on different ~s›.

PREFACE TO SHAHIDI EDITION

For those who remember this book when it was still underground I must explain the need for this rewrite. See, I no longer go under the name Tony Saunders, which name is my slave name. My righteous name is now my government name properly and formally, and that is Shahidi Islam. For this reason I am re-releasing some of my former works under my new name so as to certify them. I have lots of other writings in circulation that go under the name Tony Saunders, some of which I am quite ashamed of. If you have found or read one of them please feel free to discard it. If it is not a book or writing under the name Shahidi Islam it is not something I am endorsing. Besides, Tony Saunders is a popular name and there are so many other people under that name I just got lost in the sea of them. To separate myself from all of them and to permanently remove the embarrassment of my former works I have chosen to release this Shahidi Collection featuring a correct explication of my doctrine as it stands. Again, if it is not a work found either with the author name Shahidi Islam or endorsed by Shahidi Islam then I do not endorse what is written within, even if it is one of my own former writings, as some of them have ideas I no longer endorse or agree with. To wipe the slate clean and to endorse ideas that I do agree with look out for upcoming books and articles from Shahidi Islam, this Shahidi Collection is itself a precursor. As this book is in the Shahidi Collection not only am I endorsing it, but it is a part of my very philosophy and outlook on life. Therefore, I believe in what is written in these pages and believe the black community would benefit substantially by paying close attention to what is being said.

Black divinity is an idea that was first articulated by the ancient Ethiopians over twenty-eight thousand years ago. Its message was continued on by the ancient Egyptian mystics over seven thousand years ago and by the ancient Hebrew mystics over three thousand years ago. The message was lost to the Hebrews during their exiles but continued on in ancient Egypt and ancient Ethiopia. Finally, John the Baptist rearticulated it and began a Kingdom of God movement in which someone coming in his near future would bring the people back to a black divinity through baptism into holiness. The Messiah continued that message which splintered into separate branches. The mystics among his followers were called the Gnostics and they combine the Messiah's message with ancient Egyptian philosophy. The Gnostic message thereby continued the idea of black divinity secretly and underground while mainstream Christianity was also underground due to heavy persecution. When Christianity finally became legal it was the mainstream version that succeeded and Gnosticism remained outlawed, driving them further underground. At that time, the only black person considered divine was the Messiah (back then the only images of the Messiah were black). Black divinity re-emerged with Muslim mysticism, which combined the Gnostic oral tradition with Islamic interpretations of the Quran. Finally, black divinity reached its greatest height in the Americas when the Honorable Elijah Muhammad brought Islamic mysticism to America with his Lost-Found Nation of Islam. The truth is, we as black people have always had the potential to be divine, but thanks to the Elijah we are only now starting to realize how to actually achieve this reality. This book is a pathway to that achievement.

PREFACE TO THIRD EDITION

Within months of publishing the second edition of *Black Divinity* it became apparent that there would need to be a third; however, having already begun the process of marketing the second edition I had to let that run its course. The current third edition is by far easier to reconcile to the 5 Percent philosophy than the first two editions were. However, as the basis for all three editions was notes taken in 2006 when I was still a Christian it is not completely fair to call any of these versions of *Black Divinity* a 5 Percent book. True the first two editions were written while I was a "new born" 5 Percenter and contain some 5 Percent embellishments; but no genuine 5 Percenter would respect either of them or the current as substantial 5 Percent theory. In that sense *Black Divinity* remains somewhat of a fossil, or at least an embryo.

I have chosen to remake *Black Divinity* this third time for the purpose of opening up an avenue for those who will read my next few books to see a more unified variation of my intellectual development: that, though certain substantial changes and transformations have occurred in my personal views and conclusions, my overall interpretation of life and of the solutions to the black situation were already in existence over a decade ago. A final reason behind the current remake was to deal with certain issues that have arisen since the publication of the first edition, in particular the rising of ISIS. As the first two editions speak excessively of the Egyptian goddess Isis and her husband Isar, I felt it would be potentially confusing for future generations, and the young of the current generation, to read the word Isis so much and not associate it with a terrorist organisation;

therefore I changed all mentions of the names Isar and Isis to their proper Egyptian names Ausar and Auset.

That said, this book is relatively faithful to the second edition with, however, certain big changes that bring the ideas closer to my current development. I do not want the reader to be confused, though, the book as a whole is and must be read as a Christian book. The Islamic and 5 Percent leanings do not in any way compensate for the heavily Christian philosophy expounded throughout. Nevertheless, the heart and soul of this book is to lead to a new interpretation of life and the Hebrew prophecies thereby bringing us to a place of fulfilment and salvation. Not that some outside saviour comes from the sky and saves us. Our salvation is self-performed. We become our own saviours through knowledge of self, love of self and love of neighbour as of self. In this is found the kingdom God promised to the Hebrew people and is found the pathway to that divine nature that is opened to us by accepting the message of truth.

Finally, this book is dedicated to my Sun and Enlightener who is currently a political prisoner doing time in Oklahoma State Prison, thank you for the jewels you dropped on me: it is much appreciated. And to all the Gods and Earths out there, peace – coming straight from Tony Saunders, whose righteous attribute is Shahidi Islam.

PREFACE TO SECOND EDITION

The first edition of this book was released in 2012 for the purpose of inspiring black people to consider their potential for divinity. With the passing of time errors and inconsistencies became more evident. Also written for the purpose of representing the New York City street culture and showing some of its remarkable ideas and articulating them to the black intelligentsia of America I found it ever more difficult to get a footing in this crowd and among this audience. Finding instead a home among African professionals I found it necessary to remove some of the more immature and gang related ideas of the first edition. I also found that the general message, that of demodernization, was not respectfully disclosed or given the conspicuousness it deserves in the last edition.

I feel at this time that perhaps the French were too soon to close the coffin on modernity. Modernity cannot be wished away it must, like any existing ruling force, be overthrown. Nothing has overthrown it. Nothing has taken its place. It still exists as the central basis of life in the Western world, as no new class of people has replaced it. No new movement has stood toe-to-toe with it and won. There has been no fight, not so to speak but literally.

Socialism may fight capitalism, but socialism on its own still cannot trump modernism. It is not the overthrow of modernism or a leap into a postmodern world. Even the anti-capitalist movement and the Make Poverty History movement come nowhere near to an overthrow of the system or its proper fight back.

I myself am simply laying the foundation for such an overthrow to occur. I may not see its completion and I do not expect to be that huge, just to be a foundation is more than enough for me; a stepping stone on which many giants tread. I do not think it too wise to go ahead of yourself, and expecting an imminent demise of modernism is stepping ahead of myself. True indeed, I must walk this straight and narrow path of anti-modernism but I must go at a pace that is credible and followable.

But how does one fight against something so stable and time honoured? What does one say to send tremors down the spine of modernity? It exists virtually everywhere. It is the all-seeing, all-controlling force of all forces. Modernism is so used to being in charge it seems almost impossible to dethrone her from her pre-eminence; built, as it is, on several shaky epistemological foundations. Modernism promised the uncovering of truth but brought in the propagation of opinion. It promised the reign of reason but brought in the reign of chaos. It promised us equal rights but brought us unequal privileges. It promised uninhibited freedom but brought in disguised subjugation. It promised universal prosperity but brought in abject poverty. These have been the real benefits of our surrendering to the machineism of modernism; but it is time for a change.

In this situation the first thing that needs to be adjusted is our views of systemic indoctrination. Everything in modernity is a system and everything is a machine. Machines called systems connecting to other machines called bureaucracies, to create further machines called institutions. Different structures form into systems which then become pandemic throughout modernism as a whole.

Systems are the central disease of modernity. They suck the life out of any and every thing they touch. This soulless enterprise is all-consuming as it infects the livelihoods of all living things in the human mind. It is abstract, absolutizing and objectifying. In fact, the objectivity of modernism is the basis for all its 'sciences.' But objectivity must give way to demodernizing intersubjectivity or we may all lose our souls.

By letting go of the grand theories of science, and by accepting that everything has a soul through which it vibrates transmissions and feedback at different velocities, amplitudes, frequencies and wavelengths, and through which it interprets all events and phenomena; we can begin to overthrow the first monster of modernism: the scientific method. True indeed, we should still hold to some of its classifications but overall grand sciences create only chaos and complexity. We need to appreciate that all these things are related. Without science taking a humbler seat in the banquet of life, modern theoretical ideologies will continue getting more and more dehumanizing.

So what does this mean, the abolition of objective theories? It means we appreciate that there are two or more sides to every truth. Even if one was to have all the facts of a specific event it still would not count for half the information necessary to make a reasonable judgment on the entire case. There is the observer's past experiences, feelings, hurts, pains, wins, gains and biases to consider also along with all manner of other subjective realities that have not been mentioned. But a truth is not only subjective, it is intersubjective as it is based on the subjective realities of every living being that exists. At the same time, if the truth is intersubjective then we are left with the irony of truth and the caricature of science.

In all this French Postmodernism was right; to destroy or surpass modernity we must begin at its philosophical precursors. Philosophically and ideologically that which is called postmodern would be better called anti-modern. It challenges the edifice of modern objectivity. Thus we have the understanding on its behalf of the intersubjective realities of each individual and the understanding that grand all-encompassing truths are an impossibility. So the French school is the best place to begin a full frontal assault against modernity. Having thus overthrown modernism in the mind and moved on to the postmodern it would be fair to prepare for the next level. This book is that.

INTRODUCTION

The following chapters are based on notes originally written in 2006 and edited in 2012 for the current purpose. Also included are various outlines I had written from 2011 and 2012 for the empowering of our people, but that I have now chosen to publish due to the current circumstances. Contained within are a wide cross-section of quotations which break up a lot of the work making it seem at times frustrating and difficult to read. This annoyance was unavoidable due to the current situation, and unfortunate mistrust of those outside of the street life of the intelligence of anyone arising out of the street life. Again, hopefully no one within the street life, particularly within the 5 Percent Nation, will be too offended by some of the language that I have chosen to use throughout, as it is mainly for the purpose of speaking to the uninitiated, not to ruin our image or desecrate our culture.

From a historical context all past developments in human progress have been correlated to philosophical precursors. From Aristotle's influence on ancient Greece and Plato's influence over the Roman *res publica*; to the influence of Rousseau on the French Revolution and Marx on the Russian; it is virtually impossible to separate historical epochs from their philosophical precursors. The initial philosophical bursts of light and hope, however, usually begin to dim as the pains of reaction begin to set in. This reactionary response to the new ideas and the hostility of its opposition usually bring great sorrow and disillusionment to the representatives of the new vision and ideal.

As these realities are the historical norm for all prior to revolutionary changes it is clear that anything of this calibre will meet also its own huge bursts of reactionary opposition and rage.

From church pulpit to political gathering, from social clubs to cultural events all groups and sections of society claim allegiance to morality and against the dark cloud of the street life. True indeed, as the streets are considered a curse on society, and themselves cursed of God, we, in the eyes of those outside the streets, should have nothing to do with anything even resembling the theocentric, let alone the theocratic. In fact, our anti-establishment makes us seem to any who are not affiliated to be more nihilistic than ritualistic. This anti-establishment being a product of our rejection by the establishment and being outcasts to it, has caused us to question our place in a society that would create and tolerate such vicious injustices as occur in the neighbourhoods of this so-called Western society.

The black theocracy is itself a system based on the identifying of a black theodicy, that is, a study of God's goodness and righteousness from a black person's perspective. Having arisen from the backstreets of New York as the godbody, the black theocracy is based primarily on the use of codes and culture to find black identity amid the difficult and adverse situations of racism, poverty, marginalization, dyseducation, demonization, humiliation, and habitual incarceration.

But the godbodies are ultimately the militant vanguard of the 5 Percent Nation; keeping alive the message of Allah (Clarence 13X) and the conception of the black man's divinity, a message for which he was put in the psychiatric ward. The godbody unfortunately are not recognized by most 5 Percenters as bona fide members, but we do represent them and we represent them to the fullest. Still, we godbody do have the potential to become the major alternative to the giants of neoliberal Americanism and authoritarian Marxism in our communities; encouraging the absolute abolition of unnecessary and oppressive entities and institutions. But as we are mainly a cultural movement we should remain supra-religious and inter-faith, sticking mainly to the development of black scholarship.

As a people most of we blacks have been separated from our history and a knowledge of our history; but as Nature expresses herself through an almost ritualistic spontaneity, I feel that a knowledge of recent black history is worth acknowledging. Marcus Garvey inspired an entire generation with the thought of a black God. A God, not white like their slave-masters (or like their job-managers in this current system of wage-slavery) but a God black like them, who understood the trials and sufferings of the people and offered them the strength and power to redeem themselves from these sufferings.

This philosophy spread in Africa, America and the Caribbean in many forms. Two most obvious forms were the Rastafarians, who claimed Negusa Negast Tafari was the black God incarnate, and the Black Church, who claimed the Messiah Jesus was the black God incarnate. But you also had the Black Muslims, who claimed Master Fard Muhammad was the black God incarnate. Then you had the Afrocentrics who claimed the ancestral gods of Africa (particularly those of ancient Egypt), which manifest themselves in Nature, were the black gods incarnate. And also the Kemetic scholars, who claimed the Egyptian god Ra was the black God incarnated in all black males; similar to the 5 Percent, who claim Allah to be the God incarnated in all black males who have mastered the 120 lessons and opened the third eye of astral vision. (And though the 5 Percent – whose teachings are the basis of the theocracy – claim that the highest a black woman can become is an Earth, the theocracy here holds to the ancient teachings that for the black man to become a God he needs a Goddess, so we acknowledge that through the 120 lessons a black woman can become that Goddess.)

But to return to the Black Muslims, the circumstances under which the black Moors of the Moorish Science Temple of America developed their mystical doctrine were based on the fact that the Moors were expelled from Spain during the Reconquest. Instead of seeing it as an exodus from Mecca to Medina, they saw it as an eviction from Eden into the wilderness.

Master Fard Muhammad, being himself a disciple of the Moorish Science Temple and of Noble Drew Ali, would then found his 1st Temple of Islam in America along with the University of Islam, the Fruit of Islam, and several other semi-Sufi organizations based on their teachings; who taught the history of the Islamic Moors of Africa, Europe, and America. But in revenge for *la Reconquista*, they also spread in the new World among those ready to accept it the doctrine of the "white devil." And as any and every theory is not without evidence, the Moorish Science Temple of America began to seek and search for these proofs and make them public to their disciples.

Master Fard taught all their lessons to his closest disciple Elijah Poole, who would later take the name Elijah Muhammad, and was given control of the Master's Lost-Found Nation of Islam (NOI). For three and a half years the Master taught the Elijah the Secret Wisdom of the Reality of God, which the Elijah spent the rest of his life trying to teach to his people through the NOI.

One unfortunate tension within some of the other Elijah inspired movements was their exclusivity, which, though a necessary precaution of the times, made outsiders distrustful of them and them even more distrustful of outsiders. Ultimately, the message of these groups would bring about self-confidence, inner-strength, peace of mind, and internal dignity. These psychological victories would far outweigh Dr. Martin Luther King (Martin King)'s legal and political victories which only really bought a level of self-denial, cultural-assimilation, loss of worth, and internal dependency.

Although it did broaden the attractiveness of struggle and long suffering for the sake of restoring worth and dignity, it did not take into account the realities of life: the intimidations, demoralizations and demonizations that the world uses to destroy our sense of self-worth. But the Martin King experience would prove to be of benefit beyond politics. Dr. King was a burning and shining torch and we would do well to remember his contribution to the struggle for our empowerment.

Still, as the Elijah's message reached a predominantly black audience and Dr. King's message reached all races and countries, those inspired by the Elijah or one of the movements that sprang from his message would have conflict with the disempowered residents of the world, being kept sane only through the knowledge of self he taught them to appreciate. Thus, his disciples, with no real jealousy or inferiority but self-love and self-respect (ultimately, Black Power), would not be easily destroyed or disempowered.

But his organization, the NOI, would soon be heavily infiltrated by the FBI's counterintelligence program (Cointelpro), so that they became completely incapable of effectively organizing their now empowered disciples into a positive movement. It is well known in Black and White America the level and extent to which US neo-colonialism would go to control and pacify the people. The Cointelpro was specifically set up during the 1950s to discredit, disinform, and destroy any communistic or race-related organizations during the Cold War. By the time of the NOI's prominence the Cointelpro had mastered the art of disinformation and used it to effectively neutralize them.

However, their main method, that of divide and conquer, did backfire on them as the more black organizations there were and as divided as they were, the more the prophecies of America's imminent doom and judgment sprang from the lips of their leaders, even Dr. King. All the black organizations were united in two things: their love for all oppressed and suffering people, particularly blacks; and their hatred for US neo-colonialism and misphilosophy. The prophecies by the various black groups also had similar themes: wrath on all the oppressors, particularly US neo-colonialists and wage-enslavers; and love, peace and happiness on earth in the imminent Kingdom of God (whatever name or label they called God by).

The Cointelpro operatives' use of disinformation within the media to isolate the NOI from society at large, and from black people in particular, would also effectively cause a division between Malcolm X, the former Minister of the 7th Temple of Islam and their most outspoken representative, and the other leaders within the Nation. This division would lead Malcolm; who had effectively influenced men like Frantz Fanon, a key figure in the Algerian Revolution; Ali Shariati, a key figure in the Iranian Revolution; and Patrice Lumumba, a key figure in the Congolese Revolution; out of the

NOI and into Sunni Islam seeking protection and support from the international brotherhood.

It is said that the NOI killed Malcolm X but most people by now know that the FBI killed Malcolm X using NOI guns. Through strategic disinformation programs: phone tappings, buggings, informants, etc., they bought down a great man and effectively crushed a potential black revolution.

A year after Malcolm X's death Bobby Seale and Huey Newton founded an organization in America based on his general message called the Black Panther Party for Self-Defense (BPP). This Party was an armed and militant group that functioned similar to how the Iranian influenced Hezbollah do today, minus the religious connotations. Having come at a time when ghetto people of all races and nationalities were being targeted by the police for harassment, brutality and murder; the Panther's stand against neo-colonial capitalism and US police brutality, and their refusal to be intimidated by their persecutors became an inspiration to many who were oppressed in the ghettos of the world.

During the 1960s the BPP were the leading political organization of the American Black Power movement, and Huey Newton became the leading personality of that movement. The BPP was set up to provide protection, food, clothing, housing, education, healthcare, etc.; basically, all the services that the state should provide – and that most states, including the US, now do provide – to the poorest neighbourhoods in America. They set up programs and a ten point platform of their general mission statement; but as it had communistic and racial overtones (two very dangerous ideas for 1960s America), the FBI, led by J. Edger Hoover, sought to squash them using the already effective Cointelpro methods.

Anytime there is tyranny the people have a right to defend themselves and the BPP exercised that right, never using violence as an offensive force but only as a defensive one. Of course, the police did not like that at all so they started a campaign against the BPP to brand them as volatile, aggressive and promoters and practitioners of violence; basically, a group of thugs. This move, however, was mostly political trickery having understood the extinction of the isolated and how to bring it about.

The BPP were so heavily attacked by this program; which used buggings, tappings, and mail stealing, opening and forging; media humiliation, demonization, and ideological labelling, dividing and isolating; infiltrators, informants, and false charges, documents and evidence; political trickery, misphilosophy, and word twisting, dissecting and absolutizing; discreditings, entrapments, raids, arrests, imprisonments, exiles, and the obvious police and SWAT brutality, to effectively neutralize all Panther credibility.

Still, it would not be until they were able to destroy Huey Newton's credibility with the streets and with the BPP, that they would be able to destroy the BPP altogether, creating distrust and paranoia among the faithful. All the BPP wanted to do was help the underclass of all races (including white people) find empowerment. But considering that when even Dr. Martin King began to fight for the same ideals in his "Poor Peoples Movement" they branded him a troublemaker, it is not hard to imagine the police's response to Huey Newton.

As a result of his ongoing difficulties with Maulana Karenga, Huey Newton also rejected the idea of culturalism as counter-revolutionary, thus causing him to have few links with the real black America, which by all standards is very culturally and spiritually minded. But we godbody mainly and centrally stand on, and have created, a cultural mechanism that has changed the face and shape of the ghetto youth of the American East Coast and black American underclass to this day. We are also, however, in duty bound to explain to the bourgeois and intellectual among our brothers and sisters just what it is that we are about in a detailed theodical treatise, to gain their support and help in maintaining our cultural identity.

I hope that by the development of this theodicy we will in time be able to undercut the entire foundation on which modern society is built, thus creating a means for its most imminent transformation. In its place we practitioners of black divinity have created a structure capable of liberating all elements of society without robbing or exploiting one class for the sake of another. This divinity also allows we black people in particular to find a very natural form of self-expression in an environment which tolerates and encourages our social and human development, instead of encouraging self-loathing and self-denial for the sake of appearance or vain competition. This reality I found to be true, though not so much universal, among the body now largely represented throughout the US.

It must also obviously be noted that these ideas and practices are not those of the entire godbody of the United States, but are plus degrees based on lessons I learned in the Socialist Workers Party as an anti-capitalist and in the Black Church as a Pentecostal. As I left America as a "new born" godbody I never had the chance to fully master the 120 lessons; I did, however, take a lot of the lessons I learned in cipher with the godbody and expound on them to co-create with certain of my associates a black theocracy. This book is mainly a union of these three schools for the further empowering of our people.

Recognizing also that the Gods do not like innovation; I concluded that we stand no hope of ever overthrowing white supremacy without making certain changes to our lessons. We will never elevate until we are willing to innovate. And if we were to find that something was emphatically wrong we would be obliged to destroy it and so elevate beyond it, even as we destroy the mathematics of anyone who does not backup their lessons with proof. It is my hope that these lessons, which are mainly based on quotations, can be used by all other new borns to understand how the Gods build, and by godbodies to bring us to a place of true divinity in our ways and actions based on knowledge, wisdom and understanding. True indeed, as the highest form of understanding is love, even so the highest form of love is unconditional, it is by this kind of love that we will be able to elevate beyond local hood heroes to become global superheroes. And never forget, spiritual hells all help illusions develop internally in some lost Asiatic minds. Peace.

The Legacy of the Apostle Paul

Following I will be exploring what I consider to be just concerning the name of Paul, even as the misuse and twisting of his teachings and very revolutionary ideas by that which is called the Pauline school has led to his current notoriety in the world as of capitalistic sensitivities. Choosing instead to consider what in Paul's life and work contains the kernel of his reality and avoiding all otherworldly debates and ideological controversies, I will be, in essence, trying to recapture that social theory that Paul implanted, or tried to implant, into his early followers and associates. It is my hope that in doing this I may return us to the core reality of Paul's general vision for Christianity as a movement and as a society.

Many Christians, especially among Evangelical Charismatics, use the apostle Paul as an excuse to justify their greed. Of all the apostles he has been considered the most liberal, and certainly he needed business affairs to run smoothly as he was also a tentmaker (Act 18: 1-3). But was Paul a father of capitalist thought as many prosperity preachers claim he was?

The West has built a system tailored to imperialistic ends. Fear of failure and fear of having to trust in a mystery god has caused them to seek insurmountable wealth to maintain a healthy and productive lifestyle. They grow fat with material possessions and offer no real help to the poor. They preach prosperity through faith to a poverty ridden mass so that if they do not gain prosperity they obviously do not have the faith to believe they can. They are the rich slavemakers of the poor, who may understand some of the truth but use it to their own advantage, shaming the true and living by claiming they are serving him when they are serving only themselves.

As far as history goes the world cannot afford to maintain the West's system of implacable wealth creation. Competition inevitably turns into conflict, now open, now hidden conflict. It cannot but cause ruin because it is so disorderly and filled with contradictions. As István Mészáros points out, one of the contradictions which will prove to be, and has proven to be in the past, one of capital's absolute limits (capital being the means of production and exchange); is the contradiction between capital's national protectionism and its need to create transnational markets. Capital is of necessity private, personal and nationalistic yet it needs to become international to maintain a prosperous existence. The imperialistic tendencies within capital cause its national manifestation to seek the overpowering of other national capitals; yet it must itself maintain this international dominance to keep from competitive obsolescence.

This contradiction existed during the time of colonialism. At that time, capital's nationalist tendencies triumphed over its internationalist tendencies to a certain extent; which caused the liberation movements to fight for national sovereignty instead of international anarchism. But this internationalist tendency within capitalism has not gone away; instead it has re-emerged as globalized capital; a globalization that has provided fuel for the fire of its critics hostility. This has made the West's agenda for liberal, and indeed neoliberal, politics very difficult.

In the twenty-first century Western civilization has had only two substantial opponents: 1. Post-colonialists and 2. Religious fundamentalists. The post-colonialists are usually anti-imperialists as they were at one time subject to the Western empires in the form of colonialism. For the most part they fear a neo-colonial advance from the West as they hear them preaching globalization, but practicing the subjugation of smaller countries under the national capital, rules and power structure of more modernized countries. Based on the practice of the West, and not their preaching, these countries, having nationalized their governments, go on to nationalize a number of big properties for the native population of their location.

These countries, mostly anti-imperialist, usually believe that all national capital should be held within the nation and shared out among the people of that nation. They are unfortunately too small or weak to fight a substantial war with the neoliberal neo-colonial powers, so as potential profit margins and the possibility of gaining some desired resource could always cause the West to fight if diplomacy ceases to work, threats of overthrow or assassination are usually more than enough to keep them in line or from going too far against the wishes of their Western overlords.

With religious fundamentalism it is a different story. At this time the expansion of Western morals and the globalization of capitalist economies into religiously different countries; and liberalism's extreme lack of morality by the standards held within that country, are causing, and have been causing, the religious communities of those countries to react. So far this has led to Islamist wars between America, the bearers of Western standards, and certain Muslim nations, the keepers of religious purity. They war with America because of liberalism's lack of moral purity, and America fights back because of terrorism's potential threat.

This may explode into world war in the current clash of ideologies; and though America may be the stronger nation, in a battle over morals it cannot win. The immorality of the neo-colonialism and white supremacy they uphold will one day have to give way to a new morality. The 'gods' of the current system are lost in an ideological struggle with each other. Western civilization must snatch up as much of the world in an imperialistic scrabble for territory as it can before these territories begin their own fight back in the form of global war.

If we are to fully understand the apostle Paul in this context it is important to first recognize two things. First, the Judeans of Paul's day were not like the Jews of today. Virtually all Muslims and some enlightened blacks know that the original Judeans were black. Not necessarily dark black, but definitely a kind of dusky bronze black, as it was said by the prophet Ezekiel, "In visions of God brought he me into the land of Israel, and set me upon a very high mountain, by which was as the frame of a city on the south. And he brought me thither, and, behold, there was a man, whose appearance was like the appearance of brass, with a line of flax in his hand, and a measuring reed; and he stood in the gate" (Eze 40: 2,3). Now the word translated here as brass is *nekhosheth*, which actually means copper, thus being in similitude to mahogany, and nowhere near the olive colour most Israelis have today. The implication from this Scripture is that the man is either a man of Israel or an angel of the God of Israel, either way he would have been the colour of the people of Israel.

But if that is the case then why are the current Jews white? According to Arthur Koestler, himself a Hungarian Jew, the majority of Ashkenazi Jews converted in the eighth century from a Turko-Caucasian tribe called the Khazars, and so went on to outnumber the original authentic Jews. Sections of this tribe then migrated to "Poland, Lithuania, Hungary and the Balkans, where they founded that Eastern Jewish community which in its turn became the dominant majority of world Jewry." Many nineteenth century historians and anthropologists knew about the Khazars for decades, but some of them only used this knowledge to further their white supremacist agenda.

However, there were eminent anthropologists like Roland Dixon who had this to say of them, "The Khazar being converted to Judaism in the eighth century, thereafter seem to have spread far and wide to the west and northwest, their modern descendants probably forming the preponderant element among the east European Jews." Moreover, there is further proof that the Ashkenazim were not authentic Jews and thereby had no right to call themselves Semites, as it is written in the Scriptures: "Now these are the generations of the sons of Noah, Shem, Ham, and Japheth: and unto them were sons born after the flood. The sons of Japheth; Gomer, and Magog, and Madai, and Javan, and Tubal, and Meshech, and Tiras. And the sons of Gomer; Ashkenaz, and Riphath, and Togarmah." (Gen 10:1-3.) Ashkenaz was of Japheth.

At the same time, the Sephardim Jews: which are the Jews of Spain, Portugal, the Middle East and North Africa, represent the Jews most likely to have been the stock from which the Messiah and the first century Christians came. These Jews, although being darker than proper Europeans and Arabs, were most likely even darker – that is, they were most likely that bronze black of Ezekiel's vision – in the first century when both Paul and the Messiah walked the earth, as mingling with the Tuareg, the Berbers, the Arabs and the Europeans over the centuries would have definitely lightened their complexion; just like the Egyptians, after centuries of mingling with the Berbers and the Turks, particularly after the migration of the Turks into Egypt in the twelfth century, also lost their much darker complexion seen on the walls and in the paintings of Egypt.

The second thing that must be acknowledged is that the apostle Paul was born a citizen of Rome and therefore had an affinity to the great city and its people. Being born a citizen of the imperial city gave him privileges that would not be afforded to most other people, even white people. The apostle Paul's devotion to white people over against his own black people may make him seem a rather strange subject to start from in defining an already existing black divinity (one that probably would have an aversion to me teaching on this man in the first place) but I feel that the apostle Paul's anti-imperialism is an astonishing example for all black people to begin their own knowledge of self journey.

The apostle Paul's journey to self-discovery is an interesting one. From the biblical accounts we can gather a little information about Paul's life before he became a Christian. Paul was born Saul in the city of Tarsus in modern day Turkey, a Benjamite Judean, who was most likely black; and a citizen of the city of Rome. From this information we can gather that Paul was bought up in a middle class family from two places; the fact that he was born a citizen of Rome even though he was Judean and the fact that Tarsus was famed by early authors such as Strabo for being a very wealthy place filled with intellectuals as well as aristocrats. Saul then obviously went on to learn Judaism as well as philosophy in school, which we can gather from his letters' almost Platonian style. Saul was bought up a Pharisee. And although he was born in Tarsus, the accounts in Acts say he was bought up in Jerusalem and was taught in the way of the Torah by Rabbi Gamaliel. So Saul apparently had a good Judaic upbringing from Tarsus to Jerusalem. And from Paul's own testimony we find that he also persecuted the church when it first began in Jerusalem.

This same Saul, as most Christians would know, was converted because while he was on his way to Damascus to persecute the Christians there, he received a vision of the risen Messiah and was blinded. Then, it was a Christian who opened his eyes to see again, and who converted and baptized him. Saul, after that moment, went through a real humbling. It is very reminiscent of the conversion of Malcolm X, a pimp, a hustler and a thief, who went on to found several Muslim temples in America for the Nation of Islam.

Malcolm's conversion story is a little less well known than that of the apostle Paul's. Malcolm Little was arrested in Boston for theft and was given a ten year sentence. During the majority of his time, of which he served seven years before being paroled to his brother, his family was able to convince him they could get him out of prison. At this time Malcolm had become so depraved that the other inmates called him Satan. He would argue with the correction officers and chaplains and would pretend he forgot his prison number to get put into solitary. Malcolm's Damascus experience is when his brother told him he knew a man, a black man, who had 360° of knowledge. Soon, in a vision Malcolm would see this man as Master Fard Muhammad, the founder of the Nation of Islam. Like with Saul Malcolm was humbled and devoted the rest of his time in prison to studying and learning about the Nation of Islam. By the time he was released he was still not ready yet to preach, but, just like Saul, when the time was right Malcolm could not be stopped.

Malcolm Little was given the name Malcolm X by the Nation of Islam just as Saul was given the name Paul by the messianic community. This messianic community, predominantly black Judeans, predominantly peasant farmers and non-industrialized workers, shared similarities with the early Nation of Islam. Christianity as a movement started out in the lower classes, then it grew to gain aristocrats and merchants, and soon people from all walks of life. Paul became a poor righteous teacher in the early messianic movement even as Malcolm would become in the Islamic nationalist movement. But none of Paul's teachings say the kind of social system he believed God would approve of. To him the kingdom of God (or Nation of God) was imminent – Malcolm also shared a similar feeling of imminence about the Nation of Islam – so his form of anti-imperialism was not a violent sedition but an ethical progression.

At the height of his influence he wrote to the Roman Church, "I am not ashamed of the gospel of Christ: for it is the power of God unto salvation to everyone that believeth; to the Jew first, and also to the Greek" (Rom 1:16). As, in the apostle Paul's time, the Jews were still predominantly black, when Paul says things like, "to the Jew first, and also to the Greek", he is actually saying to the black first and also to the white, he is naming the full spectrum of racial orientation. The apostle Paul was a black man and as a black man he understood the realities of a black struggle. The sufferings he experienced as a Judean in imperial Rome were the sufferings of a black man in a white world system.

Malcolm X's understanding of the racial dichotomy is relatively different. Though Malcolm X accepted that in the struggle of the races, the black was first, in his consideration of the white man he felt more sure of their overthrow and judgment. Malcolm X wrote, "The Honorable Elijah Muhammad teaches us that since Western society is deteriorating, it has become overrun with immorality, and God is going to judge it, and destroy it. And the only way the black people caught up in this society can be saved is not to *integrate* into this corrupt society, but to *separate* from it, to a land of our own, where we can reform ourselves, lift up our moral standards, and try to be godly." Thus, the kingdom of God for him was in a separated land where black people could practice Islam freely in unity and godliness.

The apostle Paul's insistence on justice and ethics was also based on his idea that with an imminent kingdom of God judgment would rain down on the enemies of God. In perilous determination he pointed out that not only salvation but also tribulation began with the Jews and continued on to the Greeks. "For the Jews require a sign, and the Greeks seek after wisdom: But we preach Christ crucified, unto the Jews a stumblingblock, and unto the Greeks foolishness; But unto them which are called, both Jews and Greeks, Christ the power of God, and the wisdom of God." Again, where it says wisdom the word is *sophia*, as in philo*sophia* and the word used for power is *dynamis*, as in dynamism. The judgment given to each would be based on their own interpretation of the actuality of God, particularly in his manifestation as the crucified Messiah. Still, this tells us nothing of the desired social programme God, from the apostle Paul's perspective, sought for.

God's expectation of social justice and ethics in ancient Israel is more undeniable as he fought and spoke against any oppressive or self-gratifying practices among the people. Yet during the days of the prophets Israel made itself very rich through these same corrupted and oppressive practices. God said through the prophet Malachi, "And I will come near to you to judgment; and I will be a swift witness against the sorcerers, and against the adulterers, and against false swearers, and against those that oppress the hireling in his wages, the widow, and the fatherless, and that turn aside the stranger from his right, and fear not me, saith the Lord of hosts." In fact, what marked out a prophet or the prophetic was this central theme: the calling of the people from the fear and worship of vanities and idols towards the fear and worship of the one God; that is, the fear of the Lord through the practicing of his law.

Justice and ethics can also be discerned in this, for without law there can be no real justice. Still, that is not to say there is a contradiction, cause though we read in Paul, "The just shall live by faith. And the law is not of faith: but, The man that doeth them shall live in them"; justice by faith also proves to be a vain standard to fear without knowing that in which you are placing your faith. For if you place your faith in vanity to walk after that, the corruption of "sin is at the door" and it will master you. And if you put your faith in the flesh (that is, the material world) to walk after that, "the end thereof is death" and there is no coming back from that.

Therefore the prophets would cry out against practices like defrauding workers of their wages or oppressing strangers, the widow and the fatherless; all practices continued on at a much sharper level within modern Western societies, which have taken the mercantile mentality of the Middle East and turned it into a moralizing principle. But what does the prophet Amos say on this, "Hear this, O ye that swallow up the needy, even to make the poor of the land to fail, Saying, When will the new moon be gone, that we may sell corn? And the sabbath, that we may set forth wheat, making the ephah small, and the shekel great, and falsifying the balances by deceit? That we may buy the poor for silver, and the needy for a pair of shoes; yea, and sell the refuse of the wheat? The Lord hath sworn by the excellency of Jacob, Surely I will never forget any of their works."

But what we know of the apostle Paul's message is concerning the grace of God against the vanity of placing your faith even in good works, as he says to the church in Rome that "if Abraham were justified by works, he hath whereof to glory; but not before God. For what saith the scripture? Abraham believed God, and it was counted unto him for righteousness." (Rom 4:2,3.) But this saying was written to build up faith against fear; not against the total practice of just works, let alone of those unto God; and was meant to be an anchor to the weak who felt the sting of God's wrath upon them if they failed to keep his law. To show the ethical standard by which the apostle Paul felt justified he explains again, "For by grace are ye saved through faith; and that not of yourselves: it is the gift of God: Not of works, lest any man should boast. For we are his workmanship, created in

Christ Jesus *unto good works*, which God hath before ordained that we should walk in them" (emphasis mine).

Minister Malcolm X also had a predilection toward good works comprehending, "The black man in the ghettoes...has to start self-correcting his own material, moral and spiritual defects and evils. The black man needs to start his own program to get rid of drunkenness, drug addiction, prostitution. The black man in America has to lift up his own sense of values." He also recognized that it is the extent of our self-awareness that allows us to come to the full conclusion of our place in society: "My black brothers and sisters – *no* one will know *who* we are...until *we* know who we are! We never will be able to *go* anywhere until we know *where* we are! The Honorable Elijah Muhammad is giving us a true identity, and a true position – the first time they have ever been *known* to the American black man!" Thus the consideration of the black predicament is based on the self-awareness of black people as to their condition.

"For as many of you as have been baptized into Christ have put on Christ. There is neither Jew nor Greek, there is neither bond nor free, there is neither male nor female: for ye are all one in Christ Jesus." This exclamation of the apostle Paul's is a contextual mantra that eliminates all oppositions in the world: the ever faithful Manichaean conflict. With regard to the question of male and female the apostle Paul writes, "Husbands, love your wives, even as Christ also loved the church, and gave himself for it; That he might sanctify and cleanse it with the washing of water by the word, That he might present it to himself a glorious church, not having spot, or wrinkle, or any such thing; but that it should be holy and without blemish."

Malcolm X did not lose any of this in his own consideration of black women. His understanding was that based on the pathology (sickness) of the black man toward disregarding his black woman. We have not protected her, we have not cared for her, we have not honoured her. Malcolm X felt such things were a direct course to our own enfeeblement, "The Honorable Elijah Muhammad teaches us that the black man is going around saying he wants respect; well, the black man never will get anybody's respect until he first learns to respect his own woman! The black man needs *today* to stand up and throw off the weaknesses imposed upon him by the slavemaster white man! The black man needs to start today to shelter and protect and *respect* his black woman!"

But the apostle Paul also understood that for women to be respected they also had to be worthy of it. He gives an allusion to this when he writes to the predominantly female Philippian Church, saying: "Let this mind be in you, which was also in Christ Jesus: Who, being in the form of God, thought it not robbery to be equal with God: But made himself of no reputation, and took upon him the form of a servant, and was made in the likeness of men: And being found in fashion as a man, he humbled himself, and became obedient unto death, even the death of the cross." The apostle Paul was saying, in essence, that his female friends in Philippi should humble themselves, even as the Messiah humbled himself; and seek that better part that comes only from God.

As the apostle Paul's main following among the Philippians was female I feel he saw humility as a necessary attribute for them to possess. This can also be seen as an interpretation of the words of the prophet Isaiah, who said,

> "Moreover the Lord saith, Because the daughters of Zion are haughty, and walk with stretched forth necks and wanton eyes, walking and mincing as they go, and making a tinkling with their feet: Therefore the Lord will smite with a scab the crown of the head of the daughters of Zion, and the Lord will discover their secret parts." But "Fear not; for thou shalt not be ashamed: neither be thou confounded; for thou shalt not be put to shame: for thou shalt forget the shame of thy youth, and shalt not remember the reproach of thy widowhood any more. For thy Maker is thine husband; the Lord of hosts is his name... For a small moment have I forsaken thee; but with great

mercies will I gather thee. In a little wrath I hid my face from thee for a moment; but with everlasting kindness will I have mercy on thee, saith the Lord thy redeemer."
"O thou afflicted, tossed with tempest, and not comforted, behold, I will lay thy stones with fair colours, and lay thy foundations with sapphires. And I will make thy windows of agates, and thy gates of carbuncles, and all thy borders of pleasant stones. And all thy children shall be taught of the Lord; and great shall be the peace of thy children. In righteousness shalt thou be established: thou shalt be far from oppression; for thou shalt not fear: and from terror; for it shall not come near thee."

In all this we see again, the outpouring of the grace of God upon his people; for though these things are not of physical manifestation they are of symbolic. And if God has given these precious promises to a fallen and forsaken women, that they should have the beautiful and precious hope of peace and righteousness. And if this righteousness God promised is by that, his promise, then, in essence, it is not by any choice or action on their part but, as the apostle Paul also taught, it is a gift of God. For the grace manifested by God to the sinner is of his own doing, in that he loves them and desires to save them. But as Paul continues to the Roman Church, "What then? shall we sin, because we are not under the law, but under grace? God forbid. Know ye not, that to whom ye yield yourselves servants to obey, his servants ye are to whom ye obey; whether of sin unto death, or of obedience unto righteousness?" (Rom 6: 15,16.) And inasmuch then as righteousness must be the righteousness of God, it must not be that of the world or of the standards of the world. And if God, in his righteousness, was able to judge as sin that which he deemed as sin according to his own ethical interpretation then we find him all the more able to redeem from sin those whom he finds to be of genuine spirit.

But the grace and righteousness of God are by sincere design, for saving any person or group of persons makes them blameless with regards to legal precedent in an instant; and to be legally blameless is to be ethically exemplified. This exemplary behaviour, now proving to be of right and exact proportions, creates a new standard in society that destroys all old standards that came before allowing for the new group to exist to itself in its own right. At this point the advice given by Rosa Luxemburg is also exemplary, "Socialism will not and cannot be created by decrees; nor can it be established by any government, however socialistic. Socialism must be created by the masses..." Also acknowledging, "A leader in the grand style does not adapt his tactics to the momentary moods of the masses, but rather to the iron laws of development; he holds fast to his tactics in spite of all 'disappointments' and, for the rest, calmly allows history to bring its work to maturity."

Though the words Isaiah spoke to the women of Zion carried promises of beauty and of righteousness, of peace and of betrothal; indeed, that oppression and terror would be banished from their land; even so, these things are only figurative and not of literal interpretation. The great God in his grace has redeemed us from oppression and fear, but only in accordance to our acceptance of his figurative interpretation; for these precious promises are fulfilled only figuratively, that is, in the symbolic sense; for they make no sense without symbolic interpretation. In the symbolic sense there is no oppression or terror in Zion; in the symbolic sense Zion has foundations of sapphires and gems; and in the symbolic sense Zion is betrothed to her Maker as to a husband; for all these gifts they received by faith.

Regarding the question of bond and free we see the obvious question of slavery. This is where the apostle Paul *appears* to differ substantially from Malcolm X; but upon closer examination the two are not that far apart. Although in the Scriptures the apostle Paul says: "Servants, be obedient to them that are your masters according to the flesh, with fear and trembling, in singleness of your heart, as unto Christ; Not with eyeservice, as menpleasers; but as the servants of Christ, doing the will of God from the heart; With good will doing service, as to the Lord, and not to men: Knowing that whatsoever good thing any man doeth, the same shall he receive of the Lord, whether he be bond or free." He also said, "And we beseech you, brethren, to know them which labour among you, and are over you in the Lord, and admonish you; And to esteem them very highly in love for their work's sake. And be at peace among yourselves."

The apostle Paul was not encouraging slavery, he was encouraging work. The imminence of the kingdom of God to him was not cause enough to stop their secular lives. Malcolm X states in agreement, "No Muslim who followed Elijah Muhammad could dance, gamble, date, attend movies, or sports, or take long vacations from work. Muslims slept no more than health required. Any domestic quarreling, any discourtesy, especially to women, was not allowed. No lying or stealing, and no insubordination to civil authority, except on the grounds of religious obligation."

The obvious correlation here between the ideas and hopes of the Nation of Islam and Paul's conviction that the Church of God should admire those who work is intriguing. The apostle Paul also exemplifies it in his second letter to the Thessalonians, "Now we command you, brethren, in the name of our Lord Jesus Christ, that ye withdraw yourselves from every brother that walketh disorderly, and not after the tradition which he received of us. For yourselves know how ye ought to follow us...For even when we were with you, this we commanded you, that if any would not work, neither should he eat." Again, though this expresses his organizing of the messianic movement into a class structure; is there any idea more impressed upon a person than this within this current capitalist system?

In that sense how would the apostle Paul feel about the work ethic within the capitalist system? I personally do not think Paul meant that all non-workers should never eat at all, just that work was to be an inescapable reality within the messianic movement and society as a whole. The apostle Paul wanted to end the disorder among the Christians, particularly those in Thessalonica, who were becoming busybodies, as can be seen when you read a little further down,

"For we hear that there are some which walk among you disorderly, working not at all, but are busybodies. Now them that are such we command and exhort by our Lord Jesus Christ, that with quietness they work, and eat their own bread." This point is also made clear in his first letter to them, stating, "And that ye study to be quiet, and to do your own business, and to work with your own hands, as we commanded you; That ye may walk honestly toward them that are without, and that ye may have lack of nothing."

And as the prophets used to cry out in their day, "These are the things that ye shall do; Speak ye every man the truth to his neighbour; execute the judgment of truth and peace in your gates: And let none of you imagine evil in your hearts against his neighbour; and love no false oath:" "Wash you, make you clean; put away the evil of your doings from before mine eyes; cease to do evil; Learn to do well; seek judgment, relieve the oppressed, judge the fatherless, plead for the widow." For the God of ancient Israel and the God of early Christianity was a practical God. He also goes on to say through his prophet Zechariah, "Thus speaketh the Lord of hosts, saying, Execute true judgment, and shew mercy and compassions every man to his brother: And oppress not the widow, nor the fatherless, the stranger, nor the poor; and let none of you imagine evil against his brother in your heart"; so that the justice and compassion of God may be revealed in the earth; so that the widow and the fatherless, the stranger and the poor may be saved from the hand of cruel and unrighteous people; so that God's special attention shown to these groups may not go unnoticed.

Even so, the apostle Paul obviously also had no problem with these groups among non-workers receiving their daily bread and services from those who had the power to give; for when given his commission from the other apostles, as he said to the Galatians, "Only they would that we should remember the poor; the same which I also was forward to do." He even said to the Ephesians, "Let him that stole steal no more: but rather let him labour, working with his hands the thing which is good, *that he may have to give to him that needeth*" (emphasis mine); plainly showing his concern for the genuinely poor and needy, and for the establishment of a work ethic.

Again, in a modern society these four groups would be called: the single parent and single parent families, foreign migrants and the unemployed non-workers. These four groups make up the current underclass, and are the most marginalized class of all historical episodes. This is why, even though society tends to not care for them, God cares for them and sees their sufferings. As we can see, God sent his prophets and apostles to speak specifically for them and stand up for their cause.

In modern society it is a different story. Here it is political ideologues who fight for such individuals. Among them Rosa Luxemburg felt particularly compelled to promote these issues, stating "A general requirement to work for all who are able to do so, from which small children, the aged and sick are exempted, is a matter of course in a socialist economy", but still, "The public at large must provide forthwith for those unable to work – not like now with paltry alms but with generous provision, socialized child-raising, enjoyable care for the elderly, public health care for the sick, etc." This general requirement to work, being not too dissimilar from Paul's and Malcolm's, shows that the idea of people having to work is not simply a religious idea but exists within the socialist framework too. The work ethic is and will be necessary within the theocratic movement as well, giving us the chance to make a reasonable contribution to our society and our communities.

Now, it may seem strange that a ghetto theodicy should back "a general requirement to work", but street lifers – all street lifers – do work. The work ethic is already in the streets, they are just unable to find legitimate work they are able to do. All thugs and gangsters retire from the illegal life as soon as they can find fulfilling legitimate work. If it is not fulfilling they usually return to the illegal life. For which cause, Paul said again to the church at Rome, "There is therefore now no condemnation to them which are in Christ Jesus, who walk not after the flesh, but after the Spirit. For the law of the

Spirit of life in Christ Jesus hath made me free from the law of sin and death. For what the law could not do, in that it was weak through the flesh, God sending his own Son in the likeness of sinful flesh, and for sin, condemned sin in the flesh: That the righteousness of the law might be fulfilled in us, who walk not after the flesh, but after the Spirit." (Rom 8:1-4.)

This statement takes on new bounds when one replaces Paul's use of the word sin with the word crime, which is how the first century readers would have interpreted it. Here the Spirit is a privilege given to the lost to escape a life of crime and enter a life of righteousness according to the law. But while the Spirit frees us from the legal requirement, according to Paul's gospel, it still does not free us completely from just works; for we find the prophet Ezekiel crying out for God:

> "Behold, all souls are mine; as the soul of the father, so also the soul of the son is mine: the soul that sinneth, it shall die. But if a man be just, and do that which is lawful and right, And hath not eaten upon the mountains, neither hath lifted up his eyes to the idols of the house of Israel, neither hath defiled his neighbour's wife, neither hath come near to a menstruous woman, And hath not oppressed any, but hath restored to the debtor his pledge, hath spoiled none by violence, hath given his bread to the hungry, and hath covered the naked with a garment; He that hath not given forth upon usury, neither hath taken any increase, that hath withdrawn his hand from iniquity, hath executed true judgment between man and man, Hath walked in my statutes, and hath kept my judgments, to deal truly; he is just, he shall surely live, saith the Lord God."

Now this kind of justice and ethics, this very practical form of justice and ethics; is God's form of justice and ethics. That God could see justice and righteousness in such base and basic ideas shows that the great God is beyond what we have thus far assumed of him. Still, as we know, modern Western society has no concept of these practices nor does it even recognize any of these as having ethical variation or orientation. Modernity sees justice and ethics in the liberal and the popular. In fact, popular opinion is the main standard of justice and ethics in most modern societies. Here society, in its perpetual excuses and blockages, keeps itself from its own redemption, but the class of the righteous taking their stand will ultimately bring society to its own liberation through their own iron determination.

Paul, usually believed to be anti-Semitic and against the Jews, does say to the Romans, "For I could wish that myself were accursed from Christ for my brethren, my kinsmen according to the flesh: Who are Israelites; to whom pertaineth the adoption, and the glory, and the covenants, and the giving of the law, and the service of God, and the promises; Whose are the fathers, and of whom as concerning the flesh Christ came, who is over all, God blessed for ever. Amen" (Rom 9:3-5). Malcolm X also saw a divine calling on black people, saying in his own time, "We believe that the miserable plight of America's twenty million black people is the fulfillment of divine prophecy. We also believe the presence today in America of The Honorable Elijah Muhammad, his teachings among the so-called Negroes, and his naked warning to America concerning her treatment of these so-called Negroes, is all the fulfillment of divine prophecy."

The American blacks were lost in a sea of confusion having no means of achieving success in a world designed against them. Malcolm X felt that these struggling black people just needed to learn the right course, saying "The American black man should be focusing his every effort toward building his own businesses, and decent homes for himself. As other ethnic groups have done, let the black people, wherever possible, however possible, patronize their own kind, hire their own kind, and start in those ways to build up the black race's ability to do for itself."

The apostle Paul's social theory bares some similarities here as he felt that the church should take care of their own too. His statement to the church at Corinth articulates this idea, "Who goeth a warfare any time at his own charges? who planteth a vineyard, and eateth not of the fruit thereof?...he that ploweth should plow in hope;...he that thresheth in hope should be partaker of his hope. If we have sown unto you spiritual things, is it a great thing if we shall reap your carnal things?" Here the apostle Paul is stating very plainly that the early messianic movement, which was still predominantly a black movement, should take care of its own. He was also showing and proving, like Malcolm X, that it is quite respectable for the people of God to provide for their own ministers instead of waiting on some other people to provide for them. And one thing is definitely sure, if the messianic movement raised any funds, those funds were reaped and shared out among the brothers and sisters.

The unobvious thing, however, is: this is not only an open endorsement for material gain from a poor righteous teacher, it could also be one for private ownership, and thus for capitalism. So, should we black people be socialistic seeking organized common ownership of industry or capitalistic seeking competitive private ownership of industry? Consequently, Paul never mentions communal ownership in his letters, although it is implied in that in the early messianic movement all things were owned communally. Based on the above quoted letter, if someone owns a business they have the right to reap the material profits thereof. This is not only the general idea Malcolm X was striving to make clear, it is also the central argument of capitalism. Again, what did Paul and Malcolm really have in mind when they recounted their capitalistic ideas? Did Paul and Malcolm really care for big business enterprises? Another question that comes out of this letter is whether preachers, pastors and ministers have the right to be rich at all. Surely, according to what we have learned so far from this chapter they do.

Well, to the first question, the apostle Paul was speaking this argument in favour of the worker not in favour of the capitalist non-worker; we can tell by this statement, "Now to him that worketh is the reward not reckoned of grace, but of debt." Thus he shows that when somebody works they deserve to reap the benefits thereof.

Then again, we must not forget some of the more feudalistic ideas he espoused in the above, "who planteth a vineyard, and eateth not of the fruit thereof?" Surely, it is the capitalists and the feudal lords who own the vineyard and the workers who merely work it?

When the apostle Paul says, "he that ploweth should plow in hope;" he is saying in essence that the worker, the one who works the plow, should receive of what he has worked. The feudal lord is not considered for he says in a letter to Timothy, "The husbandman that *laboureth* must be first partaker of the fruits" (emphasis mine). I see the apostle Paul as talking here about those who plant *and* work the vineyard, because somewhere else he says "every man shall bear his own burden." So he was essentially saying that the person who works the vineyard is worthy of its fruits.

The importunity of the initial question also opens up a general insistence by the preachers of prosperity: There is a seed time and a harvest time. Those who wish to harvest must sow the right seeds. One who sows into financial success through their tithes and offerings will reap financial success in their lives and businesses. This is an obvious vulgarization of what the apostle Paul said to the Galatians, "Be not deceived; God is not mocked: for whatsoever a man soweth, that shall he also reap." The trouble is these preachers fail to read further on, where it says; "For he that soweth to his flesh shall of the flesh reap corruption; but he that soweth to the Spirit shall of the Spirit reap life everlasting."

The apostle Paul and Malcolm X only sought for the general improvement of their people, not the creation of an elite among their people. Yet it could still be asked, where did their hearts truly lie in their respective programmes? Firstly, the apostle Paul was not blind to the suffering of his people but sought all the more for their unification to God, saying "Brethren, my heart's desire and prayer to God for Israel is, that they might be saved. For I bear them record that they have a zeal of God, but not according to knowledge" (Rom 10:1,2), as he wrote to the Roman Church. Malcolm X saw this lack of knowledge in the black community as our greatest weakness, saying

"My homemade education gave me, with every additional book that I read, a little bit more sensitivity to the deafness, dumbness and blindness that was afflicting the black race in America."

Concerning the leaders in our community becoming rich or receiving a large amount of money for preaching the gospel, the apostle Paul does say you should give to preachers of the word, acknowledging "Now ye Philippians know also, that in the beginning of the gospel, when I departed from Macedonia, no church communicated with me as concerning giving and receiving, but ye only. For even in Thessalonica ye sent once and again unto my necessity." So the apostle Paul felt that community leaders and preachers were worthy of pay, even as any worker is worthy of pay.

There is nothing wrong with leaders and preachers getting paid for administering truth, but there are some who would prey on the gullible so as to beguile them out of their money. The apostle Paul said of such people they are lost, drowned in the "Perverse disputing of men of corrupt minds, and destitute of the truth, supposing that gain is godliness". Godliness is not a measure of financial gain. Godliness is in living a righteous lifestyle. How can the working and underclass people possibly sow their way out of financial difficulty without any capital or assets of their own to sow into? God blesses what you have, but if you have no assets or capital then your blessing will gain you nothing?

Still, perhaps the most powerful argument the prosperity preachers have is this Scripture oft quoted by them, "For ye know the grace of our Lord Jesus Christ, that, though he was rich, yet for your sakes he became poor, that ye through his poverty might be rich." What makes this Scripture so complicated is the fact that we know most of the people in the early messianic movement were poor. Whether he was talking about spiritual wealth or material we do not know for sure, but it is more likely, considering the context in which it was written, that he was talking about material. So, is this statement a bold faced assertion of Paul's to material prosperity, and if so to capitalist standards and a capitalist class. To be sure, this is the clearest socio-economic statement the apostle Paul makes; the others are all vague or out of place.

To grasp fully what Paul was trying to convey let us look at the verses preceding this one to make sense of its context. The apostle Paul says here in his second letter to Corinth, "Moreover, brethren, we do you to wit of the grace of God bestowed on the churches of Macedonia; How that in a great trial of affliction the abundance of their joy and their deep poverty abounded unto the riches of their liberality." The apostle Paul is speaking here of the churches of Macedon, which included Philippi, Berea, and Thessalonica, which, although they were poor materially and even in extreme poverty, still gave liberally. But why is the apostle Paul bringing this up? Because he wants the Corinthians to give liberally too, when Titus comes to them.

The apostle Paul continues in verses seven and eight of the same chapter, "Therefore, as ye abound in every thing, in faith, and utterance, and knowledge, and in all diligence, and in your love to us, see that ye abound in this grace also. I speak not by commandment, but by occasion of the forwardness of others, and to prove the sincerity of your love." But as we continue on we can find the true social views of Paul staring us in the face: "For I mean not that other men be eased, and ye burdened: But by an equality, that now at this time your abundance may be a supply for their want, that their abundance also may be a supply for your want: that there may be an equality: As it is written, He that had gathered much had nothing over; and he that had gathered little had no lack." So that now we see in a nutshell the apostle Paul's real social philosophy, which absolutely rubbishes the capitalist philosophy. Furthermore, we can see here the apostle Paul stating very plainly his desire for economic equality, and using Old Testament Scripture to back it up.

Moreover, in cases like where the apostle Paul said, "Being enriched in every thing to all bountifulness, which causeth through us thanksgiving to God"; he is not undermining what he previously said about equality, he is merely saying that he feels all people, especially – though not exclusively – Judean people, should have all the things necessary for life, enjoyment and development. The apostle Paul is not here justifying material wealth, and by process of elimination, material poverty. When he says, "Being enriched," he is only endorsing enrichment for the sake of self-development, that God might be thanked in the long run. We can see by the succeeding statement Paul's extreme aversion to material wealth when he says to Timothy, "But they that will be rich fall into temptation and a snare, and into many foolish and hurtful lusts, which drown men in destruction and perdition."

In like manner the apostle Paul also taught the church in Rome, saying "For I speak to you Gentiles, inasmuch as I am the apostle of the Gentiles, I magnify mine office: If by any means I may provoke to emulation them which are my flesh, and might save some of them. For if the casting away of them be the reconciling of the world, what shall the receiving of them be, but life from the dead?" (Rom 11: 13-15.) The apostle Paul's message to the Gentiles was to stir up his own Judean people towards godliness by emulation. The question at this point could therefore be, what about competition? Surely the apostle Paul had no problem with competition for he says, "And every man that striveth for the mastery is temperate in all things. Now they do it to obtain a corruptible crown; but we an incorruptible"?

If Paul had no problem with competitive striving then why should we now? Because striving leads to vainglory and as Paul said to the Philippians, "Let nothing be done through strife or vainglory; but in lowliness of mind let each esteem other better than themselves. Look not every man on his own things, but every man also on the things of others". While Paul admitted that his mission was to provoke his people to jealousy it was not for competition's sake so as to drive them into striving and vainglory but due to the fact that all living creatures learn by osmosis and emulation, and without seeing an incorruptible people how could his own people learn to be an incorruptible people?

Here Paul – like with Dr. Erasmus Darwin, grandfather to Charles Darwin, who, as the thinkers of his time were for the most part of the school of thought espoused by the Enlightenment, thereby making a lot of their "objective" scientific theories based predominantly on the aristocratic prejudices taught beforehand by the Restoration conservatives; the main and best example being Thomas Hobbes – was a real product of his time and of the world of Roman predominance. But where all the Judean revolutionists rebelling against Roman Imperialism incorporated sedition into their vision of overthrowing Rome, Paul incorporated a more socially viable form of anti-imperialism, based on re-educating the Romans.

(The naturalists also sought to re-educate the masses and so had to hide some of their more dangerous ideas, meeting in secret societies for fear of the religious and governmental authorities catching wind of their own Arian and Deist doctrines. Dr. Darwin, himself, considering a kind of evolution theory based entirely on Goethe's theories of nature and Aristotle's theories of man, perhaps achieved the greatest triumph for science by establishing the first of these societies. In actual fact, if there is an Illuminati it is most likely to be an outgrowth of Dr. Darwin's scientific gathering called the Lunar Society.)

Nineteenth century Russian geographer and social scientist Peter Kropotkin explains concerning the school of Charles Darwin his grandson, that, "They all endeavoured to prove that Man, owing to his higher intelligence and knowledge, *may* mitigate...the struggle for life between men;...that the struggle for the means of existence, of every animal against all its congeners, and of every man against all other men, [is] 'a law of Nature'", but we should also be able to see how in nature a body's unity can be the basis for its continuity. With such being a far more ultimate rule of nature than any struggles for existence, whether in species form or in the form of class or gender, we find an acceptable means of finding our own place within the natural framework.

Still, in spite of Paul's hope for Judean unity and salvation through emulation we must remember that the apostle Paul did not seek favour among the rich Judeans. Malcolm X also had no tolerance for the concept of a black bourgeoisie but believed only in black empowerment, as he said again "it is those few bourgeois Negroes, rushing to throw away their little money in the white man's luxury hotels, his swanky nightclubs, and big, fine, exclusive restaurants... proving they're integrated." Such concerns were far from Malcolm X. But Malcolm was not speaking here for segregation either, as he explained to his critics, "We reject *segregation* even more militantly than you say you do! We want *separation*, which is not the same!... To *segregate* means to control. Segregation is that which is forced upon inferiors by superiors. But *separation* is that which is done voluntarily, by two equals – for the good of both! The Honorable Elijah Muhammad teaches us that as long as our people here in America are dependent upon the white man, we will always be begging him for jobs, food, clothing and housing. And he will always control our lives, regulate our lives, and have power to segregate us."

Malcolm X is effectively stating here a desire for black people in America to have self-determination; a right given to every nationality who has fought for it. For this cause he championed the idea of black separation from the United States in their own struggle of liberation. "America is a colonial power...She's a twentieth-century colonial power; she's a modern colonial power, and she has colonized twenty-two million African-Americans." "Since the twenty-two million of us were originally Africans, who are now in America not by choice but only by a cruel accident in our history, we strongly believe that African problems are our problems and our problems are African problems." But, "We pray that our African brothers have not freed themselves of European colonialism only to be overcome and held in check by American dollarism. Don't let American racism be 'legalized' by American dollarism." Malcolm X understood here the predicament of the African black person based on his knowledge of America's treatment of the American black person. Malcolm X wanted both to be unified – the African blacks and the American blacks – recognizing that once a common accord was accomplished we would be more powerful as a people.

Kropotkin also, using his own field of expertise, explained how, at least within the animal kingdom, "numberless are those which live in societies, either for mutual defence, or for hunting and storing up food, or for rearing their offspring, or simply for enjoying life in common...though a good deal of warfare goes on between different classes of animals, or different species, or even different tribes of the same species, peace and mutual support are the rule within the tribe or the species; and that those species which best know how to combine and to avoid competition, have the best chances of survival and of a further progressive development."

Moreover, Kropotkin also states, "When I explored the Vitim regions in the company of so accomplished a zoologist as my friend Polyakoff [...] We both were under the fresh impression of the *Origin of Species*, but we vainly looked for the keen competition between animals of the same species which the reading of Darwin's work had prepared us to expect...We saw plenty of adaptations for struggling, very often in common, against the adverse circumstances of climate, or against various enemies,...but even in the Amur and Usuri regions, where animal life swarms in abundance, facts of real competition and struggle between higher animals of the same species came very seldom under my notice, though I eagerly searched for them." And again, speaking on Darwin's *The Descent of Man* he articulates how: "He [also] pointed out how, in numberless animal societies, the struggle is replaced by co-operation, and how that substitution results in the development of intellectual and moral faculties which secure to the species the best conditions for survival. He intimated that in such cases the fittest are not the physically strongest, nor the cunningest, but those who learn to combine so as mutually to support each other, strong and weak alike, for the welfare of the community."

This idea is also maintained in what could be considered a summary of Kropotkin's views of a human historiography of competition, "It is evident that it would be quite contrary to all that we know of nature...if a creature so defenceless as man was at his beginnings should have found his protection and his way to progress, not in mutual support, like other animals, but in a reckless competition for personal advantages, with no regard to the interests of the species. To a mind accustomed to the idea of unity in nature, such a proposition appears utterly indefensible." Again, "Sociability and need of mutual aid and support are such inherent parts of human nature that at no time of history can we discover men living in small isolated families, fighting each other for the means of subsistence. On the contrary, modern research...proves that since the very beginning of their prehistoric life men used to agglomerate into *gentes*, clans, or tribes, maintained by an idea of common descent and by worship of common ancestors."

Malcolm X also agreed feeling that in like manner the Nation of Islam should be and had to be the agglomeration of black people into a creditable community. "Our businesses sought to demonstrate to black people what black people could do for themselves – if they would only unite, trade with each other – exclusively where possible – and hire each other, and in so doing, keep black money within the black communities, just as other minorities did." These black communities, formulated as an expression not of instinctive aggression, self-interest or some internal need for conquest and power; but in response to the depreciation of the black population in the United States, were to uplift the people and allow us to become a non-colonized people. Obviously, Paul desired the same for the Judean black people; but for all his pragmatism, he was still an idealist, and his vision for black people never actually came into fruition during his own lifetime. Again, even as Malcolm X's anti-imperialism was in setting up a Nation of Islam, so Paul's anti-imperialism was in setting up a kingdom of God.

Yet, a curious puzzle arises from looking deeper at the apostle Paul's social theory that can be used against the idea of co-operation: the fact that the apostle Paul himself identified several different social classes in the church: "And God hath set some in the church, first apostles, secondarily prophets, thirdly teachers, after that miracles, then gifts of healings, helps, governments, diversities of tongues." If the apostle Paul acknowledges several different social classes within the church then who is to say God does not also call for different social classes within society? If there is hierarchy in the church then why can there not be hierarchy in society?

The preachers of prosperity can also cry in unison that the current capitalist system is only natural, in that classes have existed in the messianic movement from its beginnings and have existed in society since civilization began. Although these ideas will be challenged throughout this book, the understanding that Paul, being himself a moderately poor man, would not condone competition nor permit his followers to be inequitable, shows that at least the idea of social justice was a part of Paul's ethical doctrine. However, we see the understanding that some in the church are given higher positions than others, this shows that the faithful, in relation to the church, would play only one role among many.

In his letter to Rome Paul states: "For as we have many members in one body, and all members have not the same office: So we, being many, are one body in Christ, and every one members one of another. Having then gifts differing according to the grace that is given to us, whether prophecy, let us prophesy according to the proportion of faith; Or ministry, let us wait on our ministering: or he that teacheth, on teaching; Or he that exhorteth, on exhortation: he that giveth, let him do it with simplicity; he that ruleth, with diligence; he that sheweth mercy, with cheerfulness" (Rom 12:4-8.)

The fear, however, that Paul's endorsement of social classes within the church is a prelude to capitalism need not be maintained. The apostle Paul's understanding of social class is not one of superiority or one of oppression but merely one of interdependence. The different gifts and positions he speaks of are, in his view, of similitude to that of the human body. Just as some parts of our own body fulfil various tasks and not others, yet the entire body still works in conjunction to the benefit of the whole; even so, the body of messianic disciples (and by extension of society as a whole), should work together for the benefit of all. For though some are skilled for production, others for leading, others for service, and some for manual work, some for selling, while others can retain vast amounts of information and knowledge. All these gifts and abilities were given by God to specific individuals. And just as Paul says, "If the ear shall say, Because I am not the eye, I am not of the body; is it therefore not of the body? If the whole body were an eye, where were the hearing? If the whole were hearing, where were the smelling?" So we should not dismiss ourselves from the church or society due to our own inadequacies.

We can see here, through the analogy of the body, certain aspects of Paul's sociological views about life and nature; that though the analogy dates back to Plato Paul had an interdependence view of the functionings of society long before Durkheim made it popular. This view and understanding of the interconnection of the one part of the body to all the others, and their relation to how well the body functions as a whole, would effectively allow for those within the messianic movement to adopt traditions of solidarity and brotherhood that transcended race, class and gender, and even transcended the ages. It is this holistic view of interconnection that would also lay the ground work for future social and biological theorists throughout Christian history.

With this thus appreciated our relation to each other becomes no longer based on race, though race, class and gender will still exist; but on mutual interaction and support. Thus the apostle Paul was trying, in essence, to build among his followers strong chords of brotherhood. These chords would effectively allow them to escape the excesses of race, class and gender politics to become one family in the Messiah.

The economic aspect of the apostle Paul's social programme and ideas for the messianic movement was that goods, services and information should be distributed among the brothers and sisters based not on charge but on need. That if a brother within the church has a need they should make known their need to their fellow brother or sister based on what was needed. And so the eye, needing the help of the hand to see better communicates this information to the hand, who in turn provides the service. This service, for the sake of equality, is provided free of charge as the server will soon or some other time require a service from she whom she has just served.

From this we see that all labour: whether cultural, intellectual, technical, industrial, martial, social or sexual; is a service to the benefit of the whole of society and of the church. Consequently, by abolishing money we ultimately also remove that 'mediating devise' that currently blocks one person from another and turns us all into consumers. Thereby the body becomes a fully justified analogy in the full expression of economic equality to be reached from such a decision. The eyes do not pay the hand for helping them to see better. Altogether, interconnection lays the path for interdependence, which is unequivocally the definition of society the apostle Paul believed God desired for black people and for the messianic movement.

Another argument that could be used to say that the apostle Paul would at least have been an apologist for white supremacy found in the letter to the Romans is where he says, "Wherefore ye must needs be subject, not only for wrath, but also for conscience sake. For for this cause pay you tribute also: for they are God's ministers, attending continually upon this very thing. Render therefore to all their dues: tribute to whom tribute is due; custom to whom customs; fear to whom fear; honour to whom honour. Owe no man any thing, but to love one another: for he that loveth another hath fulfilled the law." (Rom 13:5-8.)

We find here a general theme articulated throughout the Old Testament. The prophets cried out for justice in human dealings and interchange and against the iniquities and inequities of unsociable behaviours and individuals. They said, "Woe to them that devise iniquity, and work evil upon their beds! when the morning is light, they practise it, because it is in the power of their hand. And they covet fields, and take them by violence; and houses, and take them away: so they oppress a man and his house, even a man and his heritage." "Woe to him that increaseth that which is not his! how long? and to him that ladeth himself with thick clay! Shall they not rise up suddenly that shall bite thee, and awake that shall vex thee, and thou shalt be for booties unto them?" "Woe to him that coveteth an evil covetousness to his house, that he may set his nest on high, that he may be delivered from the power of evil! Thou hast consulted shame to thy house by cutting off many people, and hast sinned against thy soul."

But what we have read from the apostle Paul could also be used by these same covetous to say that we godbodies have a duty to give due respect to this current white system, even as it was used by Roman Catholicism to say the same thing of the Roman Empire. God is the one who ordained its power so it is only ours to give them their due of tribute and submission. The condemnation for such ideas is levelled against white supremacy by Malcolm X in his fiery anti-imperialist retorts: "the American racists know that they can rule...the African American, only as long as we have a negative image of ourselves". And again, "The white man so guilty of white supremacy can't hide his guilt by trying to accuse The Honorable Elijah Muhammad of teaching black supremacy and hate! All Mr Muhammad is doing is trying to uplift the black man's mentality and the black man's social and economic condition in this country."

The apostle Paul's own anti-imperialism was one of psychological significance: "For though we walk in the flesh, we do not war after the flesh: (For the weapons of our warfare are not carnal, but mighty through God to the pulling down of strong holds;) Casting down imaginations, and every high thing that exalteth itself against the knowledge of God, and bringing into captivity every thought to the obedience of Christ;" "For we wrestle not against flesh and blood, but against principalities, against powers, against the rulers of the darkness of this world, against spiritual wickedness in high places." Yet what is not so clear from these Scriptures is the political significance they carried. A principality is a territory ruled over by a prince, while the Greek word used here for powers is not *dynamis* but *exoysia*, which means jurisdiction. What the apostle Paul is saying in essence is that the messianic movement was a movement against territories ruled over by actually existing authorities, against the literal rulers of this dark world maintained by corruption.

Again, the word used for imaginations is *logismos*, which basically means logic or reasoning. In casting down the reasoning of princes and authorities debate was to be the major weapon. Here the apostle Paul is challenging the Roman imperial powers through sound logic. To him the messianic movement is to represent an ethical entity so just that it puts Rome to shame. To explain this system of justice that trumps that of Rome the apostle Paul says in his letter to the Galatians: "brethren, ye have been called unto liberty; only use not liberty for an occasion to the flesh, but by love serve one another. For all the law is fulfilled in one word, even in this; Thou shalt love thy neighbour as thyself"; a gospel that was to be taken around the world in the spreading of the kingdom of God.

The stand up call to fight for our liberation is truly noble and efficacious. With the overriding conclusion to reconsider the classification of black people in the world, an anti-imperial struggle of the sort Paul is here recommending is overtly defiant. True indeed, to love thy neighbour as thyself is the path to divinity and the fulfilment of any law, but it goes against the common expression of government. It makes freedom perceptible. It makes the willingness to fight all the more venerable. As Malcolm X said, "there is a growing tendency among black Americans today, who are able to see that they don't have freedom – they are reaching the point now where they are ready to tell the Man no matter what the odds are against them, no matter what the cost is, it's liberty or death."

Malcolm X did not consider the two races as ever being able to coexist in America. "Why, when all of my ancestors are snake-bitten, and I'm snake-bitten, and I warn my children to avoid snakes, what does that *snake* sound like accusing *me* of hate-teaching?" But Paul in considering black and white in the empire of Rome felt there was the opportunity for unity through the Messiah's sacrifice, "For he is our peace, who hath made of both one, and hath broken down the middle wall of partition between us; Having abolished in his flesh the enmity, even the law of commandments contained in ordinances; for to make in himself of twain one new man, so making peace."

This argument is shown all the more credible by the words of Paul to the Roman Church: "Now I say that Jesus Christ was a minister of the circumcision for the truth of God, to confirm the promises made unto the fathers: And that the Gentiles might glorify God for his mercy; as it is written, For this cause I will confess to thee among the Gentiles, and sing unto thy name. And again he saith, Rejoice, ye Gentiles, with his people. And again, Praise the Lord, all ye Gentiles; and laud him, all ye people. And again, Esaias saith, There shall be a root of Jesse, and he that shall rise to reign over the Gentiles; in him shall the Gentiles trust" (Rom 15:8-12); this one is of particular interest to us here for, to give a more in-depth quotation:

> "And there shall come forth a rod out of the stem of Jesse, and a Branch shall grow out of his roots: And the spirit of the Lord shall rest upon him....And righteousness shall be the girdle of his loins, and faithfulness the girdle of his reins. The wolf also shall dwell with the lamb, and the leopard shall lie down with the kid; and the calf and the young lion and the fatling together; and a little child shall lead them. And the cow and the bear shall feed; their young ones shall lie down together: and the lion shall eat straw like the ox. And the sucking child shall play on the hole of the asp, and the weaned child shall put his hand on the cockatrice' den. They shall not hurt nor destroy in all my holy mountain; for the earth shall be full of the knowledge of the Lord, as the waters cover the sea. And in that day there shall be a root of Jesse, which shall stand for an ensign of the people; to it shall the Gentiles seek" (Is 11:1-10).

The union of animals and people that anticipates the kingdom of God upon the earth is, in essence, a learning of interconnected brotherhood and communal support and interdependence. These figurative realities, however, are not that far from the truth of nature;

for as the apostle James said, "every kind of beasts, and of birds, and of serpents, and of things in the sea, is tamed, and hath been tamed of mankind" (Jm 3: 7). Kropotkin also reminds us, "Association is found in the animal world at all degrees of evolution; and, according to the grand idea of Herbert Spencer, so brilliantly developed in Perrier's *Colonies Animales*, colonies are at the very origin of evolution in the animal kingdom. But, in proportion as we ascend the scale of evolution, we see association growing more and more conscious. It loses its purely physical character, it ceases to be simply instinctive, it becomes reasoned. With the higher vertebrates it is periodical, or is resorted to for the satisfaction of a given want – propagation of the species, migration, hunting, or mutual defence."

Even in a "migration of fallow-deer which I witnessed on the Amur, and during which scores of thousands of these intelligent animals came together from an immense territory, flying before the coming deep snow, in order to cross passed before my eyes, I saw Mutual Aid and Mutual Support carried on to an extent which made me suspect in it a feature of the greatest importance for the maintenance of life, the preservation of each species, and its further evolution."

To which nineteenth century social theorist and Marxist thinker Fredrick Engels, in his debates with the revisionist Eugen Dühring, replies concerning the Darwinian discussion: confessing that "the idea of the struggle for existence...Darwin himself admitted, has to be sought in a generalisation of the views of the economist and theoretician of population, [Thomas] Malthus, and that the idea therefore suffers from all the defects inherent in the priestly Malthusian ideas of over-population." But "the *fact* [that this struggle] exists also among plants can be demonstrated to him by every meadow, every cornfield, every wood; and the question at issue is not what it is to be called, whether 'struggle for existence' or lack of conditions of life and mechanical effects,' but how this fact influences the preservation or variation of species." Effectively proving, not only the obvious fact of struggle in nature by his examples of the cornfield and meadow, but also of mutual aid and mutual interaction. For it is impossible to look at these beautiful expressions of plant life and not see their sociable togetherness and unity, while their invisible struggles and fights for survival and maintenance, though real, are virtually insignificant to the senses.

He then states in a letter to his friend P.L. Lavron, "The whole Darwinist teaching of the struggle for existence is simply a transference from society to living nature of Hobbes's doctrine of *bellum omnium contra omnes* [war of all against all] and of the bourgeois-economic doctrine of competition together with Malthus's theory of population." Claiming, even "In recent times the idea of natural selection was extended,...and the variation of species conceived as a result of the mutual interaction of adaptation and heredity, in which process adaptation is taken as the factor which produces variations, and heredity as the preserving factor."

Again, to him the Darwinian contribution is best summed in what he accomplished for science, "Darwin brought back from his scientific travels the view that plant and animal species are not constant but subject to variation." And this in itself was a remarkable achievement for his time. However, "It is true that in doing this Darwin attributed to his discovery too wide a field of action, made it the sole agent in the alteration of species and neglected the causes of the repeated individual variations, concentrating rather on the form in which these variations become general; but this is a mistake which he shares with most other people who make any real advance."

True indeed, "Animals...change the environment by their activities in the same way, even if not to the same extent, as man does, and these changes...in turn react upon and change those who made them. In nature nothing takes place in isolation. Everything affects and is affected by every other thing," so that, "Even the mere contemplation of previous history as a series of class struggles suffices to make clear the utter shallowness of the conception of this history as a feeble variety of the 'struggle for existence.'" For this cause, "In my opinion, the social instinct was one of the most essential levers of the evolution of man from the ape." (And even though most blacks do not accept the idea that humanity evolved from apes the fossil record is undeniable. The fossils of the earliest hominidae – humanlike beings – bear huge similarities to large primates, while the later ones come closer and closer to humanity as we know them.)

Kropotkin also agrees with Engels by showing how, "Association and mutual aid are the rule with mammals. We find social habits even among the carnivores, and we can only name the cat tribe (lions, tigers, leopards, etc.) as a division the members of which decidedly prefer isolation to society, and are but seldom met with even in small groups. And yet, even among lions 'this is a very common practice to hunt in company.' The two tribes of the civets (*Viverridæ*) and the weasels (*Mustelidæ*) might also be characterized by their isolated life, but it is a fact that during the last century [that is, the nineteenth century] the common weasel was more sociable than it is now". And, "apart from a few exceptions, those birds and mammals which are not gregarious now, were living in societies before man multiplied on the earth and waged a permanent war against them, or destroyed the sources from which they formerly derived food."

To finalize the subject he then states "mutual aid is as much a law of animal life as mutual struggle, but that, as a factor of evolution, it most probably has a far greater importance, inasmuch as it favors the development of such habits and characters as insure the maintenance and further development of the species," for "even in those few spots where animal life teemed in abundance, I failed to find – although I was eagerly looking for it – that bitter struggle for the means of existence, *among animals belonging to the same species*, which was considered by most Darwinists (though not always by Darwin himself) as the dominant characteristic of struggle for life, and the main factor of evolution."

As for Paul's doctrine of races, that is completely different from his doctrine concerning the rich. While he did tolerate the black-white dichotomy of Imperial Rome he did not seem to tolerate the rich. Though at that time far less oppressive than chattel slavery would prove to be in later years, race was not as important to Paul's anti-imperialism as the contradictions of the rich, for which cause he said in his first letter to Timothy, "Charge them that are rich in this world, that they be not highminded, nor trust in uncertain riches, but in the living God, who giveth us richly all things to enjoy; That they do good, that they be rich in good works, ready to distribute, willing to communicate".

So he said basically that the rich should share their wealth willingly and in a spirit of humility; while blacks and whites should learn to see each other as brothers and sisters in God. The rich, in his opinion, should give up their riches and be content with little, for continuing on he says, "But godliness with contentment is great gain. For we brought nothing into this world, and it is certain we can carry nothing out. And having food and raiment let us be therewith content".

So we are now able to see the interrelation between the doctrine of Paul and the practices within the godbody. I find it necessary here then to state that though the godbodies are by personal definition practitioners of Islam we are in actual fact closer to a supra-religious culture; in that we do not hold to the beliefs of any religion, or to the god of any religion. For this cause, I feel that in most, if not all, points we have been denied our constitutional rights under US – and most Western – laws, to freedom of assembly. As practitioners of peaceful assembly, we do not feel, and have not felt, it necessary to tie ourselves down to any particular religion, but to attend whichever religious grouping we feel most connects with our spirit and personal views. And here we are also most vehement, for we are unwilling to sacrifice our own right to freedom of assembly within our own cipher. Our own religious connection is one, not based on formal institutions or dogmas, but one based on how we practice our lessons through culture.

Though ultimately, the major thing that separates us from the mainstream black cultures is not our radical views on sex, violence, knowledge or mathematics; but our respect for and acknowledgment of the prophethood of Muhammad ibn Abd Allah. Most, if not all, Gods in the godbody cipher have come to accept Muhammad as a genuine prophet, and we have also come to acknowledge that that which has been passing as prophetic is in actual fact merely just utterance as given by God's grace, or delusion as given by personal vanity.

The church's current prejudice against Islam and the Prophet Muhammad is based primarily on ignorance. It began as a result of the Crusades and not of any genuine antithesis between doctrines. Islam in its actual essence is itself a Christian sect, and had it have come after the Reformation it would have been seen as no different from the Adventists or the Jehovah's Witnesses. As to the three fundamental difficulties within Islamic Christology: that of his incarnation, death and resurrection; these issues, though troublesome, are no reason at all for the tremendous abuse given to the Muslim world to try to choke them out of existence. The almost genocidal, Islamocidal tendencies within the West to try to destroy completely the Muslim world and Muslim faith is in my view, and I think I speak for the rest of the godbody, disgusting.

As to the final stone of contention, that of Muhammad's prophethood; in the early years of the messianic movement it is well known and understood that several prophets and apostles arose out of the faithful. These pre-Nicaean prophetic movements were unfortunately too dangerous to continue after Nicaea so they were altogether snuffed out by the religious establishment of the time. Those who chose to maintain this authentic legacy were thus forced to retreat into the wilderness of Egypt, the last vestige of spiritual expression, to join one of their monasteries. Then finally, at the fall of Rome, Christian spirituality and prophecy was eradicated completely from the movement, as was anything in any ways contrary to the orthodox Catholic views, as Gnostic or potentially heretical and therefore illegal.

With prophecy outlawed and forbidden in the Western and Eastern Church, God had no choice but to look outside the Church to find one who he could speak to and work through. Thus we can see the hand of God; for Paul says, "Wherefore I give you to understand, that no man speaking by the Spirit of God calleth Jesus accursed: and that no man can say that Jesus is the Lord, but by the Holy Ghost. Now there are diversities of gift, but the same Spirit. And there are differences of administrations, but the same Lord. And there are diversities of operations, but it is the same God which worketh all in all. But the manifestation of the Spirit is given to every man to profit withal. For to one is given by the Spirit the word of wisdom; to another the word of knowledge by the same Spirit; To another faith by the same Spirit; to another the gifts of healing by the same Spirit; To another the working of miracles; to another prophecy;" all by the same Spirit and based on the same standard.

Now when the apostle Paul says, "no man can say that Jesus is the Lord, but by the Holy Ghost", he here shows that prophecy, one of the gifts of the Holy Ghost, is identifiable through acknowledging the Messiah's dominion. To carry this idea a little further the apostle John says in the book of Revelations that "the testimony of Jesus is the spirit of prophecy." (Rev 19:10.) But the basis of the idea itself comes to us from what occurred when the Messiah was at home speaking with his disciples, "And John answered him, saying, Master, we saw one casting out devils in thy name, and he followeth not us: and we forbad him, because he followeth not us. But Jesus said, Forbid him not: for there is no man which shall do a miracle in my name, that can lightly speak evil of me. For he that is not against us is on our part. For whosoever shall give you a cup of water to drink in my name, because ye belong to Christ, verily I say unto you, he shall not lose his reward" (Mk 9:38-41). So the question now remains, what was Muhammad's view of Jesus? According to the Maulana Muhammad Ali translation of the Quran Muhammad said, "We gave Jesus, son of Mary, clear arguments and strengthened him with the Holy Spirit. Is it then that whenever there came to you a messenger with what your souls desired not, you were arrogant? And some you gave the lie to and others you would slay" (Quran 2:87).

Again, the apostle John also said in his first general epistle, "I have not written unto you because ye know not the truth, but because ye know it, and that no lie is of the truth. Who is a liar but he that denieth that Jesus is the Christ? He is antichrist, that denieth the Father and the Son", to which the Quran answers, "When the angels said: O Mary, surely Allah gives thee good news with a word from Him (of one) whose name is the Messiah, Jesus, son of Mary, worthy of regard in this world and the Hereafter, and of those who are drawn nigh (to Allah)" (Quran 3:45, 46).

But to make the situation a little more difficult the apostle Paul goes on to say, "But what saith it? The word is nigh thee, even in thy mouth, and in thy heart: that is, the word of faith, which we preach; That if thou shalt confess with thy mouth the Lord Jesus, and shalt believe in thine heart that God hath raised him from the dead, thou shalt be saved" To which the Prophet Muhammad says, "When Allah said: O Jesus, I will cause thee to die and exalt thee in My presence and clear thee of those who disbelieve and make those who follow thee above those who disbelieve to the day of Resurrection. Then to Me is your return, so I shall decide between you concerning that wherein you differ" (Quran 3: 55). Many Muslims, to differentiate themselves from the Christians, have said that this death was not the death on the cross but someone took his place; but I seriously doubt that someone who admired martyrdom like the Prophet meant anything less than the common Christian doctrine. And if he believed that God exalted him after his death then he thereby believed in the Messiah's resurrection.

Concerning his virgin birth by Mary the Prophet also said, "She said: How can I have a son and no mortal has yet touched me, nor have I been unchaste? He said: So (it will be). Thy Lord says: It is easy to Me; and that We may make him a sign to men and a mercy from Us. And it is a matter decreed" (Quran 19: 20, 21). And concerning the Messiah's ministry he said, "I have come to you with a sign from your Lord, that I determine for you out of dust the form of a bird, then I breathe into it and it becomes a bird with Allah's permission, and I heal the blind and the leprous, and bring the dead to life with Allah's permission; and I inform you of what you should eat and what you should store in your houses. Surely there is a sign in this for you, if you are believers" (Quran 3:49).

In all these Scriptures we see not only the genuine prophethood of Muhammad, but also our right to claim Muhammad as one of our prophets. In fact, the only reason Muhammad was rejected from the body of prophets and saints was due to the historical foundations of Catholicism, in which the doctrine of Irenaeus of Lyon was adopted into the body of saintly doctrines. Still, Irenaeus would incorporate ideas of centralized hierarchy, ideological supremacy, Christian patriotism, and intellectual authoritarianism into the Catholic Church; while Muhammad would incorporate ideas of informal structuralism, ideological assimilation, ultra-monotheism, and intellectual development into his vision of the Islamic Mosque.

And so, concluding this beginning of interpretations into what we perceive to be the true, or at least purest and most consistent, perspective of what the early messianic movement presented to their fellowships as a social and ecclesiastical platform of righteous living, I state that this black theocratic movement is in effect a truer representation of that authentic Christian vision and reality. It has been the misinterpreting of this vision by generations of unknowledgeable people that has brought on the doom of modernity.

HISTORICAL PROGRESSION

The historical progression of Western society toward its current modern articulation has its basis in God and in a desire to know God. But if we truly desire to see God in history we must first understand, with the prophet Daniel, that "the Lord our God is righteous in all his works which he doeth" (Dan 9:14). From here we can also see an answer to that false sense of religiosity inherent in many within the religious fold. We who accept the existence of a God (doctrinally the godbodies except the idea that the only God is the Son of Man, nevertheless, in practice most of us godbodies understand that a grand intelligence holds the universe together, and formed from matter everything that exists in the universe through supreme mathematics; we call this force I Self Lord And Master) do tend every now and then to say: "O God, I praise you for who you are!" as though that is the essence of spirituality.

Though we try to accept the existence of a true and living God, we spiritual individuals can tend to abandon truth for appearances without actually meaning what we are saying or even knowing or appreciating what it is we mean. The words of this Scripture convey that it is not the title or expression of God that should be respected and praised but the reality of God, that God is righteous and therefore seeks integrity and not hypocrisy. So theocracy in its black variation represents a form of nationhood in which righteousness is instituted through God's law. We black theocrats currently have one law: the law of righteousness. Righteousness is our law, our God, our king, our enforcer, our purpose, and our destiny.

So the testament God has given us is himself as righteousness; an idea the apostle Paul takes further by saying in his letter to the

Romans, "For as many as have sinned without law shall also perish without law: and as many as have sinned in the law shall be judged by the law; (For not the hearers of the law are just before God, but the doers of the law shall be justified. For when the Gentiles, which have not the law, do by nature the things contained in the law, these, having not the law, are a law unto themselves: Which shew the work of the law written in their hearts, their conscience also bearing witness, and their thoughts the mean while accusing or else excusing one another;) In the day when God shall judge the secrets of men by Jesus Christ according to my gospel." Hence, we have the potential to become temples of the true and living God in which God himself dwells, by carrying within ourselves the presence and fullness of his law.

Following we will be exploring different time periods so as to show the place of God in historical progression from early antiquity to late modernity. We will therefore go through various historical phases of development to show how they affected human relationships with God. For example, as it has come to be appreciated the influential Greek philosopher Plato was taught and trained by the Heliopolitan schools of Khem Ta (which means "black land" but was affectionately then called Kemet, and is now called Egypt). In the Heliopolitan interpretation of science all things were considered interconnected to Ra, who himself was considered the divine essence. Ra in his manifestation as Khepera or Khepru was the transformer of matter in an evolutionary manner. Khepru represented that force which allowed raw materials to transform, evolve and motion through various phases. The realm of his existence, known to the Heliopolitan mystery schools as Pet, would be what we in our day would call phase-space, as it is the realm of all phase transitions.

As stated by Roman historian Strabo: Plato – having studied and learned from these schools for thirteen years in Heliopolis – mastered, in his own somewhat different way, the various sciences and philosophies of the grand masters of Kemet. The final paper, which he wrote at the completion of his studies, was the ground breaking Timaeus, which he reproduced in Greek in his later life and explained it as coming from a debate between Timaeus and Socrates.

The Kemetic mystery schools were second to none in learning, art, culture and science. The centre of all learning was Ra, who represented godhood, knowledge, science and perfection. To the Heliopolitan schools achieving Ra came by a mystical development and understanding of the non-physical, astral realms of Pet and the Dwat (the invisible realms of massless beings). To them Ra, or perfection, was made up of three parts: the *khat* or physical body; the *ba* or life force; and the *ka* or astral body, represented also as the complete or unified being. This school was dialectical and trinitarian in interpretation holding to the understanding that Ra was attainable only by making the three one.

The four rival cosmogonies (or creation myths) of Kemet were the Hermopolitan, the Memphite, the Elephantine and the Theban. To the Hermopolitan schools Ra was attained through a division of four groups of two: Heh and Hehet, the masculine and feminine of infinitude, respectively; Kuk and Kuket, the masculine and feminine of darkness, respectively; Amen and Amenet, the masculine and feminine of spirit, respectively; and Nun and Nunet, the masculine and feminine of ocean, respectively; as they were a school of the binary and dualistic interpretation of life striving for Ra through respecting the laws of duality. To the Memphites Ptah created the worlds through thought and through Heka (magic words); and being the grand architect of the universe, and grand master of all Kemetic grand masters, he created all things by pronouncing his word. In Elephantine, however, which was most likely the land of Goshen, as Hebrews have populated that area since the days of Joseph; their cosmogony was based on Khnum, the ram-headed craftsman, who creating the *khat* and the *ka* on his potter's wheel from clay and wind. Finally, the Theban schools were more holist and pantheist in their cosmogony holding to the interpretation that God and the divine existed in everything. Cosmogony to them was based on finding that mystical link that unifies the various sciences, thus their schools were broad based and almost entirely focused on the worship of Amen Ra. At the same time, Heliopolis had other cosmogonies: the main one being that Ra rose from the primordial flood riding on his boat of a million years with eight other powers that became known as the Paut Neteru.

To understand these Kemetic traditions in a more in-depth way one has to come to terms with their scientific interpretation of cosmogony; that all the ancient cosmogonies of Kemet viewed the universe from the perspective of primordial chaos. None of their ancient cultures saw the universe as something coming out of nothingness or being made out of nothingness by an unknown and unknowable maker; but as an unorganized chaos of primordial matter (ocean of energy in chaotic motion) which through Ra Atum, or knowledge of self, was able to self-organize into an orderly universe.

The Kemetic term for the primordial chaos was Nu, the process of self-organization from Nu to Ra they called Khepru, and the enlightened self that woke him they called Tum. Tum, meaning self-creation: the self-created, self-sufficient one; represented the great manifestation of Ra that paradoxically set on course the process of Khepru (evolution). The theory of Tum is similar to a concept just recently discovered called self-organization: the process by which all things move from chaos to order. This works not just on a universal level but also works on an individual level too. For each individual within Nu to reach the level of Ra or godhood it would also have to go through the evolutionary process of self-discovery and self-creation to reach it.

The Greeks expressed this in their concept of potentiality and actuality; where the unknown and unactivated potential of a body becomes actualized when it is used. However, ancient Kemet had a much more unified definition based on the process of self-organization. Under their interpretation a being goes through several phases of development until it reaches self-actualization or self-realization, where it is fully real and fully self. This was not based on a distinction between potential and actual but of unconsciousness and self-consciousness.

Ultimately, to them it was the gaining of self-awareness (knowledge of self and of the potential of self) that allowed the primordial universe to begin the process of self-organization by which the waves of energy, being connected to other waves, were able to form bodies and create novae, nebulae, stellar, solar, lunar and planetary bodies. As these self-similar energy waves formed smaller and larger subatomic bodies they began to converge also into smaller and larger celestial bodies. This evolutionary process of self-creation within the astronomical bodies they called Khepru. However, it was in defining and interpreting the apocalypse of the self-created Ra that the different Heliopolitan mystery schools sought to prove their worth.

All occurrences within the Heliopolitan cosmogonies were represented in the symbolic story of Nu, the primordial chaos. From the midst of Nu comes Tum, in the form of Nefer Tum, representing luminosity, rising upon a lotus flower (obviously symbolic of meditation), who through self-copulation (i.e., masturbation) produces Shu and Tefnut, that is, gasidity and liquidity respectively. Once these two were produced they immediately fell into the primordial chaos, where they mutually copulated together. Their copulation then produced Geb and Nut, that is, solidity and lucidity respectively. Tum, now alone in Pet, the realm in which he resided, and in which he brought order to the chaos; sent out his left eye (or *maat*) to find his two children. As she took a long time to find them he replaced his left eye. When Maat finally returned with his four offspring Tum was very overjoyed and made them all divine with a glance from his eye. As for Maat, having already replaced her he put her at the centre of his forehead to oversee all things in the universe as his third eye.

The obvious conclusion from all this is to view this story as pure fantasy; but this hardly stands the test of time as the Kemetic people were far too advanced in science and technology to believe in mere fairy tales. The next conclusion is to view it as symbolic, which allows us to see the parallels between the fantasy and reality. In Kemet all the leading schools saw the universe as being unified by its *ka*. This *ka* or being when fully understood becomes Ra. When the *ka* of Nu becomes fully understood he also becomes Ra and through Tum, or self-creation, he begets or births or produces Shu and Tefnut, who themselves produce Geb and Nut. At this point these five concepts become the representative elements of molecular physics: massless light, fluids, liquids, solids and lucids. From the teeming of Geb and Nut, that is, earth and sky, you eventually get organic matter: Ausar and Auset, Setek and Nebthet. Ausar and Auset representing vegetation in its masculine and feminine forms; Setek representing aridity, harshness and desert; and Nebthet representing civilization and matriarchy. These nine: Ra Atum, Shu, Tefnut, Geb, Nut, Ausar, Auset, Setek and Nebthet are again the Paut Neteru, the nine great powers, who in the former myth rose with Ra Atum out of the waters of Nu in his boat of a million years.

In his Timaeus Plato expresses his own views about metaphysical development: eternity and the beginning and end of time. The ideas he expressed were mainly from an idealistic standpoint. Here ideas in their perfect form represent a much greater image of truth and reality than physical forms in their imperfections. Plato also reasoned that fully perfect being: being that is both scientific and real, is represented by the ideal, that is, by Absolute Truth. It creates all things through ratio, ration or Rational Mind, birthing non-perfect things through thought. Wherefore all physical and ideal realities are a product of Rational Mind, which – although being Absolute Truth and also perfection – being perfect, is based on ideals. They are received and interpreted by us through our thoughts, which themselves are all ideas considered over by Absolute Truth. As these thoughts are acted out by us they move from potential to actual and through activism from actual to physical. In the process they lose more and more of their essential reality the closer they get to the physical, at least according to Plato's theory.

Plato's views reflected the times he was in and the political upheavals taking place in ancient Greece during his lifetime. The first glimpses of democracy were beginning to shine through in Greece and Plato, being moderately aristocratic, did not like the changes taking place. Plato hated democracy, not because of the liberties but because of the hypocrisies, the fakeness and the crowd-pleasing it encouraged. To him even a democracy could be unjust and majority rule could be oppressive. This was the world of politics, a word also fully defined by his day, in which the *polis*, or secular city, was run by the freedmen, that is, the *demos*. To Plato better suited to run the *polis* was the wise and the philosophical, the cultured and the educated. For this cause Plato retreated into his realm of the Ideal (a word which he is attributed to having created) and the psyche, in which perfection was real and was realizable.

Another to study at the Kemetic schools was Moses, whose Kemetic name was Djehutmosu, but who many Egyptologists know as Thutmose, the brother of Akhenaten. He was bought up under the Theban tradition and initiated into the cult of Amen. But he obviously was so impressed with the other Kemetic cosmogonies that he incorporated them all into his own Hebrew cosmogony. Hence why the Hebrews have five creation myths that follow in succession. Remember also that, "Moses was learned in all the wisdom of the Egyptians, and was mighty in words and in deeds" (Act 7: 22), thus one can see how powerful an influence Kemet was on him before he ventured to Arabia where he learned the Bedouin culture of animistic monism. The elemental and naturalistic culture of both the Bedouin and sedentary of Arabia, would have also had a lasting effect on the man, who in later life returned to Arabia to enjoy life as a Bedouin shepherd and tribal chief before beginning his own school and tradition in Kemet as a prophet.

Moses definitely derived his Hebrew tradition by combining all the patriarchal Kemetic cosmogonies into one, this is, firstly, evident when one considers that the first words the Hebrew God uttered were, "Amen Ur" (which has been translated as "Let there be light"), and is, secondly, evident when one considers that verse 2 of Genesis 1 could have easily been excluded from the text and gone straight from, "In the beginning God created the heaven and the earth" to "And God said, Let there be light" but Moses was determined to also include the Hermopolitan cosmogony regardless of how out of place it was there.

The Moses tradition had a sharp sense of racial identity. The Hebrew God is seen as choosing Israel, particularly, of all the races of the earth. The confirmation of the Testament at Mount Sinai in Arabia is then the sign that Moses' school is the successor to the Kemetic schools and that God has elected Israel as his own chosen people.

The Hebrew school showed God as a deliverer, a mighty God, and a warrior God. He is a God who fights for his people and destroys mighty nations (indeed the mightiest of nations at that time) on their behalf. Again, if one considers Israel after the conquest of Khem: they had no prophets and no apostles; but God chose some to be Judges and some to be Nazarites from among the people. Then came Samuel, who was a Judge, a Nazarite, and a prophet according to the Mosaic tradition. After Samuel came David, who completed the Samuel Testament by fully organizing the Nation of Israel. The Davidic tradition that followed maintained the electoral status of Israel, but this time not merely in regard to their status as a race of people but also in regard to their status as a nation. To a certain degree this gave the Israelites confidence and self-assurance in the day of battle, or at times of conflict or crisis; but it also produced haughtiness, false pride, racial patriotism, and nationalistic insensitivity.

Nationhood in the Davidic tradition came by conquest and governmentality so that war, conflict, and self-confidence would come part-and-parcel with his testament. With conquest, conflict, and confidence also came celebration, thus the Davidic tradition also included the birth of the psalmists. David, being one of the first real psalmists, made the use of psalms to praise, celebrate, congratulate, mourn, and entreat into a national pastime. So the Davidic Testament was confirmed in Jerusalem where God would fill his followers with a spirit of rapture. But as the racial patriotism and nationalistic insensitivities made Israel very closed-minded to outsiders the God of Israel chose to use the Isaiah tradition to reconcile the fallen nations of the world to himself. Here the God of Israel becomes the ruler over the nations through a form of government in which the people of Israel teach the nations, and the whole creation, how to live in peace.

David and the Davidic kingdom may have brought in and allowed for beauty through religious praising and dancing for God, but by the time of Jeremiah they had become so lost in delusion, with their romantic view of God that they were on a collision course right into the Isaiah school's testament of God's government over the whole of creation. By this time the Davidic kingdom had also lost all its original godliness and become a complete caricature of itself, being corrupted by idolatry and the luxurious lifestyle of a wealthy, at ease nation. They even lost that warrior spirit of David and the Judges, which made the name of Israel great among the nations. Babylon, by this time, was far more war ready with an experienced leader like Nebuchadnezzar as their king. The defeat of Judea was inevitable, forcing the Judeans to retreat into the heart of Egypt – that is, until civil war broke out in Sais – when the Judeans fled even deeper into the African continent.

By the time the Prophet Muhammad arrived on the scene all trade through Asia was controlled by the Desert Arabs, as all trade from East to West and from West to East in Asia had to go through Arabia, this made Arabia in itself one of the trading capitals of the world. So Mecca, being one of the wealthier cities of Arabia, controlled virtually all trade in Asia by controlling all the Desert Arabs.

At that time, conflicts between the Orthodox Catholics and the Roman Catholics, the Catholic Christians and the Nestorian Christians, and between the Christians and the Judeans, raged throughout the Middle East. Muhammad himself took a somewhat neutral stance choosing rather to follow the instructions given him by the angel that spoke to him. Ultimately, his main goal was never to found a united Arabian Empire but simply to de-clutter the then current Arabian religion and dethrone its many gods.

However, his fledgling Muslim movement was too small and unstable; so that it was always in danger of annihilation. Even from its beginnings it was the constant threat of annihilation from the many Arab tribes that forced the Muslims to fight and fight and fight until they had conquered most of Arabia unifying them under Muhammad's monotheism, though most of these tribes never fully unified under Islam until after the death of the Prophet.

With this now unified Arabia on the map other unified nations began making plans to seize this new gem for themselves: First Syria, then Iraq, then Persia, then Egypt. One by one they all came, one by one they all fell. The only threat to Islam that the Muslims were not able to conquer was their Byzantine forebears. The only reason for this was that Byzantium called on the newly established Holy Roman Empire for help against the Muslim Turk.

Now sometime after Charlemagne, the founder of the Holy Roman Empire, had passed away, the various 'Caesars' of the Empire fell into different estates and principalities, each one ruled over by an executive officer or magistrate. These fighting men would organize fighting units with which to govern their newly acquired feudum, receiving taxes and services from those under their authority.

The highest magistrates of these medieval days were the knights, a class of ruthless and aggressive warriors who pledged their loyalty and service to Church and Crown. In those days chivalry, service and loyalty were the chief virtues. Through these they developed a complicated structure and lifestyle based on fabled legends like King Arthur and of course Charlemagne.

They also had highly protected places of residence, which meant that should troubles arise or war threaten the people of that area could flee to the home of their bishop, baron, prince or knight and find refuge. At the same time, these heroes were obliged to fight to defend those of their principality and be examples to them of 'good manners.' However, nearing the end of the Crusades against the Muslims trade began to revive and grow, literacy was encouraged and taught, mercenaries and cold-blooded killers blurred the rules of combat and guns were available making the knights somewhat obsolete.

The medieval church was also still rife with infighting, though their biggest enemies were the Muslims. The Christians considered Islam to be anti-Christ while the Muslims considered Christianity to be polytheist. Just as Christians were united against Muslims so Muslims were united against Christians.

The Christian opposition was itself fuelled and strengthened by the apocalyptic visions of the prophet Daniel and the apostle John, which were given new life and interpretation through the light of the then current events. These reference points used by the Catholic clergy as a means of demonizing the Muslims became the most helpful tools of propaganda in the crusader period.

But the Muslims, still being the best warriors of their time, maintained rule over their different territories being the benevolent chiefs of their vast empire. Still, having conquered everywhere from Senegal and the Andalus to Persia and the Indus they needed to make their mark and stamp on those under their authority so they would charge them *dhimmi* or protection tax. These non-Muslim taxpayers were also, to a certain degree, segregated from their Muslim rulers. It was this and their isolated and aloof demeanour that allowed the non-Muslims to feel secure enough to plot a Reconquest.

Yet the Islamic Empires themselves were unlike any empire that had come before. As with their Arabic predecessors the Muslims were a warrior/trader culture so that these fierce conquerors were also shrewd merchants. As some of them began to settle into small groups in the free areas they had conquered one of the first things they did was build a mosque to establish a worship base with which to praise and worship Allah.

The architecture of the mosques were extravagant and beautiful. They had a minaret from which the call to prayer could be made; they had outdoor facilities from which to do their *salat* or prayers towards Mecca; they had flowing waters and pools from which to do *wudu*, that is, daily washings; and all was designed to look like their image of paradise.

Having built their centre for worship, which was their religious base, these Bedouin merchants began to set up trading areas, bazaars, from which to buy, sell, and trade merchandise. The forming of these marketplaces soon allowed these Bedouin settlers to start building houses for themselves and their families. Within a matter of time these Muslim settlements had become full-fledged cities with highly sophisticated technical and experimental knowledge. From there they went on to develop schools of Islamic law and schools in Islamic theology integrating both within the science of jurisprudence.

This is perhaps where German religious reformer Martin Luther made his biggest error, his belief that governance and law were separate from theological issues. Luther believed that God and spiritual matters had no part in any legal or governmental issues and that the empires of the world were to be run by a worldly hierarchy which would replace the religious hierarchy of the Catholic priesthood. This bureaucratic theory was mainly due to his being supported by the German princes against the Catholics, and their protest movement against the Catholics was the pretext that instigated Protestantism.

Luther also believed in a priesthood of all believers in which everyone had access to God without the need of a mediator. This was his definition of the government of God; a church in which all members had immediate access to God. Further, through this perspective Luther was able to open up spiritual and religious powers to the people, a revolution that would reach its climax in the Enlightenment. But their spiritual and intellectual empowerment had no serious effect on their material, political or psychological development or empowerment.

Henry VIII soon took the two governments theory a stage further in maintaining his own political power and creating a political hierarchy while also maintaining in his new Anglican movement the religious hierarchy of Catholicism. He would then name himself the head of both trends so that he, in a sense, replaced the Pope in all things but one: the allowance of biblical group formations for those who would join his Church of England.

At the same time, the Puritans had a much more radical theory of the government of God believing that it instead was a more levelling and egalitarian establishment. This idea was further radicalized by the persecution inflicted by Mary Tudor after Henry VIII and his son Edward VI passed away. Started in Geneva by John Knox, the Puritan settlement of English speaking Calvinists came to influence most of the radical and communitarian movements around the world, including capitalism.

Having their roots in Calvinism the Puritans had the opposite definition of Reformation to Martin Luther, the movement's founder. Where Luther saw two governments Calvin saw one, the government of God, and he fought to unify the two governments of Luther, spiritual and secular, into one.

Calvin's movement was steeped in rebellion, revolutionism and defiance, but not of God, only of the governments of man, any man, over the government of God. As this doctrine entered into England by the returned settlement it would ignite a civil war, which would challenge the British decree of the divine right of kings. This war was effectively between two powers: that of the royalty, represented in the Crown, and that of the commoners, represented in Parliament.

It is during this time that we see the markets of Reformation economics, where the small-holders, farmers and artisans each trading their goods at a price reasonable to the times or putting all their strength to the service of the noble and warrior class, really come into play. The nobles that could afford larger properties or land masses would buy and use them to gain more wealth and prestige among the peasants and artisans. From here slavery and the socialization of labour allowed the Medieval system to give way to the Restoration system. The European Restoration – based primarily on what was going on in the Americas, particularly with the slave trade and the slavery system – was a Restoration of the monarchy after the social upheavals caused by the Reformation and the civil wars it produced.

Socialized labour in the form of slavery created and generated great amounts of wealth for its owners; who could use their wealth to purchase either more slaves or greater land masses. It also allowed the slave-owners to sell larger amounts of a product being sold by a small or middle peasant for a much lower price. The aftereffects of this revolutionized sales, enterprise and the market as a whole. Thus, the market of the Restoration, as it moved out of the Dark Ages, was slowly becoming the shopping market, in which the street and town contained shops (as opposed to the stalls of the bazaars) for the selling of their products. Also the enterprise, a technically non-existent entity pre-Reformation, was expanded by selling directly to a shopkeeper or shop-owner, instead of to a purchaser or feudal lord.

As slave-exploitation gave way to machine-exploitation products could be made faster, cheaper and more economically. This economizing of labour allowed the owner of a good machine to earn twice the wealth and prestige of the slave-owner; who was already facing the difficulties of social outrage inspired by the Abolition movement. Thus with the ability to access greater wealth, prestige and public support the machine owner out flanked the slave-owners and overthrew them as a class. This decisive victory was in spite of the bitter and grief stricken conditions of the labourer in the factory. It seemed that while the gentry were decrying the sufferings of the slave in the field they were ignoring the sufferings of their own labourers in the factory. This cynical and hypocritical reality (that they obviously noticed but chose to ignore) caused the air of both hypocrisy and cynicism to mar the church and Christianity ever afterward.

So we see with Kropotkin, by studying and considering these origins of modernity, the peaceful agricultural communities, who allowed the history-makers: the caliphs, chieftains, knights and nobles, to rule over their territory so long as they were left in peace. This formation of the class of rulers allows us to understand that though class struggle did exist it existed on a relatively invisible level in Medieval and pre-Medieval societies, and so was a lot less prominent than our history books and records would allow us to appreciate.

The clear evidence of social history when understood in its proper context puts the current ideology of self-interested struggle for existence on its head. In actual fact, the historical development of bourgeois production cannot be explained by natural phenomena, but only by the socialization of labour. The puritan idealists who practiced this form of economic development anticipated modernity, devoting their lives to God in the hopes of reaching his kingdom in the afterlife.

Though many among these puritans started life as petty shopkeepers or as small industry and estate owners; such shops and ownerships, due to their religious devotion to the work ethic and their practice of socialized labour, grew substantially over the years to become enterprises. The growth, development and transformation of these small industries into large corporations allowed for the demise of slavery and the rising of the new class to the top of civilization. The best workers among them – again, to prove their election from God – would also seek to outwork and swallow whole the businesses of their fellow bourgeois contemporaries; thus showing themselves that in the kingdom of God they would be the higher in rank, as in the kingdom of England, Prussia, etc., they were more successful than their peers.

This competition for rank in the kingdom of God would soon evolve into competition for competition's sake as a Darwinian logic and greater technological progress began to replace Christian sensibilities and moralistic devotions. With the coming of an almost carnivorous kill or be killed mentality within modern civilization a Darwinian animalism of labour and a Marxian dialecticism of society began to take precedent in the lives and minds of the people, drawing them into the hostile social classes we have today. Moreover, the current class struggle and the current algebra of productive development, being divorced from their historical and ideological precursors, have now become separate from, and so transcendent to, history and all historical conditions.

At the same time, while it cannot be denied that the puritans inspired the English Civil War that itself brought about the short lived British Republic, it also cannot be denied the influence this British Republic had on the American revolutionaries. In Washington, Adams, Jefferson and Franklin's vision of a unified and fully independent America they included independence of the mind, conscience, speech and expression. They believed in the freedom not only of the religious, spiritual and intellectual; nor yet only of the practical and legalistic, but of the total man: militarily, with the right to bear arms; socially, with the right to freedom of speech and assembly; morally, with the right to freedom of religion and expression; and hierarchically, with the separation of powers and democratic and electoral rights given to the people.

Again, if we trace this reality to its earliest foundations we can see that from William Wilberforce and the Abolitionists; Maximilien de Robespierre and the Jacobins; George Washington and the Republicans; John Locke and the Empiricists; John Lilburn and the Levellers; John Knox and the Puritans; and Thomas Münzer and the Mühlhausens the transition from utopian idealism to the demand for social improvements has always begun with some form of philosophical precursor.

Even at the first stage of human history it can be seen how humanity, having first begun to consider some of the best qualities in nature, manifested or expressed these as knowledge. At this time Ra, in the form of enlightenment, was the personification of all-knowledge and of that deeper mysterious knowledge of the inner science of things. The disciples of this new breed of mystery lesson, however, disliked the idea of a perfect knowledge or the idea of humanity aspiring to reach such heights.

Moreover, due to economic meltdown in the Kemetic social superstructure; Ausar, the Kemetic god of vegetation, i.e. the agricultural god, became a greater model to aspire to for the Egyptian peasant masses. Ausar was perfect for the farming and peasant economy in development in Kemet at the time, so that the Asarian Revolution – in which the intellectual upperclass of priests and elite mystics were overthrown by the peasant and artisan – was a prelude to all future revolutions. Here the abuses of the establishment had reached their climax along with the social and intellectual climax of the general system. With this climax having already occurred in the

IV Dynasty the VI Dynasty was doomed to feel the revenge of history. All established orders upon the ending of the V Dynasty were called into question and crumbled under the might of the peasant militia.

According to Cheikh Anta Diop: "The disclosure of administrative and religious secrets; the dispersion of tribunal archives; the numerous attempts to destroy the bureaucratic machine that was crushing the people; the proletarianization of religion, which extended the Pharaonic privilege of immortality of the soul to all the people; the profaning of religion itself; and the extent and violence of the social upheavals as they are recounted" all tell of "the suppression of royalty [and], the profaning of its symbols". These changes to the social fabric of Kemet did not reflect the birthing of the Asarian apocalypse, but its use to justify and quench the uprising of the time. Ausar, whose name also meant blackness in ancient Kemet (but black in the good sense as in perfect, beautiful, powerful and happy); was the figurehead used by the farming and peasant masses.

Again, from this Asarian Revolution can also be understood the social irregularities of any revolutionary experience, including its counter-revolutionary element. Here Ausar, the figurehead of the revolution, was soon replaced, nearing the end of the "First Intermediary period," with his son Horu as the personification or model of divinity. The Horu (which was a title of the king) being himself the physical manifestation of Horu, the son of Ausar, on earth; was again hailed by the people. What happened was the people and priests alike took those which were the best qualities in man and projected them onto Horu, thus making *the Horu*, his representative on earth, to have to imitate these qualities in person, while the priests and people imitated him.

Thus Ausar was used by both the masses and by the returned monarchy in response to the social conditions of the time; conditions under which, as Diop states again: "The destitute of Memphis, the capital and sanctuary of Egyptian royalty, sacked the town, robbed the rich, and drove them into the streets. There was a true reversal of the social conditions and the financial situations. The movement rapidly spread to other cities," a theme itself very reminiscent of the great French Revolution of more recent times.

According to Engels this revolution, of and in itself, was the direct result of the French philosophies and ideals propagated during the Enlightenment. The idealists of that time, in Engels' view, who, "prepared men's minds for the coming revolution, were themselves extreme revolutionists," "everything that ran counter to eternal reason was to be remorselessly done away with." However, the realization of their vision would accomplish exactly that which was accomplished from Ra in Kemet: The class of proprietors, having completed their revolution, found that to stifle the anarchic impulse brewing at the bottom from the peasants and paupers, needed to use the propagation of more nationalistic ideas to quench the anarchistic ideas then being spread. This would continue until the brute force and eventual nepotism of Napoleon took place. Hence, the eighteenth century proprietors, still becoming a bourgeoisie, rather than creating an enlightened government where reason was the only king, created a chaotic society where wars of conquest were the only king.

During this same period Britain was going through her own, though less violent revolution, the Industrial Revolution. The effects of this revolution brought about changes to the social fabric unimagined and unplanned by its architects, as Engels explains: "the herding together of a homeless population in the worst quarters of the large towns; the loosening of all traditional moral bonds, of patriarchal subordination, of family relations; overwork, especially of women and children, to a frightful extent; complete demoralisation of the working class, suddenly flung...from the country into the town, from agriculture into modern industry, from stable conditions of existence into insecure ones..." all telling of a time of unsettled and almost ruined equilibrium.

But like with the Asarian Revolution the re-instituting of the privileged brought about the removal of the anarchic chaos at the cost of re-instituting religious and social prejudices and superstitions. (The most notable prejudices of Victorian Britain were based on manners, particularly in regards to marriage and property). All these realities would prove to be a wall that would block any social revolution from blossoming proper in Britain. The counter-revolution in the form of prejudice allowed the revolution in Britain to remain only an industrial one, while in 1848, at the height of the global industrial revolution, came several social revolutions to compensate for the new radical developments.

Again, according to Engels, "The revival of commercial prosperity, natural after the revolution of 1847 had spent itself, was put down altogether to the credit of Free Trade. Both these circumstances had turned the English working class, politically, into the tail of the 'great Liberal Party', the party led by the manufacturers", the main strength of which was the power of petition and confrontation of parliament. Prominent and very effective among these lobbyist manufacturers was the Anti-Corn Law League. Determined to achieve for the manufacturing class what the Anti-Slavery Society did for the slave class, the League set out from 1838 to loosen some of the political and economic powers held by the landed aristocracy and demand for the liberation of trade and industry. Their victory in 1846 was at the outset of crash.

Engels, retelling of those times, states: "The repeal of the Corn Laws was the victory of the manufacturing capitalist not only over the landed aristocracy, but over those sections of capitalists, too, whose interests were more or less bound up with the landed interest – bankers, stock-jobbers, fund-holders, etc. Free Trade meant the readjustment of the whole home and foreign, commercial and financial policy of England in accordance with the interests of the manufacturing capitalists – the class which now represented the nation. And they set about this task with a will. Every obstacle to industrial production was mercilessly removed. The tariff and the whole system of taxation were revolutionised. Everything was made subordinate to one end...the cheapening of all raw produce".

From this we see in a stroke the transformation of industry and of the rules of the game. With trade now liberalized within Britain, the big bourgeoisie, now, for the first time, had their own system, liberal capitalism. "But while England [had] thus outgrown the juvenile state of capitalist exploitation...other countries [were] only just [attaining] it. France, Germany, and especially America, [were] the formidable competitors who, at [that] moment – as foreseen by me in 1844 – [were] more and more breaking up England's industrial monopoly. Their manufactures [were] young as compared with those of England, but increasing at a far more rapid rate than the latter; and, curious enough, they [had] at [that] moment arrived at about the same phase of development as England manufacture in 1844."

Again, Engels provides the basis for the best explanation of this situation when he states:

> *The revival of trade, after the crisis of 1847, was the dawn of a new industrial epoch. The repeal of the Corn Laws and the financial reforms subsequent thereon gave to English industry and commerce all the elbow-room they had asked for. The discovery of the Californian and Australian gold-fields followed in rapid succession. The colonial markets developed at an increasing rate their capacity for absorbing English manufactured goods. In India millions of hand-weavers were finally crushed out by the Lancashire power-loom. China was more and more being opened up. Above all, the United States – then, commercially speaking, a mere colonial market, but by far the biggest of them all – underwent an economic development astounding even for that rapidly progressive country.*

All these great changes to business that were occurring within the British Empire allowed Britain, the then chief manufacturer of the world, to slowly expand even as other markets began to open up. But unbeknownst to all of them a new storm was starting to brew at the bottom, the labour movement. This still very adolescent movement was able to capture the emotion and the sorrow of the time experienced by the industrial labourer. For while the manufacturer shot to new bounds of fancy around the world, the labourer sank to new depths of desperation and depression in the slums.

The chilling scenes of a Dickens' novel were the masterful description of social realities for these now urbanized, now ghettoized individuals. And though the Peoples' Charter of England (founded at the same time as the Anti-Corn Law League) did affect small bursts of political enthusiasm among the radicalized workers, there was no way the landed aristocracy were going to allow them and the manufacturing class both to have their demands met at once. Both being, in their case and in their mind, their 'natural inferiors', the surrender of power even to one of these classes would have to come by struggle and determination. Difficult though the plight of the labouring class was, with no articulate spokesperson outside of Robert Owen to defend their cause, they continued in their squalid, depressed and impoverished lives without the means to emancipate themselves.

However, things were able to improve in their conditions, even if ever so slightly. Engels mentions how, "the repeated visitations of cholera, typhus, small-pox, and other epidemics have shown the British bourgeois the urgent necessity of sanitation in his towns and cities, if he wishes to save himself and family from falling victims to such diseases. Accordingly, the most crying abuses...have either disappeared or have been made less conspicuous. Drainage has been introduced or improved, wide avenues have been opened out athwart many of the worst 'slums' I had to describe." "Thus the development of production on the basis of the capitalistic system has of itself sufficed...to do away with all those minor grievances which aggravated the workman's fate during its earlier stages. And thus it renders more and more evident the great central fact that the cause of the miserable condition of the working class is to be sought, not in these minor grievances, but in *the capitalistic system itself*."

Notwithstanding, in both their industrial and social forms the revolutions of the eighteenth and nineteenth centuries were a direct or indirect result of one man's hard work and effort; that man was Sir

Isaac Newton. Newton's *Principia* would produce two motivations for the two revolutions in political economy. First, his discovering of the "laws" that governed the motions of the planets and the cosmos would present other philosophers with the challenge of finding laws in other natural systems as well as justifying them with reasonable or mathematical arguments. The natural philosophies and natural sciences that were produced as a result of this gloriously ambitious project gave way to the Enlightenment with regards to philosophy and the industrial revolution with regards to science.

It would be this searching for the laws of nature and for the underlying reason behind existence in its multifaceted manifestations that would produce within the Enlightenment thinkers a desire to overthrow what they held to be the irrational, unjustifiable, royal establishment, for a more justifiable and reasonable establishment in which they that ruled justified their right to rule and, with reasonable argument, proved their worth as rulers to the grand jury of the electorate. The masses, being both judge and jury, would pass sentence through the *electoral ballet*, and democracy would present the final verdict. Like manner of thinking would exist in all institutions of this "enlightened" world system, where all things from top to bottom were put on the election block of either the market or the ballot to decide its usefulness and thereby its worth and fate.

Indeed, the "kingdom of reason", birthed by the Enlightenment, instituted what we would now call modernity; however, at the heart of modern civilization stood that ever present dichotomy: the struggle between the classes. Though this struggle has existed in all historical epochs of recorded diction, what has existed since the dawn of modernity has been far more prominent, far more pronounced, far more obvious than ever in the history of humanity.

As Engels also said, in the eighteenth century it soon became apparent that the basis of enlightened reasoning was propriety, or the equal rights of propriety. This being obvious by the manifestation of their "equality of all men," being actualized only as the equality of all proprietors under the law and to redress and change the laws as so suited their need to maintain property; and of their "reign of eternal rights" being actualized only as the right of proprietors to own and maintain property and to pass it on or dispose of it as so suited their desire to maintain social propriety.

With the decaying of the French Revolution into the Reign of Terror, on the one hand, and Napoleonic nepotism, on the other, the voice of social conscience would have to come from the grass-roots. Saint-Simon and his new Christianity and Charles Fourier and his phalanges, were the first reasonable criticisms against the decadence of the times. Modern industry was still virtually non-existent in France and only just developing in England so the proper bourgeoisie and proletariat (gentlemen and workingmen) classes had not yet been created, therefore the class antagonisms of that time were mainly between the propriety and the peasantry. Indeed, the peasants and paupers of this pre-industrial phase were slowly beginning to develop the capacity to vision for a better world: a world, not based on the extravagances of the treacherous proprietors but on the taking of power by the poor and administering social wealth orderly and equally to the people. In essence, these utopians of the interim period began to envision a proto-socialism in which all social and economic problems and wrongs could be balanced and smoothed out by reason.

These children of the French Revolution, for the most part lower and middle class small-holders, feeling dispossessed by the revolution they played such a strong role in helping and now being either petty-bourgeofied or proletarianized were to a certain degree hostile to the same beautiful revolution. Their love for the revolution was matched only by their hatred for its betrayers in the proprietor class. This would ultimately lead the proprietors to seek the strong arm of the Napoleons to quench the fire brewing within these semi-proletarian forces. This is, again, in accordance with all prior to revolutions. In the time of revolution a strong hand must bring stability to the masses at the bottom or chaotic disorder is inevitable. In these instances, if the revolutionary leaders do not quench this then the counter-revolution will either use it for their own benefit or quench it themselves. Either way they will overthrow the incapable and incompetent revolution in an instant.

That said, as a result of France's great Revolution the cry for liberty, equality and fraternity was now shouted from the rooftops. These calls were, however, unanswered after its victory and instead only a Reign of Terror in which the guillotine was the only king caused many an idealist and social reformer to go into the wilderness of the urban desert, then not yet industrialized, to seek to devise new change inspiring literature.

The first to do this was Henri de Saint-Simon an impoverished aristocrat who found himself incredibly wealthy at the turn of the century and decided to devote himself to study. His first published work was in 1803 and expounded the first socialistic critique of the great French Revolution. All other future French social reformers and socialist thinkers would ultimately take their ideals from a more developed version of what Saint-Simon produced during this time. To be sure, socialism started out as a purely and exclusively French movement.

On the other side of the Channel, where the industrial movement was in full swing, the only real movement for genuine social change was that of Wilberforce's Abolition of the slave trade. The working class as an entity, or at least as a substantial entity, did not as yet exist as Robert Owen had not yet organized them into one.

Owen, who coined the term socialist, would in his time gather the scattered workingmen's associations to form the first significant Trade Union movement of workers. Inasmuch as English Trade Unionism, though in essence self-formulated, was first organized into a movement by Robert Owen, all existing TUCs owe a huge debt of thanks to what Owen did in his time to organize the first version of it.

Thus French socialism, radical and moderate; and English trade unionism, political and economic; were the two major forces of class reform going on at that time in Europe. Only one piece was missing from the puzzle: German communism.

This entity would begin as an idealistic version of French radical socialism stretched beyond the realms of realistic argument. In the hands of its idealist element German socialism became somewhat of a caricature making little sense to actual human realities. The idealism of the German socialists would strangely enough be contrasted with the activism of the German communists. Here, German speaking workers, predominantly tailors scattered across Europe; were a force of substantial conspiratorial revolutionaries.

These men, who took mainly from the radical French literature of the time, formed a small French movement in the form of the League of the Outlaws. This group then later evolved into the League of the Just as it began to grow into a European-wide movement. While the first died out pretty quickly, the second League, by collaboration with Marx and Engels' worker's committee, rebranded itself as the League of the Communists, and thus maintained a level of immortality through Marx and Engels' *Manifesto of the Communist League*.

German Communism, as communism was, again, predominantly a German movement, was sort of like a synthesis of the French socialist movement and the English labour movement. It took its grit and toughness from the workers associated with it and its theory and programme from the intellectuals who were involved in it (for the most part French inspired socialists). And as an international communist movement it incorporated Germans from Germany, France, England, Belgium and Austria.

Now, what distinguishes us theocrats from all these progressive movements is our determination to express our interconnection to the deity through the incorporation of political, economic, psychological, sexual, spiritual and cultural enrapturement, which makes us more and more divine. We are also against the social inequalities and injustices that seem to be everywhere in the world today. We are against a corrupt materialist system and a corrupt imperialist system; against corrupt communism and corrupt capitalism.

Karl Marx, the founder of the Marxian schools of communism, invented the modern conception of materialism. His materialism simply says that matter is the only reality and that anything non-physical can only be either based on matter or pure delusion. In other words, the only reality is the physical, "let us eat and drink for tomorrow we die," and "gather all the possessions you can cause if you don't someone else will." Oh yeah, and "God and religion are the opiate of the people."

Materialism is the basis of modern Marxism, but it does nothing really but offer false hopes of a paradise on earth justified only by scientific reasonings and theoretical phraseologies. Those countries that ever actually achieve a Marxist society, however, come to find in practice the outcome of this form of social organization is either disillusion after the desired ends fail to materialize, or fanatical self-delusion when those who refuse to let go try to justify its failure with scientific and historical inaccuracies and deceptions.

The materialism of Marxism and its boast of scientific superiority combines to produce global covetousness and competition on a grand scale. Due to the nature of Marxism this global competitiveness is on a materialistic and scientific basis. But materialism has a capitalistic component too – so that, while one ideology claims superior scientific validity, the other claims superior material benefits and possessions – and considering that both are to a reasonable degree interconnected to and interdependent on money-capital and commercial competition, capitalist materialism will always look superior to any form of Marxian materialism.

Leninism would go on to compound and exacerbate these contradictions of Marxism by legitimizing and internalizing authoritarian dictatorship for utopian purposes into its structure. Through him all successive states could and would be willing to use authoritarian dictatorship to coerce society into their utopian vision. Thus with the legitimation of authoritarianism for the purpose of bringing about some materialistic paradise, whatever the ideology be, authoritarianism would prove not only to be a Marxist reality but also a fascist, socialist, militarist, pan-Arab, pan-African, and even an anarchist reality. That coupled with the ruthlessness of the Leninist regime, and with the scientific justification of that ruthlessness, made it ever more appealing to non-Western leaders who were educated in the West.

Leninism and Leninist-inspired Marxism in themselves have only two central flaws in their systems leading to their own self-destruction. These flaws could be articulated as being their rigid authoritarian structure and command system based on bureaucratization; and the disproportionate power given the state with the diminishing of the powers of the market. Basically, any intelligent communism should divorce itself from Leninism and design a proper critique of modern society emphasizing ideas like interdependence and co-operation, and the prevailing of social empowerment and universal brotherhood.

These failures within Leninism are perhaps best told in Lenin's own words: "Dictatorship is iron rule, government that is revolutionarily bold, swift and ruthless in suppressing both exploiters and hooligans," he also decreed that individual executives in the rail industry should be given *unlimited* powers, saying "Today, however, the same revolution demands – precisely in the interests of its development and consolidation...that the people *unquestioningly obey the single will* of the leaders of labour."(Emphasis Lenin's.) This form of dictatorship would create crisis throughout the Marxian world.

Marxism's history in Asia and Latin America is altogether a lot less tragic than in its Russian form. Though having some similarities both are divided by two strands that evolved to meet the national climate of their area. Their similarities are based on the Leninist orthodoxy of Marxism applied to their historical conditions. Their differences stem from the merging and combining of this application to other variants within the Marxian circle. In Asia this took the form of merging Leninism with a Maoist variation of Trotskyism. In Latin America it came by merging Leninism with a distinctly Latin American variation of Bernsteinian revisionism.

Although both were relatively Trotskyist, neither condoned nor tolerated Trotskyism; and while Maoist and Vietminh philosophies were increasingly more Leninist in regard to politics and governance; Sandinista and Zapatista philosophies would prove more increasingly Trotskyist (though denying his relevance). Walking the delicate balance and tight-rope between the two extremes would be Castroism, which would be inspirational to all variants of Marxism the world over. Though a Latin American definition Castroism was influenced by Maoism as well as by the Soviet Union; however, it would not submit to either having any control over the Cuban Revolution nor allow either to dislodge its distinctly Latin American style and origins.

The three realities, Asian Marxism, Latin American Marxism and Castroism had the two specific flaws of applying a Leninist programme to their locations of habitation, and the idea that it is possible to be both nationalist and internationalist at the same time. A true nationalist is nationalist through and through only playing lip-service to internationalism, anti-racialism and anti-discriminatory ideas. A true internationalist is internationalist through and through only playing lip-service to nationalist, patriotic or what could be perceived to be racist or offensive sentiments.

By contrast Euro-Communism and African Marxism remained distinctly continental in their affinity to Marxian ideas. Hence their nationalism was lip-service but only towards a broader more continental Marxism. As both continental movements failed to realize a cohesive Marxian structure in their particular habitat, and within their distinct continental localities; they would both either fade away with time or decay into military dictatorships and self-destruct.

What was agreed within the Euro-Communist circles was the idea of parliamentary development and the methodical transgressions of the Third International, while in Africa it was economic inability and the one party rule of several charismatic leaders that triumphed in their movements. Both strands were conducive to the conditions of their environment. As Europe is excessively pro-parliamentarianism such had to be preached for its communism. However, Africa, being filled with huge personalities and revolutionaries was destined to produce leaders meet for inspiring the masses, even as in colonial and pre-colonial times – but as a desire to keep up with the West and as the pressures of radical modernization confronted these states they soon became too heavily dependent on the IMF, World Bank, and Eastern and Western powers to finance their ambitious projects, thus they eventually accumulated huge debts and ended up economically ruined. But again, in both cases the fundamental flaw of Leninism played a huge part in their theoretical framework and effective demise.

Perhaps the biggest flaw, however, has to be given to Western Marxism. Though as a reality it is nothing more than the philosophical bickerings of small intellectual circles of whiners and complainers, it loves to present itself to the masses as a practical programme for change, producing nothing really but bloated words and bloated terminology. Further, it has seemed to become nothing more than a moral, almost religious, church decrying the bourgeois system and its faults with the same fervour a Pentecostal preacher or religious fanatic decries the outrages of sin. Even as some religious leaders are known for personally involving themselves in certain social and political issues for the sake of their religious convictions and consciences, even so, Western Marxists, in an almost hypocritical way, decry capitalism and Stalinism for their evils while neglecting the goods capitalism has been able to accomplish through the acceptance of certain Marxian ideas, on the one hand, and the goods Stalinism has also carried out trying to enforce other Marxian ideas.

Western Marxists try with all their might, like their Muslim, Christian and Judaic predecessors, to dissociate their leader's theories from their practical failures, claiming it was the devil in the detail that ruined the system. What they have failed to appreciate is that there is not, and can never really be, a perfect social theory or reality. Social life will inevitably be marred with imperfection. Marx, as with his predecessors, presented to his followers an idealistic kingdom just as much a utopia and Shangri-La as that of those he so mercilessly critiqued in his day. Such things should therefore be left to the imaginary and dream world of fiction and not enforced by greedy or delusional philistines desperate to make a name for themselves. We all have a yearning for liberation and liberation is achievable in life as well as in the world, but it must be a liberation of the mind first then it will manifest itself outwardly.

The philosophical reasoning of Western Marxists have no bearing on practical reality, nor do the solutions they offer: as any solution that arrogantly claims to have found the keys to heaven on earth based on something outside of genuine righteousness, which has its basis in unconditional love, never contains any substantial add-ons but heartache, frustration, disillusionment and disappointment. Human imperfection and mortal fallibility distort the practical realities of Marx's theories, and as these theories claim a scientific and objective (almost divine) justification, rather than surrender the theory and its inevitable implosiveness, Marxists instead surrender the imperfect humans who sought to implement its 'scientific' realities. The constant mockeries, trials, marches, demonstrations, debates, and conflicts they experience as a result of Marxism are blamed on the capitalist, the state, the bureaucracy, Stalinism, reformism, the boogerman, etc., anyone worth blaming, in an almost fundamentalist zeal.

As a whole, Western Marxism is not a Marxism of movement: whether revolutionary or reformist; it is a Marxism of demonstration, in the laziest degree, and of philosophizing, in the most complex degree. Technically speaking, Western Marxism is 'all talk and no trousers.' And those that come to the West from the post-colonial areas expecting action usually only get met with contradiction, debate, discussion and disappointment, from a bunch of smug individuals with a vast intellectual knowledge of history and academics, but with no real or concrete experience of struggle. In fact, if they have been involved in any revolutionary activity at all it is usually insignificant. This is why most Western Marxist movements only end up deteriorating into right-wing counter-revolutions and takeovers: From the far Left becoming the far Right, to the new Left becoming the new Right, even to the centre Left becoming the centre Right; and now we have the hard Left becoming the hard Right.

All this is because these Western Marxists know how to critique, debate and complain about sufferings, but know nothing about the actual struggles of the working or underclass. They know how to bellyache and boo-hoo but have no real or serious attachment to the struggle that is experienced by those in the actual circumstances of poverty or oppression; so they are likely to betray the revolutionary cause when it reaches boiling point. That is not to say that they are evil, just complacent. Having no experience of the pains of real poverty we find they may therefore "have a lot more to lose than their chains." For this cause they tend to take a back seat and allow the masses to do all the work while they jump on the bandwagon at the last minute and give themselves excessive glory over the part they played in the almost insignificant fight. Wherefore, those in the ghettoes of the West or of the non-West would do well to avoid it at all costs.

Nevertheless, even as the basis for Marxism has been materialism, so the basis for imperialism has been capitalism. Imperialism is nothing more than the international form of capitalism, and is the policy and practice of dominating the political and economic affairs of weaker countries by conquest, the establishment of colonies. Capitalism in itself has two central flaws to its system leading to its own self-destruction. These flaws could be articulated as being the disorder in the distribution of goods, services and information, which they call laissez faire. The second being the division of labour into capital owners and capital producers. In ancient times the producers of goods also owned and traded them, so as capital is produced communally so it should also be owned communally. These two difficulties cause crisis to occur in periodic cycles making crash somewhat inevitable.

However, to solve the problem of these mysterious breakdowns the system devised the use of money-capital (particularly fictitious money like stocks, shares, assets, credit, etc.) as a means of regulating and coordinating economic affairs. The money capitalists (bankers) would ultimately make their profits through interest, while the circulation of their capital would save the system. But far from solving the problems of production and distribution money-capital, particularly in its fictitious form, only exacerbated them by prolonging the inevitable and by creating inflation.

Imperialism has turned out to be no different from its initiator in all ways but one: it is politico-military in orientation. But with the rising of global wars with the Muslim nations politico-military subjugation seems to be the inevitable path history is taking us. It does always seem to start with economic factors first and move on to more overt forms of subjugation as the situation suits the time. Obviously, the European empires have fallen, now the GUSE (Great United States Empire) takes hold. US imperialism is perhaps the last of the great empires. Americanism takes its grip on the world's economy and uses that to justify a military presence. But resistance fighters, who saw the same thing from Europe, now stand up to the GUSE in hopes of stunting its historical march.

This path of self-discovery has seen the West achieve many great accomplishments that we would do well to remember. They have made of themselves a class of individuals unseen beforehand. This is because their ancestral doctrine celebrates the new and the young. They thrive on making and doing more new so newness follows with them. But newness in its modern variation is self-destructive. It leads to explosion or implosion. Modernity creates the fuel also for the destruction of other systems too.

This Eurocentric obsession with newness is the driving force behind modern society, while liberation seems to be the driving force behind postmodernism. This move is one geared towards assisting modernism in its own self-destruction. It pushes forward the march against the evils of modernity (colonialism, World War I, the October Revolution, the rise of Fascism, World War II, the Holocaust and the Atomic bomb). Liberation doctrines are a start in the conquering of the vices of the modern system. Also necessary is a strong sense of self, a determination to not lose the part of you that makes you who you are.

This current system has a tendency within itself to distract you with so many unnecessary preoccupations that you lose sight of who you are and what your potential is. This is especially true of we blacks, who have submitted to subhuman definitions instead of the semi-divine definition we at one time demanded. We no longer see ourselves as capable of touching the fringes of divinity. Modernism has made us static, inert and indifferent. That godhood that we as a people used to possess is now lost. We now see self as mundane, humdrum and awkward. The cloudy consciousness we now possess is based on what we lost, only it is the reverse. We see white people as the brink of science and spirituality and ourselves as the fallen race, lost through four hundred years of slavery, both chattel and wage-slavery.

The liberation of the whole black person from our physical, mental, spiritual, psychological, sexual, social and economic bondage will come at a cost. We must fight for these victories. Interestingly, while modern society struggles to stay afloat black people struggle to stay alive as black people. Our black essence is constantly called into question, our ancestral pride is constantly put to shame and our unified God is constantly depersonalized. The fight back has been an exhausting one on the part of the black. We seem to stay under the heel of a kind of segregated interpretation. There is no right or wrong only white and non-white.

The black predicament is currently one of mental segregation on a global scale. We are subject to racial self-consciousness that causes us to not appreciate that though white people may be at war with us we have the right and the power to fight back. We have spent so long under white people's heel that we have become unwilling to do very much to change the situation. Although some of us are willing to fight and do something about white supremacy and white racism many of us see no hope as to solving the problem of racism and thereby resolve themselves to just blaming the system for all the problems of the world. We may no longer see ourselves as niggers and bitches but as Martin Kings and Winnie Mandelas; but our sufferings have not led the way to our self-glorification. The one time black view of inferiority may be dying away but we unfortunately still have the chains of mental segregation clouding our judgment in certain cases.

Indeed, to be black nowadays is to be extremely black, to be black beyond belief, as Gordon says. The level of blackness a person possesses is basically determined by the extent to which they themselves are conscious of it. One who is proud of their black skin and black body may still manifest non-stereotypical behaviour based on how far they have come in assimilating the West's ideas and normative behaviours into their mentality. This is not black racial self-consciousness, this is black pride. Black racial self-consciousness is the acute awareness that your black skin and black body makes you different, stands you out, makes you a target for abuse. These realities, though true, should not hold us back as a people or stop us from accepting our true place in society. The black person who uses our current lack of acceptance as being a primary cause for social inhibition is in fact a victim of their own racial self-consciousness.

At the same time, we have cultural distinctions that separate us from white and other non-black people. These cultural inhibitions also play a part in our mental segregation as to be white is more than having a skin colour, it is a set of values and ideas that enforce stereotypical behaviour. The same is also obvious with being black. A black person has a set of prescribed and proscribed actions and activities that we must maintain in order to be safe. These activities usually involve the use of our body or our sensuality. Rarely is a black person called upon for their intellect or even their spirituality. Black is physical, to be sensual and sensational. This is another segregated stereotype. But rather than focusing too long on the colonial remnants in the ideological world I will devote the rest of this chapter to explaining actually existing realities within the theocratic experience.

The interpretation of ethical distinction and contradistinction produces no social or active reality with regard to God, or in which he can manifest himself as righteousness and love for us in the social world. We are merely taught to fear and worship an unknown and unknowable God in the great beyond who has no relation to man but as his judge and better. This 'great God,' superior to humanity in every way but sin, we are also taught is not to be questioned or challenged, as to do so may anger or disappoint him, and thus block our path to his glorious heaven, or cast us into his terrifying hell.

The divine honour bestowed upon this god, though higher than that bestowed upon monarchs and rulers, has historically caused humanity to fall into the shadow of idolatry and hypocrisy in their semi or false devotion to him. However, if God himself were to prove unrighteous or corrupt, I believe it would be the duty of every person who believes in righteousness or justice to disobey God. Again, even if God were simply good and nice, perpetually wrong and nasty humanity would not be worthy to represent him or be represented by him. In this the God of the Messiah shows himself perfect by manifesting himself as *agape* (pronounced a-gaw-pae), that is, unconditional love.

Now I recognise that saying that we should keep from worshipping, honouring and praising a god for being God may seem blasphemous to those who seek to please the religious establishment; however, the worship of God simply for being God is the root of the global controversy as it stands today. We – who would challenge the authority of world rulers and leaders should the slightest touch of human imperfection manifest itself – dare not challenge that which is beyond the realms of human judgment; showing ourselves to be a product of the same internal hypocrisy. Yet we would only honour a leader or manager for being a capable leader or manager, even if it is only by our own personal biases. But the identity of an evil God who does not judge or act according to love or righteousness we fail to call into question.

Again, the argument among the populace that God is the Creator and Father of all the living, and thereby deserves honour, even if only on that note, crumbles with regard to oppression. In this the absent father is to be honoured above the oppressive father. But only in a figure, are not all fathers considered oppressive? Oppression when it is unbearable means to cry out for salvation. In this the adopted father is more of a father than the biological, for the cry of the heart was heard and the misery abated. Furthermore, to honour a god who oppresses you is fine but in my view is completely unnecessary; in fact, I would hope for the day he perishes or is killed if he were oppressive.

But a similar argument could also be made with regard to his power; that an all-powerful God should above all be feared. I would say, yes, fear him, but you have no reason to like him if he is oppressive or unjust. As a matter of fact, I believe it would be better to burn for an eternity with those who love and care for me as I really am than to spend an eternity in fear and surrounded by those who hate and despise me or only love me in hypocrisy. You can get used to the fire, used to the cell, used to whatever tortures the unjust god dreams up, but to be in a place without real or genuine love, without trust and with only fear is in my view a real hell. At least those in hell have no reason to fear any more so they would be surrounded by genuine love.

In fact: the absolute power of God makes him all the more someone to be despised, as the old aphorism says, "Power corrupts, and absolute power corrupts absolutely." Any omnipotent god, in that sense, is thereby rendered malevolent. But power is influence, and it can come by either persuasion or coercion. Though to a degree God uses both, if we consider how the *real* God persuades we get a glimpse of how he gets his power. God is both, on the one hand, omnivisional (all-seeing) and, on the other hand, panopathic (all-sensitive). These two create the illusion of omniscience and omnipotence. For those who are confused at this point, let me point out: panopathy is empathy but on an extreme level, it is an empathic connection to everything in the universe. Thereby, an omnibenevolent God has influence, but it is not through coercion as much as through empathy.

It therefore becomes possible, even desirable, for us to seek to attain to a personal godhood through developing an agapic/ empathic connection to everything in the universe. For without an agapic/empathic connection heaven would prove nothing more than a Hobbesian hell of all against all, blind self-interest, cut-throat competition and hypocritical using; in such jealousy, hatred, selfishness and abuse would be the norm, as well as fear (especially of the omnipotent god). Again, an omnipotent god who lacks agapic and empathic love is no better than a monarch or leader who lacks pity: cruel, harsh and uncaring.

Still, it is my hope that the reader will not be too discouraged by the idea of a personal godhood, for, inasmuch as we all carry the Spirit and presence of God, we carry within ourselves that divine nature, even as it is written: "Whereby are given unto us exceeding great and precious promises: that by these you might be partakers of the divine nature, having escaped the corruption that is in the world through lust" (2Pt 1:4). For the mystery of the divine nature was revealed when "Jesus answered them, Is it not written in your law, I said, Ye are gods? If he called them gods, unto whom the word of God came, and the scripture cannot be broken; Say ye of him, whom the Father hath sanctified and sent into the world, Thou blasphemest; because I said, I am the Son of God?"

But in the resurrecting of our black divinity two gods were chief in all Kemetic traditions: the sungod Ra and the nightgod Ausar. That which the global West called worship of the sun or of the dead ancestors was in actual fact the honouring of these two concepts respectively. Again, Hethor (who in Kemet was the goddess concept), in her form as the divine cow that carries and marries Ra, is both lover to Ra and mother and sister to Ausar and Auset. And being goddess of love, joy, pleasure, sex, dance, music, sensuality, wisdom, intelligence and virtually every other good thing, Hethor also passed a lot of these attributes to her daughter Auset.

From here we can see that the resurrection of the father is in the son and of the mother is in the daughter. And as knowledge and sexuality both represented male and female divinity, respectively; so Ra and Hethor embodied these two concepts personally. For though Hethor was the second thing Ra created (the first being himself as Ra Atum), as the skygoddess Nut (who in Kemet was the Nature concept) Hethor was mother, daughter, and lover to Ra. Yet not to justify incest – which was a lot less practiced in Kemet than most Egyptologists appreciate – or any Oedipal ideas, but merely to represent the interconnection of the black family. In similar vein, Ausar and Auset were the male and female equivalent of the Kemetic concept of the Black: *Asr* and *Ast*, but mean black in a much more divine manifestation, as in Black god and Black goddess. Here the words conveyed to the Kemetic people a sense of black divinity, black sensuality, black prosperity, black beauty, black strength, black intelligence, black soul, black magic, black rapture, black power, black erotica and black love.

Black divinity, for both male and female, is rooted in love, and as the apostle Peter said, "Seeing ye have purified your souls in obeying the truth through the Spirit unto unfeigned love of the brethren, see that ye love one another with a pure heart fervently: Being born again, not of corruptible seed, but of incorruptible, by the word of God" (1Pt 1:22, 23). To which the apostle Paul continues: "And though I have the gift of prophecy, and understand all mysteries, and all knowledge; and though I have all faith, so that I could remove mountains, and have no charity, I am nothing. And though I bestow all my goods to feed the poor, and though I give my body to be burned, and have not charity, it profiteth me nothing. Charity suffereth long, and is kind"; and this charity he speaks of, being by interpretation agape is thus our key to theocracy, and by extension, divinity. It also manifests the black divinity of the black family, inasmuch as we all suffer long and suffer hard.

The apostle John also adds, "My little children, let us not love in word, neither in tongue; but in deed and in truth." The soteriology of this statement being undeniable, because our God, who seeks the truth, desires to boast over us, even as it is written, "And the Lord said unto Satan, Hast thou considered my servant Job, that there is none like him in the earth, a perfect and upright man, one that feareth God, and escheweth evil? and still he holdeth fast his integrity, although thou movedst me against him, to destroy him without cause" (Jb 2: 3). So it is always necessary to remember the power of God, for he said again through his prophet Isaiah:

> *"Behold, I have created the smith that bloweth the coals in the fire, and that bringeth forth an instrument for his work; and I have created the waster to destroy." "When thou passest through the waters, I will be with thee; and through the rivers, they shall not overflow thee: when thou walkest through the fire, thou shalt not be burned; neither shall the flame kindle upon thee. For I am the Lord thy God, the Holy One of Israel, thy Saviour: I gave Egypt for thy ransom, Ethiopia and Seba for thee. Since thou wast precious in my sight, thou hast been honourable, and I have loved thee" (Is 54: 16; 43: 2-4).*

The obvious question to ask at this point is who then is God? God is agape (agape in itself being rooted in the Greek word gape – which means earned, merited or deserved kindness – and meant undeserved kindness). This term is undeniably the combination of two concepts: beneficence (kindness) and mercy (undeservedness) thereby becoming omnibenevolence, which exonerates the apostle John, saying "God is love" (1Jn 4: 8) by defining God as agape, which is unending love.

With a God like Agape, which is omnibenevolence, or love unconditional, there is neither good nor evil, blessing nor curse, life nor death; as the one who acknowledges and practices unconditional love will still be filled with love regardless. But if our acts of unconditional love have no willingness to suffer and to suffer long for them, they are not agapic. Even Ausar himself suffered in the humiliation of imprisonment, death, scattering, castration, hell and the daemons of hell; and Auset in the humiliation of widowhood, slavery, wandering, single-motherhood, excommunication and beheading; but by the powers of agape they both overcame them all. The apostle Peter says in his first letter to the churches, "Beloved, think it not strange concerning the fiery trial which is to try you, as though some strange thing happened unto you: But rejoice, inasmuch as ye are partakers of Christ's sufferings; that, when his glory shall be revealed, ye may be glad also with exceeding joy."

So now, understanding that the deity of the Scriptures is of little relation to that being preached around the world as God; and understanding that the accountability of the monarch, which was always dependent upon their preservation of rightness (and even the modern "patriarch" now has to prove himself worthy by the standards of rights in order to maintain his position in the household), is now found for the *monotheos* so as to put any theism seeking to capture the social sensitivities of the people under the balance of agape. Even so, now we can see the theodical perspectives present, for if we desire to honour God in accordance to agape, how do we authentically honour one we know so little about? Truly, a genuine honouring of God must consist of more than songs and prayers and kneeling and prostrations.

Consider now the evil Christian who worships God amazingly but treats his fellow human beings with contempt, even to the point of shooting and killing those he views in his warped mind as evil; then consider the gracious atheist who loves her fellow people, does all she can to help the poor, gives to several different charities out of her own pocket, works as a part-time nurse and in her spare time volunteers as a dance teacher for inner-city youths. She does that with a higher genuineness than the Christian, who is obviously motivated by delusions of grandeur and hypocritical self-obsession. Christian standards of "original sin" or "Adam's curse" are absolutely ridiculous arguments on the part of any religious theologian to justify that woman's place in hell for all the good she has done in her life out of her genuine love for humanity. The secret to her salvation is neither the Christian God nor the Muslim Allah, but is the God called Agape, the God of the Messiah.

ESCHATOLOGICAL JUDGMENTS

The book of Revelations is a very prophetic book. Written by the apostle John while on Patmos Island, it contains what most people believe to be the road map for the last days of the universe, or at least of humanity's existence in the universe. In order to understand some of the inherent symbologies behind the traditions of Christianity and the mysticism of what physicists call phase-space we will have to venture into a school of thought quite alien to most Western thinkers of modern times. Perhaps the best place to begin in this school of thought is with the basic premise of traditional religion: "Now it is by faith that we know what we believe in will happen, being completely assured of a reality that is invisible" (Heb 11:1 my rewording).

Now although this idea has the potential to create mystery gods, the ancient Egyptians did not have a problem with the idea of hidden realms which the third eye could tap into. In these realms, which are astral realms, dwell as much of the deity's many manifold manifestations as in the physical if not more. The obvious question from here is: if an invisible and basically astral realm exists where is the proof of its existence? Naturally, we godbodies understand that the symbolisms of the book of Revelations are just that: symbols, yet we also see them as having their representation in the astral, the causal and in the concrete. With this understanding in mind we acknowledge that the book of Revelations has not yet been completely fulfilled, therefore we try to show and prove that the terrible plagues spoken of within it need not happen. To large sections within the godbody of the street life, judgment can be averted through respecting the life and teachings of Muhammad, Jesus and the Prophets.

This chapter will not be dealing with everything written in the Revelations; that would take a book of equal or greater size than the current to deal with. However, this chapter will limit its range to those judgments experienced from the opening of the seals of the great book of God. God willing, I shall also be able to show the relation and correlation between the prophecies in the book of Revelations and those in the book of Prophets. This will also prove not only a continuity but also show a remedy for the current complacency within the world of today towards ethical righteousness. God can change his mind, he can change his word, he can even change his laws; but God cannot change his nature. He is the same yesterday, today and forever. In Hebrews it is also written of him, "Thou, Lord, in the beginning hast laid the foundation of the earth; and the heavens are the works of thine hands: They shall perish; but thou remainest; and they shall wax old as doth a garment; And as a vesture shalt thou fold them up, and they shall be changed: but thou art the same, and thy years shall not fail."

Three things must be mentioned from the outset of this expedition which biblical Theologian Marcus Maxwell points out in his commentary on Revelation: First of all, "...that the book of Revelation would have been perfectly well understood by the first century readers, and therefore [is] not a detailed blueprint of the plan of God for the Second Coming. It primarily addresses the churches of the Roman province of Asia Minor," so it is not to be accurately interpreted to mean everything must and will happen exactly as it is written by the apostle John, nor that its fulfilment was merely a last days thing and not a very current and in the moment thing.

Secondly, "John recounts the same events several times, expanding the detail and providing fresh viewpoints. For instance, there are three series of seven judgments: the seals (beginning in chapter 6), the trumpets (from chapter 8), and the bowls (chapter 16). At first sight these are successive events but on closer examination turn out to be different perspectives on the same thing, since all end at the last judgment." The book is basically telling the same story seven times and in seven different cycles (if one counts the seven thunders and the seven letters); thus by the studying of any one of the three judgments we should, generally speaking, be able to understand the whole Revelation.

The third thing that must be understood about Revelations is that based on the eschatology of it. Maxwell says, "In recent years some scholars have begun to argue that the images of cataclysmic change in apocalyptic language are not really about 'the end of the world.' Instead, they should be seen as predicting, or even calling for, great changes in the social order." "It seems to me that to a great extent, both views can be held together."

Prior to the advent of the Messiah the prophets were the ones who taught the people about ethical living, crying out to the children of Israel and Judea and of all the Middle Eastern nations telling them to administer justice and practice righteousness. The prophet Isaiah, who is called by many the Prince of the Prophets, was, in his day, the leader of a Prophetic School in Judea, where he prepared others to preach the message of justice and the fear of the Lord. The prophet Isaiah preached to the corrupted people of Judea, saying "None calleth for justice, nor any pleadeth for truth: they trust in vanity, and speak lies; they conceive mischief, and bring forth iniquity." During the same time period other prophets and contemporaries of Isaiah raised their rallying cry against corruption, saying: If "He is a merchant, the balances of deceit are in his hand: he loveth to oppress. And Ephraim said, Yet I am become rich, I have found me out substance: in all my labours they shall find none iniquity in me that were sin". "And I said, Hear, I pray you, O heads of Jacob, and ye princes of the house of Israel; Is it not for you to know judgment? Who hate the good, and love the evil".

Understanding from here and elsewhere within this theodicy the genuine righteousness of God, that he pleaded the cause of the poor and vulnerable in society even back in ancient times, we can have a better understanding of the reality and the cause for fear over the imminent "Day of the Lord" spoken of by all the prophets with fear and trembling. For the wrath of God is manifested against humanity for all their corrupted ways and all their corrupted views and all their corrupted lies. Wherefore the imagery of the book of Revelations is simply a graphic and symbolic depiction of social and astral realities and not the fantasies of illusionary status.

Obviously, other prophetic voices speak of this situation in a little more detail, the prophet Joel says, "Blow ye the trumpet in Zion, and sound an alarm in my holy mountain: let all the inhabitants of the land tremble: for the day of the Lord cometh, for it is nigh at hand; A day of darkness and of gloominess, a day of clouds and of thick darkness, as the morning spread upon the mountains: a great people and a strong; there hath not been ever the like, neither shall be any more after it, even to the years of many generations." This army which is gathered across the mountains is clearly gathered for the purpose of fighting. But what are they fighting for and who are they to fight against? Well, from Revelations we get an idea: they are fighting to, simply put, conquer; and they are fighting against the people of Israel.

Yet the prophets say concerning their battle:

"And the remnant of Jacob shall be among the Gentiles in the midst of many peoples as a lion among the beasts of the forest, as a young lion among the flocks of sheep: who, if he go through, both treadeth down, and teareth in pieces, and none can deliver. Thine hand shall be lifted up upon thine adversaries, and all thine enemies shall be cut off."

And *"I will make Jerusalem a cup of trembling unto all the people round about, when they shall be in the siege both against Judah and against Jerusalem. And in that day will I make Jerusalem a burdensome stone for all people: all that burden themselves with it shall be cut in pieces, though all the people of the earth be gathered together against it...In that day shall the Lord defend the inhabitants of Jerusalem; and he that is feeble among them at that day shall be as David; and the house of David*

shall be as God, as the angel of the Lord before them. And
it shall come to pass in that day, that I will seek to destroy
all the nations that come against Jerusalem. And I will
pour upon the house of David, and upon the inhabitants
of Jerusalem, the spirit of grace and of supplication:
and they shall look upon me whom they have pierced,
and they shall mourn for him, as one mournest for his
only son, and shall be in bitterness for him, as one that
is in bitterness for his firstborn. In that day shall there
be a great mourning in Jerusalem, as the mourning of
Hadadrimmon in the valley of Megiddon. And the land
shall mourn, every family apart; the family of the house of
David apart, and their wives apart; the family of the house
of Nathan apart, and their wives apart; The family of the
house of Levi apart, and their wives apart; the family
of Shimel apart, and their wives apart; All the families
that remain, every family apart, and their wives apart. In
that day there shall be a fountain opened to the house of
David and to the inhabitants of Jerusalem for sin and for
uncleanness..."

But we mainly get an understanding from the allusions painted in the Revelations of a coming warfare that, though appearing as a social upheaval or conflict, may in actual fact be a symbolic or figurative conflict. The reality of this view, though not yet very convincing, is given another thrashing by the prophet Ezekiel when he says quite plainly in his own astral journey: "And the word of the Lord came unto me, saying, Son of man, set thy face against Gog, the land of Magog, the chief prince of Meshech and Tubal, and prophesy against him, And say, Thus saith the Lord God;...After many days thou shalt be visited: in latter years thou shalt come into the land that is brought back from the sword, and is gathered out of many people, against the mountains of Israel, which have been always waste: but it is brought forth out of the nations, and they shall dwell safely all of them. Thou shalt ascend and come like a storm, thou shalt be like a cloud to cover the land, thou, and all thy bands, and many people with thee." All these words, being clearly the picture of conflict and war as painted by the prophet Joel, tell of Israel having just returned from conflict only to enter into an even harsher conflict.

So from all these things we can see the harsh realities of God bringing his theocracy to earth, and not some fantasy of beauty and peace. The Messiah himself said, "Think not that I am come to send peace on earth: I came not to send peace, but a sword." Thus, like with the idea of the "Day of the Lord," in most Judean minds, so with the "Second Coming" of the Messiah in most Gentile minds; heavily romanticized and whitewashed by its 'prophets'. For someone to come along and destroy all worldly power and authority is for someone to come along and destroy everything that the world stands for, believes in, and has held as most sacred.

But the ultimate triumph of the theocratic movement will not come as a result of people saying the right words or being absolutely perfect in all their ways. The fact of the matter is, a person has a better chance of converting real people by being their real selves, and not trying to put on an over moral show. And even in those times when it appears as though the person is still unyielding, they do have a memory system and through this the mind of God gets revealed to them in the night. Hence we find a necessity, not necessarily to relearn all the early Christian symbols, at least not yet anyway, but to explore the judgments expressed in the revealed drama concerning the execution of this wrath, and it's averting.

All this is where theodicy meets theocracy. For in the fifth chapter we find the unravelling of a heavenly crescendo of praise, in which the symbolic Lamb figure is found to be worthy of that which is found at the right hand of the heavenly throne, and in its Greek variation is given the name *Biblion*. It is the opening (or unsealing) of this *Biblion* that brings about the manifestation or realization of the apocalyptic cataclysms that follow.

At the opening of the first seal (6:1, 2) a white horse and its horseman appear before the apostle John and the four living creatures that stand before the throne. This horseman, who at the time was holding a bow, was then given a crown and told that he must go out to subdue and overcome. We find later on that the one sent out to subdue and overcome could be an allusion to the very Messiah who – in 19:11-16 – leads the armies of heaven, also riding on white horses. To fully explain this paradox Maxwell makes clear concerning the book of Revelations that "there are repetitions, visions within visions, and themes that seem to disappear only to reemerge later." The truth is, the book of Revelations, like all things in the astral realm, does not actualize in a linear fashion, straight from one event to the next. Or, as Koester says, "visionary time has no straightforward connection to chronological time". The same is also true of a dream. Time in a dream does not necessarily move forward, and events can occur or reverse as the dream progresses; such is the case with Revelations. Still, the reason I see the rider of the white horse as the messianic hope actualized as opposed to Maxwell's theory of an imperial conqueror is that the heathen do not rage until the light has first come to them; and because "the Lord God does nothing before he first reveals his mysteries to his servants the prophets" (my rewording).

To get to the bottom of all this we might need to venture into one of the influences behind the apostle John's Revelations, that is, into the book of 2Esdras:

> "And it came to pass after seven days, I dreamed a dream by night: And, lo, there arose a wind from the sea, that it moved all the waves thereof. And I beheld, and, lo, that man waxed strong with the thousands of heaven: and when he turned his countenance to look, all the things trembled that were seen under him. And whensoever the voice went out of his mouth, all they burned that heard his voice, like as the earth faileth when it feeleth the fire. And after this I beheld, and, lo, there was gathered together a multitude of men, out of number, from the four winds of the heaven, to subdue the man that came out of the sea.... And, lo, as he saw the violence of the multitude that came,

he neither lifted up his hand, nor held sword, nor any instrument of war: But only I saw that he sent out of his mouth as it had been a blast of fire, and out of his lips a flaming breath, and out of his tongue he cast out sparks and tempests. And they were all mixed together; the blast of fire, the flaming breath, and the great tempest; and fell with violence upon the multitude which was prepared to fight, and burned them up every one, so that upon a sudden of an innumerable multitude nothing was to be perceived, but only dust and smell of smoke: when I saw this I was afraid" (2Esdras 13: 1-11).

It is undeniable the influence this apocryphal work had on the apostle John for he wrote in his Revelations: "And I will give power unto my two witnesses, and they shall prophesy a thousand two hundred and threescore days, clothed in sackcloth. These are the two olive trees and the two candlesticks standing before the God of the earth. And if any man will hurt them, fire proceedeth out of their mouth, and devoureth their enemies: and if any man will hurt them, he must in this manner be killed" (11: 3-5). And just in case the reader is unable to see the relation between these Scriptures and the rider on the white horse the Messiah himself said: "this gospel of the kingdom shall be preached in all the world for a witness unto all nations; and then shall the end come." Before the end can come God must first send out his witnesses to speak the message of the theocracy; when this is happening then we know judgment will follow.

To complete my explication I will now go to the prophet Zechariah, "then answered I, and said unto him, What are these two olive trees upon the right side of the candlestick and upon the left side thereof? And I said again, and said unto him, What be these two olive branches which through the two golden pipes empty the golden oil out of themselves? And he answered me and said, Knowest thou not what these be? And I said, No, my lord. Then said he, These are the two anointed ones, that stand by the Lord of the whole earth." All leading us to the interpretation that the two witnesses are in fact two messiahs who will be opposed by the people of this world when they share their witness of the theocracy. However, it is a little more complicated than that. The Hebrew word used by the prophet Zechariah is not *mashiakh* as in Messiah, but the word *yitshar*, which means oil producers; yet I will here be translating it as little messiahs.

Thus, the rider of the white horse is not the Messiah as such, but is instead symbolic of the two witnesses, even as it says later on in the Revelations, "And the armies which were in heaven followed him upon white horses, clothed in fine linen, white and clean" (19: 14). It also says concerning the two witnesses, "these have power to shut heaven, that it rain not in the days of their prophecy: and have power over waters to turn them to blood, and to smite the earth with *all plagues*, as often as they will. And when they shall have finished their testimony, the beast that ascendeth out of the bottomless pit shall make war against them, and shall overcome them, and kill them" (11:6, 7; emphasis mine).

Now the word used in Revelations for witnesses is *martys* which is rooted in the word *martyr*. Basically, the two witnesses are two martyrs, but what is truly different about them is that they have the power to "smite the earth with all plagues as often as they will." And as the Revelations are predictive specifically of the *eskhaton* (last things), these plagues called forth by the two witnesses must be the seven last plagues of the wrath of God (16: 1-21) – seven obviously being a symbolic number as the two witnesses have a virtually limitless number of plagues they can call forth. Therefore Revelations 16 provides a template of the kind of plagues the two witnesses shall call forth – sores; turning seas into blood; turning rivers and fountains of water into blood; power over the sun; turning the Beast's kingdom to darkness; drying up the Euphrates to prepare the world for Armageddon; and earthquakes, thundering and hail.

What is of extra interest is that there is a relation between the seven last plagues and the seven trumpets. The first trumpet and the first plague affect the earth. The second trumpet and second plague affect the seas. The third trumpet and third plague affect the rivers and fountains of water. The fourth trumpet and fourth plague affect the sun. The fifth trumpet and fifth plague cause darkness to fill the land. The sixth trumpet and sixth plague affect the river Euphrates. The seventh trumpet and seventh plague cause earthquakes, thundering, voices and hail. Rather than look at all these plagues individually I shall simply say that the first five trumpets and first five plagues coincide with, and come as a result of, the first seal – which brings the two witnesses.

It could now, however, be asked why these two witnesses or two martyrs are here considered to be two little messiahs and not in fact the Messiah and his bride? The answer is that the two witnesses die "where also our Lord was crucified" (11:8); and again, "Wherefore they are no more twain, but one flesh. What therefore God hath joined together, let not man put asunder." What we get from these two Scriptures is that the two witnesses are very likely to be not the Messiah who was crucified, but one little messiah: that is, one witness. Besides, it makes more sense if it is a little messiah and not the Second Coming as that could turn out to be relatively different.

The witness thus carries the last plagues, because in him or her is filled up the wrath of God, and when he or she has finished his or her testament he or she shall be martyred (killed) for having martyred (testified) their message. So then what is the message? To be sure, it is not "For God so loved the world," which carries neither wrath nor judgment. It will be a message, not of salvation, but of vengeance. Then again, vengeance for what? This is a good question: the answer is most likely the blood of the prophets and righteous people of the earth who died unjustly, and the suffering endured by the victims of any iniquity or inequity that has transpired since the time of the original people. Basically, the days of vengeance come when the witness brings down the wrath of God on humanity and thus begins the *eskhaton*. And finally, this dramatic tale, or group of tales, will lead inexorably to the great deliverance of the righteous when the Messiah returns and destroys the mythical Beast character at the end.

Again, this Beast, a borrowed symbol from the scroll of Daniel, in the vision and astral journey of the Revelations is also, like with Daniel, used to symbolize a kingdom "which shall arise out of the earth"; or as Daniel also said, "The fourth beast shall be the fourth kingdom upon the earth, which shall be diverse from all kingdoms, and shall devour the whole earth, and shall tread it down, and break it in pieces." This kingdom (or Beast), so it was understood, would then be conquered by the messianic King of Israel prophesied afore time by the great visionaries of old. Then finally, according to the book of Revelations, the King of Israel would bring about a resurrection of the soul, to be spoken of in succeeding chapters. And as the apostle Paul makes very clear concerning the situation, it will all be in a case of; "every man in his own order: Christ the firstfruits; afterward they that are Christ's at his coming. Then cometh the end, when he shall have delivered up the kingdom to God, even the Father; when he shall have put down all rule and all authority and power. For he must reign, till he hath put all enemies under his feet."

So from this image we get an idea of government, not by kingdom but by dictatorship, even as the ancient Roman dictatorships were instituted by a general until order had been restored to the Roman provinces (of which all the apostles, including Paul and John, were observers); so it was acknowledged by their time that when the Messiah came he would have to seize and maintain power until all power and authority were crushed and order restored to the world. The idea of this seizing of power by God and his Messiah – with the witness as perhaps a captain in his army – though foretold long before the first century, was never as graphically depicted except by the apostle John's Revelations.

Rosa Luxemburg also agrees, stating that the revolutionist "should and must at once undertake socialist measures in the most energetic, unyielding and unhesitant fashion, in other words, exercise a dictatorship, but a dictatorship of the *class*, not of a party or of a clique – dictatorship of the class, that means in the broadest public form on the basis of the most active, unlimited participation of the mass of the people". However, whereas modernism – in the form of socialism and capitalism – sees dictatorship in the form of the class, theocracy sees dictatorship in the form of the Messiah and his dominion: the human heart. Far from the dictatorship being that of a class over the rest of society, whether that class be a majority or a minority, theocracy allows for self-government, trusting each to be ruled by their own principles of justice and ethics based on who they consider God to be and what they consider to be righteous. Therefore it is ultimately neither the rule of the rich nor the rule of the mob but the rule of righteousness and based on love.

What makes the horseman of the white horse distinct from the other horsemen is that he is given a crown and goes out to *nikao*, which means overcome, and is the exact thing the Messiah encourages the churches to do. Though there are many who consider him to actually be symbolic of 'Pestilence', there is no clue to this in the description given of him. There is actually more proof of him being the Messiah than of him being pestilence in any form. Yet there are nevertheless some who claim that the bow he carries portends to something sinister. These individuals seem to forget what David and Job said concerning God, "Yea, he sent out his arrows, and scattered them; and he shot out lightnings, and discomfited them." "For the arrows of the Almighty are within me, the poison whereof drinketh up my spirit: the terrors of God do set themselves in array against me." If God himself has arrows and bow then it is quite fitting for his servants to also have such, even if only symbolically. In all, the first seal represents the first five trumpets and first five plagues; the next five seals represent the sixth trumpet and sixth plague; and the seventh seal, trumpet and plague all represent the same end: earthquakes, thunderings, voices and great hail.

From here we can see not so much a warring as such but a brewing and preparing, the rising of a new form of government to take the place of all former ones. We can also find a deeper meaning to Ezekiel's astral drama: "Therefore, son of man, prophecy and say unto Gog, Thus saith the Lord God; In that day when my people of Israel dwelleth safely, shalt thou not know it? And thou shalt come from thy place out of the north parts, thou, and many people with thee, all of them riding upon horses, a great company, and a mighty army: And thou shalt come up against my people of Israel, as a cloud to cover the land; it shall be in the latter days, and I will bring thee against my land, that the heathen may know me, when I shall be sanctified in thee, O Gog, before their eyes. Thus saith the Lord God; Art thou he of whom I have spoken in old time by my servants the prophets of Israel, which prophesied in those days many years that I would bring thee against them?"

Even so, as the Israel of Ezekiel's vision meet with huge opposition upon their return from conflict, so the tide of conquest begins to turn as the Lamb opens the second seal (6:3, 4). At this point a fiery red horse and its horseman come to stand before the apostle John and the four living creatures. This horseman is at this time given the express authority and power to take peace from the earth and to start wars. He was also given a large sword with which to allow men to slay each other. The usual name given to this angel by those lay Bible traditionalists is 'War,' as it is believed that this angel represents the violent inclination within the human spirit.

But war has existed from time immemorial, and though modernity has brought with it more wars than any period in human history, this manifestation is more a result of vain ideologies than of that violent instinct within people's minds. Even during the time of the great empires and their religious vanities there were less wars than have happened in modernity, and the great killings that have occurred as a result of even the smallest modern battles far exceed those of any of the biggest ancient wars. In considering the reality of this situation we can understand that in modernity the intensification of wars has been deeper than at other historical epochs.

Imperialism and capitalist globalization have taken on a semblance of respectability in modern definitions, with Western elites pursuing ever wider capitalistic visions of expansion and development.

Countries such as the US and the countries within the EU and UK are currently all in the process of repackaging the brand of imperialism, at least in the sense of corporate imperialism. These business and commercial empires of the great Western powers have been on an unrepentant mission to carve up the world ever since the first modern industries came into being in Great Britain in the late 1700s.

The competition between all these various bourgeois powers and the rush to open up markets in order to strengthen hegemony is obviously a very familiar idea within the current mechanisms of the system. In the 1870s and 1880s this situation would resurface among the great Western powers driving each to expand their individual spheres of influence; thus causing overseas investment to rise substantially as land, labour and other raw materials were cheap and capital was scarce. This would ultimately produce the first string of commercial empires: those of industrial capital. Soon, as leading editor and socialist, Chris Harman, explains, "Those powers with empires sought to strengthen them by building up their military forces. Those without empires sought to take colonies and influence from those with. And, when it came to the crunch, they were prepared to wage world war against each other with Britain, France and Russia on the one side, and Germany and Austro-Hungary on the other."

That which would eventually lead to World War I was conflict and competition over the carving up of the economic have-nots between the haves, and of the political non-powers between the powers. Wars in 1898 between the US and Spain over Cuba and the Philippines; in 1899 between the British and the Boer settlers over southern Africa; in 1905 between Japan and Russia over Korea and northern China; in 1911 between Italy and Turkey over northern Africa (with a brief rivalry between France and Germany over Morocco in-between); and the war in 1912 between Russia and Austro-Hungary over the Balkans, which eventually led to World War I; were not national or ideological wars as such, but wars for ever broader economic and political spheres of influence.

With the global expansion of economic empires, arises the need to strengthen their military presence within those global territories to deter any abuses or mishandling of finances by the occupied territory or the capturing and annexing of the occupied territory by a rival empire. Economic imperialism therefore inevitably leads to military colonialism. This reality also brings a new light to the complex reasonings behind the need to go to war in Iraq. When the West speaks about the need or desire to preserve "our way of life," they are actually speaking of the preservation of capitalist and corporate spheres of influence in Iraq. This corporate influence is more than just with oil, though that did play a huge factor; this influence is with regard to the commercial and financial development of Western powers as a whole, into the Middle East. It was very likely, or at least should have been, well understood by Corporate America that expansion to the Middle East, in spite of the ending of the Cold War, would remain blocked as long as Saddam Hussein remained in power. The war was not to make the world a safer place for the West or the people of Iraq but for Western capitalism's presence in the Muslim Middle East. Therefore, while Iraq may not be a formal colony, being a semi-occupied territory, it is an informal one.

Colonialism after it has fully blossomed must inevitably lead to racism, as after the difficult phases of the struggle have been overcome the only means to justify their continued presence and occupation in the informal colony is to revert to the people's 'inherent inferiority,' but obviously in more politically correct wordings so as to hide their intensions from the masses. The painting of Muslims as inherently evil or as all a bunch of fanatical terrorists is the current strategy for justifying the continued 'War on Islam.' I say this mainly concerning those Muslims that are independent or unindoctrinated, these such Muslims and their countries are given the title 'rogue' while themselves being terrorized by the big Western powers.

Racism and classism are the inevitable outcome of the current system of economic development. It is the best means of keeping the masses on side along with the overstated ploy of 'spreading civilization'. Yet the ever more obvious reality to those of us who have for 400 years been the victims of their civilization is that modernity has brought with it nothing but war, kidnap, captivity, slavery, colonization, segregation, ghettoization, exploitation, criminalization and genocide. The transforming of human beings into the daemon of fanatic or extremist for their opposition to these things is no different from labelling them nigger or monkey for fighting racism.

This was the "New World Order" Bush Sr. spoke of at the end of the Cold War. War machines like NATO, although no longer necessary, were not abandoned, in actual fact, they were enlarged. The US after the ending of the Cold War actually spent more on arms and nuclear weapons up to September 11, 2001. Then with the incoming of September 11, and the 'War on Islam', they went on to spend a total of $379 billion in their military budget. So the US has sought to create the current imperialism that exists in the world today.

Going further still one very obvious truth to any keen observer is that the earnest manifestation of prophecy is not by the hand of human beings, nor is it the duty of humankind to fulfil, but is by the hand of God, who does these things by his own power. Again, the many small battles, wars and disputes of global history have really just been preparation for God's big showdown. The fact that to this day wars are still present within our world is in itself proof positive that the "war to end all wars" was just a prelude to something far more dangerous. Lately, as we all can now see, there has been emerging one monopolistic superpower over all of global politics.

At the opening of the next seal (6:5,6) there came to stand before the apostle John and the four living creatures a black horse and its horseman. This horseman himself carried a pair of scales in his hand, and there came a voice from the midst of the living creatures which gave the impression of a scarcity of food and of near famine conditions. For this cause this horseman has usually been called by those who know of his existence 'Famine.' A reality that is given broader explication in Ezekiel's astral vision, "Thus saith the Lord

God; It shall also come to pass, that at the same time shall things come into thy mind, and thou shalt think an evil thought: And thou shalt say, I will go up to the land of unwalled villages; I will go to them that are at rest, that dwell safely, all of them dwelling without walls, and having neither bars nor gates, To take a spoil, and to take a prey; to turn thine hand upon the desolate places that are now inhabited, and upon the people that are gathered out of the nations, which have gotten cattle and goods, that dwell in the midst of the land."

By all modern economic interpretations famine is a time of economic downturn when the demand for food is greater than the supply. However, that could never be the case in modernity. Sometimes what happens is the food that is available is too expensive for the poverty stricken inhabitants of a country (in which case most of the food gets dumped out and wasted); but ultimately there is food enough to feed the populations of the world easily. So where is the problem? There is not money enough in any country to feed all its people easily, whether through consumer shopping or state sponsorship. However the economic system of the apostle John's time worked one thing is obvious; their slavery system and marketplace economy also had fluctuations and famines of their own. So we see that famine conditions come about due to the fact that the purpose of food had, from the time of money coinage, been to make a profit and not to feed or help the hungry.

Yet modernity has seen three moments of economic downturn that it has called Great Depressions in which famine conditions have affected not only a country but the whole world. That is because the modern system has integrated all monies into a universal market system, yet all monetary systems from the first formation of the ancient states of the African and Asiatic regions have gone through cycles of famine and plenty. The problem is that this integrated money-capital, far from saving the system from the brunt of difficulty only exacerbates the difficulty through what socialists have dubbed *the falling rate of profits*. Simply put, the increasing wealth of the few super-rich bourgeoisie inevitably takes money from the moderately rich or not as rich bourgeoisie. So that all monies get concentrated into the hands of fewer and fewer people, while those who were rich today become moderately affluent tomorrow, and those who were moderately affluent today become poor tomorrow, etc.

To go with this the devaluation of money through inflation and interest rates has meant that money by today's standards can do far less than money by the standards of five years ago, let alone ten or twenty years ago. Again, this is due to the rising of the profits and capital gains of the very few super-rich, which must be compensated for by taking profits and monies from the not as rich. These stolen funds, though increasing the wealth of the bourgeois individual, cause the average rate of profits for the *class* of the bourgeoisie to steadily decrease. In order to make up for this difficulty the national system of the country is forced to print more money to curve out this discrepancy. This solution may dupe the people, it may even dupe the struggling bourgeoisie, but it cannot dupe the system, which to balance out the losses devalues the excess money-capital produced. This devaluation of national currency in turn leads to rising prices, which is the by-product of inflation, which itself precedes recession.

To solve this problem of the falling rate of profits companies do one or two of three things: 1. Expand the market overseas 2. Lengthen the hours of exploitation, 3. Get more out of the workers in the time they have through improved technology. Lately, employers have been doing the third but as they have not confronted the central issue of the monetary system the rate of profits are still decreasing. This issue is one of delicacy though, as most people in society are willing to fight and die to preserve the current system failing to appreciate that the system itself is a time bomb of economic chaos and degeneration. Unfortunately, neither the labourers nor the bourgeoisie are willing to abolish the system fearing that the loss of money means the loss of wages and thereby the loss of incentive, social disorder and economic impoverishment; while the improvement of these means the overall improvement of life. They fail to see that the improvement of these are an impossibility and, under the current system, disorder and impoverishment on an ever grander and grander scale are an inevitability.

But the system was able at one time to sustain a somewhat stable economic growth period from the 1940s to the 1970s, doing this via two ways: Firstly, through the massive state subsidies given to industry as a result of nationalization and the large amounts of revenue received by the government through the removal of the super-rich capitalists, thus allowing all their funds, that would have ordinarily been used for personal profits to go to the state instead of only the small percentage that the state would have normally acquired through taxing the individual capitalist. Secondly, through the fact that money during those days was valued under the gold standard. Basically, before the 1970s all Western monies were measurable economic units; only for that system to fall apart in the 1970s when Richard Nixon took the US off the gold standard. These two: nationalization and a measurable monetary system, held capitalism together during its heyday. Then, as money needed to fund the Vietnam War was running low, and as the workers and unions started getting greedy for revolution without actually being prepared to fight a revolution, the economic system took a downturn. That revolutionary spirit, which was a remnant of the 1960s, eventually turned to clouds of hostility and disillusionment as the world did not change nor become a better place. To make up for this the people began to march and demonstrate, but not to actually fight, thus the cities of the West ground to a halt, but with nobody seizing power crisis was inevitable.

When an economic crisis does happen it only clears the way to allow bigger businesses to expand overseas or globally, or to consume smaller local businesses. These smaller businesses must either accept being consumed to save their lives or go completely bust during the economic downturn. Among the workers, however, we find nothing but a mass of layoffs and wage decreases. All this inevitably leads to a concentration of wealth into fewer and fewer hands and thus to monopoly capital; and monopoly capital is really just another form of imperial capital, as these corporate empires begin to take over the game. Again, as capitalism gives way to corporate imperialism jobs and wages are not only at stake but are unsaveable. And so, like it or not, the labourers of today will be the underclass of tomorrow, even as the intellectuals of today, though unsuited to manual or service sector employment, in order to make ends-meet, will either have to take such or suffer complete joblessness.

This is all due to a process that economists call *the business cycle of bust and boom,* or famine and plenty. To give the standard economist explanation of this process and why they say we go through it to those who have never heard of it I shall now take the reader through their version of what it is. To start with booms are when businesses are doing well; profits are good; prices are reasonably set; wages are decent; companies are able to expand, make more branches, and invest in more productive property. With more companies expanding raw materials get scarce and their prices go up, which leads to prices going up all around, thus to inflation. Inflation soon leads to bust or "recession", where unemployment rises along with bankruptcy; companies close down the new branches, lose millions or get bought-out by larger businesses.

Life in these times is pretty much miserable for everybody and they seem to be unbeatable, but eventually there will come a time when smaller businesses will feel comfortable investing again and soon they will grow, and as they grow other companies will grow through them. A furniture store is doing well enough so they invest in more furniture. This gives work to more carpenters, who in turn give more work to loggers, who in turn give more work to truck manufacturers, who in turn help the steel and tire industries, who help other industries grow and eventually the whole system begins to grow again leading to another boom. So the *business cycle* is bust-boom-bust-boom.

This is the standard economist interpretation, however, a comparative analysis of the situation is: chaos in consumer habits and consumer choosing causes businesses that are faltering due to the concentration of monies to then panic. Simply leaving choice in the hands of the ordinary consumer, then hoping that the manipulation ploy of cunning advertisements will help or allow the product to sell, only creates greater problems for the pricing system. Without a coordinated operation to provide to the people what they need, while allowing them the option for more through a non-intrusive, non-centralized distribution mechanism, whatever programme that is put into place will either limit the capacities of the system, in which case chaos, or limit the freedom of choice of the individual, in which case oppression. The two must work together, that is, limited state *and* limited market; to take power from the one without at the same time taking power from the other leaves an imbalance and inequality in the social superstructure where power resides in either wealth or force.

However, for lack of this form of social superstructure and due to the inefficiency of the monetary system modern economists have been forced to resort to the now obsolete, now reviving, methods of their forebears: imperialism and monopoly. From here the current and continuing war crisis is the inevitable and persistent outcome. To use the same faulty solutions to the age old problems of the system will only produce the same faulty outcomes. Moreover, we can now perceive that the imperialistic wars of 1914-18 and 1939-45 were merely a prelude of good things to come if we do not start looking harder for better solutions. The current global expansion of corporate enterprises is reminiscent of those of the late nineteenth and early twentieth centuries before the outbreak of global war. Here again, the stage is set for a very dramatic and climactic conclusion.

With the opening of the fourth seal (6:7,8) the apostle John saw standing before him a pale horse whose horseman was called 'Death,' and Hades followed with him, probably riding his own pale horse. Death is then given power over the fourth part of the earth to kill by sword, famine and plague, and by the wild beasts; and with a partner like Hades, who makes a far more suitable 'Pestilence' than the rider of the white horse, he is completely prepared for what is to take place. The mission before him he has had in mind from the creation;

he has been watching and waiting for the onslaught he is sent out to inflict. The pursuit of his vision and his destiny is declared all the more forcefully as Ezekiel's drama continues, "Therefore thou son of man, prophesy against Gog, and say, Thus saith the Lord God; Behold, I am against thee, O Gog, the chief prince of Meshech and Tubal: And I will turn thee back, and leave but the sixth part of thee, and will cause thee to come up from the north parts, and will bring thee upon the mountain of Israel: And I will cause thine arrows to fall out of thy right hand."

But the prophet Ezekiel makes another statement that shows that Death is actually merely a servant used by God to bring about the demise of systems he is ready to judge: "Though Noah, Daniel, and Job, were in [a land], as I live, saith the Lord God, they shall deliver their own souls by their righteousness. For thus saith the Lord God; How much more when I send my four sore judgments upon Jerusalem, the sword, and the famine, and the noisome beast, and the pestilence, to cut off from it man and beast?" For this is the way of God. He uses Death to bring an entity to its fullest manifestation. True indeed, these last four horsemen: War, Famine, Death and Hades could in fact be the mysterious four angels "bound in the great river Euphrates" (9:14) that have been prepared for that very hour, and day, and month, and year. Thus while the first horseman is most likely the witness, prepared to bring the last plagues upon the earth, the four horsemen that follow are likely a symbol for the sore judgments God intends to inflict upon the earth nearing the end of their testimony.

Now Death itself exists in virtually every entity carrying them through to a new transition. The death of an entity is its moving from one state to another. Non-being is actually an absurdity. All things have life as all things have energy. Energy exists everywhere and energy cannot die. It merely changes from one state to another. This is how it is with humanity also. We do not die in the sense of ceasing to be, we merely transition from one state of being to another. From this we see the day of the Lord as a time of severe change, when the world shall meet God face to face and shall be changed, even as the apostle Paul said, "the dead shall be raised incorruptible, and we shall be changed."

But the changing of the world has occurred many times historically; the latest being the rise of modernity. Yet modernism will also have to stand face to face with Death, being in actuality nothing more than a European version of Americanism. American neo-colonialism has thus been backed and supported by European idealists who understand that the system itself currently stands by the power and dominance of American imperialism. All nations that are subject to the White House, IMF, World Bank, US Treasury and USAID (which all make up the Washington consensus) are subjects of the GUSE (Great United States Empire) and of US neo-colonialism. By transcending modernism one effectively transcends the imperial seat of the US and may even rouse their displeasure. True indeed, Europe is not officially subservient to the US as such, but they are still a part of its empire as they too follow the modernist agenda.

The intellectual fight back of the twentieth century led up to postmodernism; but modernism seems to have only been triumphed here. Nonetheless modernity will not reach its full demise until theocracy has become the new establishment and democracy is left in the darkness. This is the revolution that sets off a true postmodernism: a revolutionary theocratism. It sets in place a new standard of living and perceiving. When intellectual movements have reached their height then comes the tipping point at which time anything can set off revolution. The main motivating force behind modernism was humanism. We need a new motivating system in place of humanism's failed mission to improve our lot. And while Existentialism seems to be the motivating force behind postmodernism, it cannot account for the pneumatological realities that exist in the cosmos.

From the inauguration of humanism during the Renaissance to the present, everything white people have done and said has been and still is in their best interests as a race. Even their anti-racist and charitable deeds and statements are in their best interests as a race, though in the name of humanity. They universalize personal truths and broaden them to all people and races. Post-slavery black people have not been able to develop a philosophy so racially endemic as humanism. Notwithstanding, it was theorized by postmodernists that society had outgrown humanism and its grand narratives of liberation, actualization and ideology, and imploded into an all-encompassing simulation where all truth is subjective truth, if that. The fact is, however, that for society to demodernize in truth it must do just that: abolish its scientific truths.

Modernism's strength is in its monopoly on intellectual/scientific representation. It seems all intellectual and scientific achievement flows directly from modernists and modernizers. The inferiorizing of ancient customs and traditions, the rejecting and neglecting of what is essentially real and true subjectively to other races and people has brought about the humiliation of tribal knowledge, secrets and remedies and the glorification of the Western sciences. As race begins to get triumphed by ethnicity so modernism is slowly getting triumphed by an ever growing anti-modernist movement. But anti-modernism should not be a shift back to a past nirvana, it should be a shift into a bright interdependent future. It should recall nature in that all natural beings know their place in nature and operate within that sphere. This more naturalistic future is based on demodernization into something less intellectually based.

But as any true postmodernism brings on the death pangs of modernism, which is centred on democracy, such an actuality may seem contemptuous, even blasphemous, to most modern minds. The movement from the rule of the people to the rule of God means a transition from democracy to theocracy must occur. True indeed, far from creating a world of freedom, democracy has produced a fundamentalism of surveillance in the name of security. Not giving people the freedom to rule themselves is the only way for democracy to ensure it does not collapse into the pernicious malaise of chaos. This is the psychologic of self-disclosed humanity: not the freedom of humanism but the oppression of dehumanization. Here democracy is not the aspiration of subjected humanity but the imposition of modernist effectuation.

Nevertheless, the theocracy to the children of Israel and Judea was supposed to come with the Wrath of God: when God judged the nations of the world, and Gog and Magog, through Israel and Judea, his rod of punishment. To the Judeans, the armies would first be gathered for the great battle, "Then shall the Lord go forth, and fight against those nations, as when he fought in the day of battle. And his feet shall stand in that day upon the mount of Olives, which is before Jerusalem on the east, and the mount of Olives shall cleave in the midst thereof toward the east and toward the west, and there shall be a very great valley; and half of the mountain shall remove toward the north, and half of it toward the south. And ye shall flee to the valley of the mountains; for the valley of the mountains shall reach unto Azal: yea, ye shall flee, like as ye fled from before the earthquake in the days of Uzziah king of Judah: and the Lord my God shall come, and all the saints with thee."

As to this splitting of the Mount of Olives: just as Moses split the Red Sea so the Messiah symbolically split the Mount of Olives creating a valley for the nations to flee through, the valley of tribulation, as the apostle Paul also said, "we must through much tribulation enter into the kingdom of God" (Act 14: 22). What we learn from all this is that the people who individually flee through the valley of suffering will find salvation when Death meets modernity and will enter a new resurrection as they walk with the true and living becoming enraptured by his presence to grow more and more into his image. So we can conclude that the conquering of Death is not meant to be taken literally in the physical sense but is an individual experience we all receive through understanding death as an inevitability, a prelude to elevation. Here Death, though prepared for the great battle of God, is also a messenger of God to bring humanity to the point of divinity. The warfare of Death against God's authority is really just a ruse for the war of the nations against God's authority. If there was no fight before, there is definitely going to be one now.

At this point the Lamb opens the fifth seal (6:9-11) and the souls of those who were unjustly murdered for the sake of God and for their testimony cry out to God for justice, for vengeance, for revenge. It is here that Death and Hades, already prepared for battle, and having gathered and assembled their armies and their captives, are about to challenge the sovereignty of the Messiah, who has subdued and overcome all principality and power in the astral and has been preparing to subdue governments and lordships in the physical – the last being Death's. It is this subduing of Death that crystallizes his victories; lest having overcome in the astral he surrenders it all to Death.

Therefore the stage is fully set for the great battle of Death and Hades; as the prophet Isaiah also exclaims in his own scroll: "And in this mountain shall the Lord of hosts make unto all people a feast of fat things, a feast of wines well refined. And he will destroy in this mountain the face of the covering cast over all people, and the veil that is spread over all nations. He will swallow up death in victory; and the Lord God will wipe away tears from all faces; and the rebuke of his people shall he take away from off all the earth: for the Lord hath spoken it."

This final victory over Death allows for the freeing of the captives belonging to Death and Hades and clothing them with the clothing of God's people. The white robes given to them symbolize a sealing of righteousness and gives them a place among those who come later at the opening of the sixth seal. As these suffering and executed martyrs get clothed in their white robes and covered with the blood of the Lamb, they also find satisfaction and overcome the adversity and captivity they are then suffering. This would have been a message of comfort for the early messianic movement that was under persecution at that time from the Roman Empire.

But persecution from imperial powers is nothing new, the book of Daniel and the books of Maccabees are filled with them. Yet our hope takes on new bounds when we return to the prophet Ezekiel's astral drama, "Thou shalt fall upon the mountains of Israel, thou, and all thy bands, and the people that is with thee: I will give thee unto the ravenous birds of every sort, and to the beasts of the field to be devoured. Thou shalt fall upon the open field: for I have spoken it, saith the Lord God. And I will send a fire on Magog, and among them that dwell carelessly in the isles: and they shall know that I am the Lord."

There is, however, within our modern situation a new level of persecution and torture with psychological warfare that deserves recognition. The growing reality within colonialism and its present neo-colonial manifestation as the GUSE is that torture is inescapable to maintain political hegemony. But whereas in ancient times they tortured the body and put the body through the extremities of physiological pain, now they torture the mind and create newer means of psychological pain.

The political and indeed philosophical dimensions of torture reveal that the problem is deeper than the use of implements to cause pain; it is found in the ruling ideas of the imperial state. Deculturation methods, with the ruse of integration hopes, are applied to foreign countries with the distinct expectation of isolating and removing any form of political challenge to the imperial agenda. Disciplining defiance to the imperial doctrine is of course the essential aim of the neo-colonial government. However, the use of what Lou Turner calls "enhanced interrogation techniques" to acquire compliance calls the ethical superiority of the imperial power into question.

To further explain the realities of the tortured Turner tells of how, "To break down his resistance, police or military personnel arbitrarily round up ten to a dozen local residents and torture five or six of them to death while the suspected insurgent observes. After several homicidal tortures, the real interrogation begins. According to this method, torture, indeed murder, is used as an agent to condition the response of a detainee and also as a ruse for the dual concealment of the official nonknowing of intelligence and the possible knowing of official nonknowing by insurgents." These extremes to which the state is willing to go to maintain its form of hegemony are problematic as they do more to radicalize individuals than police them. At the same time, torture is not isolated to a few scattered individuals in the lower orders of the system. It is a standard procedure within the context of war. And with this legitimation method Wars on Terror, Wars on Drugs, Wars on Crime and other nondescript wars can descend into such enhanced interrogation methods to break *suspected* opponents.

According to Turner a "second method of torture is affiliated with nondirected conditioning, in which a suspect is tortured without being asked any questions....The suspect undergoes multiple episodes of torture sans explanation and questioning. Instead, when questioning begins, the suspect is told, 'we're listening,' whereupon he is supposed to tell everything he knows." These extreme means of interrogation bear similar relation to the sufferings of the early messianic movement in which they were tortured to force a renunciation of Christ and the kingdom of God out of the individual.

Yet within the current battle of the civilizations, the on-going War on Terror, there is something brewing at the bottom. Torture has done more to turn people against the West than for it. But it is from within this clash of the civilizations that a new ethics will develop, one that will be a theocratic counter to the Western modernist project. How it will look I do not know, but one thing is for sure: from within this War on Islam will emerge a doctrine that will trump modernism as it will present ideas and an ideal that modernity cannot resist. Its whole foundations will be shaken and it will lose all its strength. At the same time, just as the imperialistic wars of 1898-1912 led on into the world war of 1914-1918, so the wars on Islam of 2001-present have the potential to lead on into an Armageddon War. Thus, ultimately, the rivers and seas of blood shed by the Western world will be avenged by blood at the hands of historical developments.

There is, however, a hope for a new form of social integration that has taken hold in the global South. Especially in Africa, where democratic dreams have become the disillusion of repressed activism. US imperialism has set the pace for this tragedy of black people, whether in Africa or the Diaspora. The saints and martyrs in the quest to overthrow modernity and neo-colonialism will thus have to bring about a change in the system to eradicate this tentative absurdity through coordinated evaluation. Though coming from Islam or as a result of the on-going War on Islam, the movement to overthrow modernism will have to begin with intellectual debate. As all systems start in the philosophical and then organize into social change, this anti-modern rush will have to continue in its philosophical variation until the time of theocratic activism, when warfare, both intellectual and physical, is unleashed upon the world.

But those who take a stand against the iniquities of democracy always seem to find themselves called into question or treated as criminals or extremists for their troubles. This invokes arrest, torture or even murder at the hands of a state that is said to serve the people. This state, being a two-party, bureaucratically run, demagogically mandated, chaotically enforced mechanism; is able to repress and transgress in the name of freedom. Freedom, thus, has become a watered down excuse and cover for persecution of dissidence. Any opinion that runs counter to the hegemony of the GUSE and its modernist system is callously targeted for invective and abusive exclusion. We know this for sure: US neo-colonialism, in its current globalization form, is everywhere prevalent. The GUSE has military bases in virtually every country on the planet. One thing is for certain, imperialism is very much so still present in our world today.

Following the opening of the sixth seal (6:12-7:17) great and wondrous cataclysm occur upon the earth and in the heavens. All that can be shaken is shaken, that which is called "the wrath of the Lamb" is unleashed, and all people are held to account for their sins. The great Day of Judgment and vengeance prayed for by the martyrs of God has finally arrived and the Lamb takes his revenge for all the blood that has been spilled by the ungodly.

Here the astral vision foreseen by the prophet Ezekiel finally comes to its desperate conclusion: "And, thou son of man, thus saith the Lord God; Speak unto every feathered fowl, and to every beast of the field, Assemble yourselves, and come; gather yourselves on every side to my sacrifice for you, even a great sacrifice upon the mountains of Israel, that ye may eat flesh, and drink blood. Ye shall eat the flesh of the mighty, and drink the blood of the princes of the earth, of rams, of lambs, and of goats, of bullocks, all of them fatlings of Bashan." "And it shall come to pass in that day, that I will give unto Gog a place there of graves in Israel, the valley of the passengers on the east of the sea: and it shall stop the noses of the passengers: and there shall they bury Gog and all his multitude: and they shall call it The valley of Hamon-gog."

For even though these Scriptures are a confirmation of the prophet Zephaniah's message: "Hold thy peace at the presence of the Lord God: for the day of the Lord is at hand: for the Lord hath prepared a sacrifice, he hath bid his guests. And it shall come to pass in the day of the Lord's sacrifice, that I will punish the princes, and the king's children, and all such as are clothed with strange apparel"; the Christians of the early messianic movement would most likely have interpreted this as a distortion of the Armageddon War. (For the Armageddon War will be a world war fought between the bringers of theocracy and the keepers of democracy. The empire of Gog, the last imperial power, will be the keepers of this democracy.)

So who is Gog and where is Magog? To answer this we must consider the imperial power in the world today, the power most likely to be a hindrance to the coming of God and his theocracy. As for the man Gog, he will be the one who drives the people to war against the bringers of theocracy. The intellectual and physical warfare that occurs as a result will be eschatological to the point that the dead will not be given a proper funeral but will be left out for the animals and birds to devour. The messianic movement experienced this kind of Crusade at the hands of Nero Caesar when he began his imperial witch hunt of Christians.

The knowledge of governmental persecution was very apparent to first century Christians who faced death for their messianic devotion. At that time the messianic movement was condemned as a terrorist movement even though they most likely were non-violent. The theocratic movement of today, however, does not share this restriction;

therefore we will likely face an even heavier media onslaught than them. Here war, famine, death and pestilence are plagues sent by God to judge the world, particularly the GUSE, for their persecution of us. But for God to pass his final judgment and vengeance on the world he must first send out his angel, "having the seal of the living God," to seal those who are to be labelled for glory. Ezekiel expresses or gives a similar picture in another of his astral visions, stating:

> *"He cried also in mine ears with a loud voice, saying, Cause them that have charge over the city to draw near, even every man with his destroying weapon in his hand. And, behold, six men came from the way of the higher gate, which lieth toward the north, and every man a slaughter weapon in his hand: and one man among them was clothed with linen, with a writer's inkhorn by his side: and they went in, and stood beside the brazen altar. And the glory of the God of Israel was gone up from the cherub, whereupon he was, to the threshold of the house. And he called to the man clothed with linen, which had the writer's inkhorn by his side; And the Lord said unto him, Go through the midst of the city, through the midst of Jerusalem, and set a mark upon the foreheads of the men that sigh and that cry for all the abominations that be done in the midst thereof. And to the others he said in mine hearing, Go ye after him through the city, and smite: let not your eye spare, neither have ye pity: slay utterly old and young, both maids, and little children, and women: but come not near any man upon whom is the mark; and begin at my sanctuary" (Eze 9:1-6).*

Obviously, this mark, being the very seal of the living God carried by the angel, is a sign and proof of affiliation to the people of God to be glorified at his coming. This proof being in similitude to the blood of the Passover lamb saves those who have it from the judgment to come upon the earth from God. It is therefore more than merely an awkward mysticism but is a transcending of both mysticism and traditionalism. It is the stuff that dreams are made of.

For even as Queen Makeda of Sheba said in the Song of Songs, "Set me as a seal upon thine heart, as a seal upon thine arm: for love is strong as death; jealousy is cruel as the grave: the coals thereof are coals of fire, which hath a most vehement flame" (Song 8:6). Now the Hebrew word used here for love is *ahab*, which, though true indeed, is defined as love, is not so much the love a child has for their parent, nor even the love a soldier has for their people. *Ahab* is mainly, though not always, denoting love in the sexual sense, as in making love. On the other hand, the Hebrew word used here for jealousy is the word *qinah*, which comes from the root *qana* and actually means zeal or passion, not jealousy in the sense of wanting what someone else has or bitterness over a lover's betrayal. It only got translated as jealousy due to a misinterpretation by the Greeks in the Septuagint Bible. Still, these issues are only being brought up not to encourage people towards having more sex, or to say that women are not allowed to be abstinent, or again, to say that we godbody do, or even should, force our female members to give it up more. The issue is brought up because though marriage is rejected by most godbodies, sex is not; and to show that sexuality itself, far from being condemned by God, is in actual fact the very seal of God.

Most people have been bought up with a view that sex is carnal and unspiritual, that sexuality is secular and even vulgar, but what the Song reveals, and the Revelations confirm, is that sex plays a much more vital role in God's plan than we presumed. That is not to say that other interpretations of the seal do not exist. Ephesians 1:13, 14 says: "In whom ye also trusted, after that ye heard the word of truth, the gospel of your salvation: in whom also after that ye believed, ye were sealed with that holy Spirit of promise, Which is the earnest of our inheritance, until the redemption of the purchased possession, unto the praise of his glory." Could the seal not simply be the holy Spirit? in which case Revelation 14: 4 makes a lot more sense, where it is written of those who have the seal of God on their foreheads,

"These are they which were not defiled with women; for they are virgins. These are they which follow the Lamb whithersoever he goeth. These were redeemed from among men, being the firstfruits unto God and to the Lamb."

The seal of the living God, which is apparently the Holy Spirit, apparently has no connection to the seal of sexuality or passion – but on closer examination the two coincide. The apostle Paul says, "Would to God you could bear with me a little in my folly: and indeed bear with me. For I am jealous over you with godly jealousy: for I have espoused you to one husband, that I may present you as a chaste virgin to Christ. But I fear, lest by any means, as the serpent beguiled Eve through his subtilty, so your minds should be corrupted from the simplicity that is in Christ. For if he that cometh preacheth another Jesus, whom we have not preached, or if ye receive another spirit, which ye have not received, or another gospel, which ye have not accepted, ye might well bear with him." When Revelations says they are virgins, it is most likely in the symbolic sense, as in having no other God, Messiah or Spirit. But in that sense, the spirit in itself could hardly be the seal of God as it is undefined. What is the true holy Spirit if there are false ones that can beguile us?

First of all, I am not suggesting that the true Holy Spirit is sexuality as such; however, the seal – which is strong as death – does appear to be such. For there is a distinction between sexuality and lust: the central difference being refinement. This is what distinguishes the holy from the unholy, the clean from the unclean. At the same time, what is sexy without being tasteless? The apostle John articulates, "And to her was granted that she should be arrayed in fine linen, clean and white: for the fine linen is the righteousness of saints" (19:8). To be sure, when this Scripture says fine linen it uses the word *byssinos* which is what the Greeks called transparent linen, something worn very frequently by the ancient Egyptians, Greeks and Romans. Then again, the early church's wearing of this fine spun linen was as much a sexy act as it was a holy through the fact that they wore no underwear and so were naked underneath, as shown in Mark 14:51,52. Again, what is the purpose of mentioning this out of place story in Mark if not to subtly reveal this now lost tradition?

Indeed, this light exhibitionism of permanently not wearing underwear would have also been considered a form of black erotica, something practiced very often in ancient Egypt even as stated by Barbara Watterson, "Ancient Egyptian women wore their revealing dresses without much in the way of underwear". The same can be said also of the ancient Kushites. Even the ancient Hebrews would have practiced it, as can be seen by the Hebraic concept of *qodesh*, which means holy, though in a sexual sense (the Hebrew words *qadesh* and *qadeshah* were respectively the male and female equivalents of: refined one, holy disciple and saint; and were also the equivalents of sexual one, shrine prostitute and seducer. Basically, the holy men and holy women of the ancient Hebraic culture were like Tantrics, understanding the value of their sexuality. And though the translators in the days of King James I translated the word *qadesh* as sodomite, such a mistranslation was an expression of the times. Its proper translation as sexual one helps us to understand why the only Scripture in the Bible to translate it as sodomite, Deuteronomy 23: 17, condemned its practice in Israel: due to the excessive practice of sexuality in Judea just before its fall, as can be read in Jeremiah). It is also clear that the *qodesh* (the holy men and holy women) were instituted into religious service by King David after he entered Jerusalem, which goes a long way in explaining why Jerusalem was called "The Perfection of Beauty" and "The Joy of the Whole Earth" (Ps 48: 2; Lm 2: 15).

Notwithstanding, the seal of God is given several names throughout the gospels; of greater significance to us though is when the Messiah calls it a wedding garment – like with the white robes given to the martyrs and the white robes of the multitude, so is the clean and white *byssinos* of the wedding garment – for he said, "And when the king came in to see the guests, he saw there a man which had not on a wedding garment: And he saith unto him, Friend, how camest thou in hither not having a wedding garment? And he was speechless. Then said the king to the servants, Bind him hand and foot, and take him away, and cast him into outer darkness; there shall be weeping and gnashing of teeth" (Mt 22:11-13). For the wedding garment was a symbol of something far more powerful to the early messianic movement, it symbolized this sexy holiness that we godbodies call refinement. But fine spun linen (that is, transparent linen) in itself is not holy nor could it be a seal of anything; it is the fact that underwear was not worn in the early messianic movement – thereby making them naked underneath – and obviously the ritual and ceremonial bodily cleansings that were also performed by them in those days, that made them both sacred and sexy.

Now these remarks may seem surprising, even spurious, to some readers; but that is only due to the modern Western mindset. We have been raised to view our bodies from a purely sexual perspective, whether towards the positive or the negative. Those that view it towards the negative usually only fuel those that view it towards the positive to be more filthy and more over-the-top when it comes to their sexuality. We cannot hope to encourage better sexual practices and mentalities by avoiding the question altogether. At the same time, we should not look to the GUSE to teach us about sexuality, sexual temperance, or even hygiene since the practice of wearing underwear has no genuine hygienic value, even for women; it is far more hygienic to wash thoroughly and continually your private areas than to wear extra clothing to cover up filth.

Nevertheless, for those who feel that such a requirement is far too base for an exalted God to be concerned with I will remind them of the covenant that God made with Abraham of circumcision, the covenant God made with John of water baptism, and the covenant God made with Muhammad of the hijab. The covenants of God have a requirement in our flesh that becomes a sign of refinement and distinction. Thus, while wearing transparent jellabiyas and abayas may be holy, in that it denotes class; it is not here considered the righteousness of the saints, that is, the seal of the living God – especially when we take into consideration colder climates – however, the light exhibitionism represented in not wearing underwear (which a lot of women in the street life already do, and which I, being myself an exhibitionist, also do); is here considered the seal, as it is both sexy and it forces us to clean ourselves thoroughly, even as the messianic movement used to encourage. But that did not mean the early messianic movement did not have intruders, as the apostle Paul said, "false brethren unawares brought in, who came in privily to spy out our liberty which we have in Christ Jesus". The danger coming from the seal of the living God is that lustful minds will always want a piece.

Still, all this has not been an entirely honest account, though: when Revelations 14: 4 speaks of the seal of the hundred and forty four thousand what it says in actual fact is that the Father's name is written on their foreheads. Basically, it is the Father's signature: and God's signature has historically been a demonstration of power. So, the actual question should be asked: what then is the significance of the forehead? The only apparent answer would be that it is the location of the third eye. The signature of God is thus the opening of the third eye allowing for the ability to see into the astral realms at will. This truth is apparent in that the Lamb that they walk with has seven eyes. Still, like with all signatures there is a double signing. The godly sign with light exhibitionism, God himself signs with the opening of the third eye.

And after the godly, both male and female, have signed themselves up with sexy refinement, and God has signed back with astral vision, things start to get heavy as the world now prepares for the coming of the Wrath of God; that is, the final showdown between God and humanity. So far humanity has fought zealously against God producing symbolic horsemen carrying plagues. They have vexed themselves, destroyed themselves, subjugated themselves, and bought Death and Hades to the seat of dominion over the earth. Therefore, whereas before they had to face the wrath of the Lamb, now they are about to stand naked and face to face before a holy and righteous God.

When the Lamb opens the seventh seal (8:1-5) silence grips the heavens for about a half an hour. This prolonged silence is not one of worship or duty but one of intensity. And then it is unleashed: the Wrath of God longly waited for comes upon the earth and tries the hearts of the people. Here they stand face to face with their greatest fear and their greatest judge, themselves. The uncleanness and injustice of their ways has been hidden from all creation and nothing on earth knows someone like they know themselves. As they see themselves in all their filthiness, all their vanity, all their corruption, all their weakness, and all they have caused to happen in the world; if they can look on and still see the good behind the veil of Death, then when they are sent to an eternity with likeminded individuals, they will praise God for their victory. To them that see failure, misery and disappointment; that see ruin, sin, wickedness and shame, there will be horror and plague when God sends them to an eternity with likeminded individuals, such that their plagues may never end. When all the voices, and the terrors, and the thunderings, lightnings and earthquakes have come to pass on earth and there is nothing left to stand on that cannot be shaken, then comes the time when we must run to He who cannot be shaken, and running there we know he sees us and has seen us as we are.

In the day the baby bird is about to take to its first flight it calls out to and can call out to none other than he who is Beneficence and Mercy. When the war-horse or chariot charges into battle there is only one who it prays to for victory. When the rain-clouds gather and the storms brew there is only one whose command they await. When the rivers rush toward an aggressive coast, or are parched for lack of supply, there is only one who they depend on for strength and support. When the strong winds threaten to rip the tree from its place, or to dash the rocks and mountains with a mighty blast, only one gives them comfort and eases their fears. When the mountain lion is hungry and becomes famished from the hunt he stretches out his hand to no lower being. When the mountain goat is pregnant on the hills, and in pain to be delivered, she cries out to no lesser power to deliver her kids. When the crocodile storms through the swamps and takes his seat in the cloudy marsh there is only one who he fears, and only one to whom he will submit. When Satan is lifted up in victory and in pride of his capture there is only one who makes him tremble and only one who makes him shake.

In the final analysis, when the people are through with all their fighting and all their arrogance and all their vanities, they will have to stand, alone, before his seat; and they will have to give an account to none other than he who is Beneficence and Mercy, the Ruler at the Day of Judgment, the Lord of all the Worlds. Here we see that the only wall left for the people to hide behind is blatant stupidity; for anyone, after knowing they are emphatically wrong and corrupted, who persists in unrighteousness is doomed to the chaotic existence of perpetual hopelessness. Worse still "if we sin wilfully after that we have received the knowledge of the truth, there remaineth no more sacrifice for sins, But a certain fearful looking for of judgment and fiery indignation, which shall devour the adversaries. He that despised Moses' law died without mercy under two or three witnesses: Of how much sorer punishment, suppose ye, shall he be thought worthy, who hath trodden under foot the Son of God, and hath counted the blood of the covenant, wherewith he was sanctified, an unholy thing" (Heb 10: 26-29).

It is the declared intention of the theocracy to overthrow American style democracy: replacing the rule of the people with the rule of God. But to be sure, democracy will not lie down to theocracy, it must be overthrown. But this overthrowing need not involve terrorism or coercion. The mature system (if that is really what you desire to call it) is based on socially and theologically ethical people living to manifest their divinity. This is not the democratic "rule of law," which amounts to nothing but the rule of the bourgeoisie; this is the rule of love, which amounts to the rule of God.

Saint Augustine helps us understand more the realities of bringing about this rule of God, when he says "God is the Author of all measure, form, and order...He left no part of His creation without its appropriate peace, for in the last and least of all His living things the very entrails are wonderfully ordered – not to mention the beauty of birds' wings, and the flowers of the fields and the leaves of trees. And above the beauty of sky and earth is that of angels and of man." God basically rules over nature and the universe. It is only humanity that rebels against his rule, which is what forces him to respond with a heavy hand.

The apostle Paul states along these lines, "Now this I say, brethren, that flesh and blood cannot inherit the kingdom of God; neither doth corruption inherit incorruption." Basically, the flesh corrupts, and the completely fleshly are completely corrupt; but as the spirit is incorruptible, only it can inherit the kingdom. Again, in the Second Coming the Messiah will not be flesh and blood like he was the first time but spiritual. Now recognizing how abominable this statement must seem to the godbody I will show and prove. Many Christians love to say God will fix all the world's problems at the Second Coming, when God has already given us the means to fix them right now thanks to the First Coming. Nevertheless, the apostle Paul says concerning the Second Coming, "For the Lord himself shall descend from heaven with a shout, with the voice of the archangel, and with the trump of God: and the dead in Christ shall rise first: Then we which are alive and remain shall be caught up together with them in the clouds, to meet the Lord in the air: and so shall we ever be with the Lord" (1Th 4:16, 17).

Now Paul already said flesh and blood do not inherit the kingdom of God so it is not a physical resurrection Paul is talking about. Considering these things perhaps the best way to answer this Scriptural question is through further Scriptures. The apostle John provides a good answer to the riddle, "After this I looked, and behold, a door was opened in heaven: and the first voice which I heard was as it were of a trumpet talking with me; which said, Come up hither, and I will shew thee things which must be hereafter. And immediately I was in the spirit: and behold, a throne was set in heaven, and one sat on the throne. And he that sat was to look upon like a jasper and a sardine stone" (4:1-3). Now while, on the one hand, this Scripture presents an entirely different description of God from the images shown around Europe (seeing that jasper is a reddish brown very similar again to mahogany and sardius is an orange brown in sight like garnished oak); on the other hand, it also shows that all these things which were to take place happened in the spirit.

Yet, at the Second Coming Christ was supposed to bring about a resurrection of humanity and a dissolving of the present universe, along with all the evil within it; and as the apostle Peter said, "Seeing then that all these things shall be dissolved, what manner of persons ought ye to be in all holy conversation and godliness, Looking for and hasting unto the coming of the day of God, wherein the heavens being on fire shall be dissolved". Clearly, to hasten unto the day of God, a godliness of lifestyle and holiness of spirit were considered the practical realities we ought to be walking in.

That is primarily why the current systems of global Americanism and US neo-colonialism only hinder the true day of the Lord. A day that the prophet Zephaniah perhaps gives the most accurate description of, "Therefore wait ye upon me, saith the Lord, until the day that I rise up to the prey: for my determination is to gather the nations, that I may assemble the kingdoms, to pour upon them mine indignation, even all my fierce anger: for all the earth shall be devoured with the fire of my jealousy. For then will I turn to the people a pure language, that they may all call upon the name of the Lord, to serve him with one consent. From beyond the rivers of Ethiopia my suppliants, even the daughter of my dispersed, shall bring mine offering. In that day shalt thou not be ashamed for all thy doings, wherein thou hast transgressed against me" (Zep 3:8-11).

Basically, the day of the Lord comes after the Lamb has judged the nations of the world, led by Gog and Magog, by the hand of his once dispersed, and even now still dispersed, people of Israel in warfare. This day of God, being preceded by the Second Coming of the Messiah, should not be considered interchangeable with it. At the same time, the Second Coming is itself in accordance with individuals setting up Christ and his spiritual dictatorship in their hearts and overthrowing all the vanities of this world and of the modern state in their hearts. Then, ultimately, with the dissolving in their hearts of this present corruptible universe and everything in it, comes the day of God. Any neighbourhood that adopts a theocratic programme experiences the Second Coming, and from that moment begins to dwell in an actually existing millenarianism. But the realities of the theocracy coming into the neighbourhoods of this world and overthrowing the democratic and modern state will cause the rulers and governments of this world, and of Gog and Magog, to fight back in the form of Armageddon Wars; and when this occurs we will need to employ the help of the God you now.

THE FIRST RESURRECTION (THE RESTORATION OF THE BLACK SOUL)

In the book of Revelations there is presented a brilliant and beautiful story so grand that people for the most part consider it to be a millennium of grace: "And I saw thrones, and they sat upon them, and judgment was given unto them: and I saw *the souls* of them that were beheaded for the witness of Jesus, and for the word of God, and which had not worshipped the beast, neither his image, neither had received his mark upon their foreheads, or in their hands; and they lived and reigned with Christ a thousand years. But the rest of the dead lived not again until the thousand years were finished. This is the first resurrection. Blessed and holy is he that hath part in the first resurrection: on such the second death hath no power, but they shall be priests of God and of Christ, and shall reign with him a thousand years" (Rev 20: 4-6; emphasis mine). And again, "For the priesthood being changed, there is made of necessity a change also of the law" (Heb 7: 12).

The unobvious part that has been overlooked by so many people over the past few hundred years is that it is not the physical body that is resurrected in this *First Resurrection* but "the *souls* of them that were beheaded". This misinterpreted symbology of the book of Revelations by most recent theologians and preachers of apocalyptic peril has unfortunately led to many great tragedies and modern acts of horror. If given its genuine and proper interpretation it could have easily been seen where the interpretation of this Scripture can be found; for the apostle Paul explains, in a language the early messianic movement would have completely understood, how God, "Even when we were dead in sins, hath quickened us together with Christ, (by grace ye are saved;) And hath raised us up together, and made us sit together in heavenly places in Christ Jesus" (Eph 2:5,6). Clearly, it is the resurrecting and rapturing of the soul that is of importance, because if we fall from this grace given us by God, this grace that has saved us, then our souls have not been raised from death into resurrection life.

Basically, the first resurrection is a resurrection of the black soul. Furthermore, as the word used for soul in the Revelations is psyche; if we consider, firstly, that *psychikos* was translated in the Bible as the word sensual, and, secondly, that the Freudian interpretation of psychic activity was far more sensual than cognitive; then we see that the first resurrection should actually be called a sensual resurrection. For which cause, and for clarity's sake, I have chosen to call it a resurrection of Afrosensuality and not a resurrection of the black psyche, as such would be misleading. The secret and clue is found in the gospel of Matthew, where the Messiah says to the Sadducees who test him concerning marriage, "in the resurrection they neither marry, nor are given in marriage, but are as the angels of God in heaven," which parallels completely with the godbody's own restriction of marriage. Effectively, we godbodies prove to be the children of the resurrection, having a more messianic form of lifestyle than even the church.

Still, we are not hermits, monks or nuns. We do not take a vow of celibacy, we just do not follow the bourgeois form of marriage, but consider ourselves able to have free sexual relationships, as the Messiah also said concerning marriage, "Have ye not read, that he which made them at the beginning made them male and female, And said, For this cause shall a man leave father and mother, and shall cleave to his wife: and they twain shall be one flesh? Wherefore they are no more twain, but one flesh. What therefore God hath joined together, let not man put asunder." This standard of free love that the godbody used to practice, and have lately been abandoning; though seeming somewhat unimportant to most people by Western and modernistic standards, carried with it a huge weight of responsibility, as from here it could be seen to have played a vital role in the sensuality and development of the original people.

Moreover, if we wish to properly understand the resurrection of the black soul, that is, of Afrosensuality, we need to first understand that the life and death of the soul is interconnected to the marriage relations that exist among the individuals of that community and the oneness they share with each other. Secondly, we need to understand that these marriage relations in the first resurrection will be similar to those that existed in the beginning with the first lovers; as it says in the book of Genesis: "And the Lord God took the man, and put him into the garden of Eden to dress it and to keep it" (Gen 2: 15). Now for those who do not know: the word Eden in its Hebrew original means delight, luxury, pleasure and voluptuousness and in its Hebrew feminine is the word Edinah, which means sexual pleasure. Basically, Eden is and was always a sexual paradise.

Here we find the words of Peter Kropotkin ringing ever truer: "The first thing which strikes us as soon as we begin studying primitive folk is the complexity of the organization of marriage relations under which they are living." Indeed, Engels writes, "[John] McLennan knew only three forms of marriage – polygamy, polyandry and monogamy. But once attention had been directed to this point, more and more proofs were discovered of the fact that among undeveloped peoples forms of marriage existed in which a group of men possessed a group of women in common; and Lubbock (in his *The Origin of Civilization*, 1870) acknowledged this group marriage ("communal marriage") to be a historical fact."

Based on this theme we understand that God, in his infinite glory and power, could not have been alone in the universe; not with the potential for so much great beauty and wonder. The Bible says of the creation, "And the Lord God said, It is not good that the man should be alone" (Gen 2:18), well, nor is it good for the Lord God to be alone, hence the term Elohim. For those who do not know, the word Elohim in Hebrew is the plural form of the word El or Elah. Here the name Elohim should actually be translated: *the Elohim*, as in, the gods – or better still, the divine – which would change the Hebrew creation story dramatically.

Remember, Moses, who is the most likely author of the book of Genesis, was a master of the Kemetic mysteries, therefore the Hebrew cosmogony actually shows great similarities to the Kemetic cosmogonies, where from the one god Tum came all the Heliopolitan gods, who through Khepru (evolutionary motion) in turn created the heavens and the earth at the origin. And the Hebrew people would also have learned the Kemetic traditions while they were living in Kemet for four hundred and thirty years. (This Hebrew experience in Kemet, being of similitude to the African experience in the West, where they lost their freedom, their religion, their culture, their language and their traditions; also demonstrates an unconscious link with the past as in both cases it was black people being enslaved.)

The fact is, every time the Bible says the word *gods* in the Hebrew language it uses the word Elohim; and there is an actual distinction from where the Bible says *God* and where it says *the Lord God*. When it says the word God the Hebrew word is usually Elohim, as in the gods, whereas when it says the Lord God it is usually Adonai Elohim, which is, the Lord of the gods, or Adonai Jahvih – as in Lord Jahveh. Even the Scriptures call him, "The Lord God of gods," "For the Lord is a great God, and a great King above all gods" (Jos 22: 22; Ps 95: 3). But the Scriptures also reiterate that the gods, who in the beginning created the universe, also made humanity in their image, saying "And God [Elohim] said, Let us make man [Adam] in our image, after our likeness and let them have dominion over the fish of the sea, and over the fowl of the air, and over the cattle, and over all the earth, and over every creeping thing that creepeth upon the earth. So God [Elohim] created man [Adam] in his own image, in the image of God created he him; male and female created he them." (Gen 1:26, 27.) Thus, the gods, or to give a more suitable translation: the angelic beings, made we human beings in their own image and after their likeness, male and female: Or two separate genders, even as they are in two separate genders in the Kemetic traditions; and to be sure, there was a kind of free love institution among them.

Again, to go back to Engels, "group marriage, when observed more closely, does not appear quite so horrible as is fancied by the philistine in his brothel-tainted imagination." For even "[Lewis] Morgan, in agreement with the majority of his professional colleagues, arrived at a primitive stage at which promiscuous intercourse prevailed within a tribe, so that every woman belonged equally to every man and every man to every woman." In all this, "Mutual toleration among the adult males, freedom from jealousy, was, however, the first condition for the formation of those large and enduring groups in the sole midst of which the transition from animal to man could take place." "If anything is certain, it is that jealousy is an emotion of comparatively late development."

Now concerning our present knowledge and information on these ancient familial and societal customs Engels says, "We are indebted to the English missionary Lorimer Fison for the most substantial enrichment of our knowledge of group marriage...He found the lowest stage of development among the Australian Negroes of Mount Gambier in South Australia. The whole tribe is here divided into two large classes – Kroki and Kumite. Sexual intercourse within each of these classes is strictly proscribed; on the other hand, every man of one class is the born husband of every woman of the other class, and she is his born wife." To further explain how this system worked in practice Engels goes on, "In all forms of the group family it is uncertain who the father of a child is, but it is certain who the mother is. Although she calls *all* the children of the aggregate family her children and is charged with the duties of a mother towards them, she, nevertheless, knows her natural children from the others. It is thus clear that, wherever group marriage exists, descent is traceable only on the *maternal* side, and thus the *female line* alone is recognised."

And as Kropotkin reminds us, "The natives of Australia do not stand on a higher level of development than their South African brothers."

To further explain this system more in depth he uses the words of, "Lumholtz, a missionary who sojourned in North Queensland:

> 'The feeling of friendship is known among them; it is strong. Weak people are usually supported; sick people are very well attended to; they never are abandoned or killed...The parents love their children, play with them, and pet them. Infanticide meets with common approval. Old people are very well treated, never put to death. No religion, no idols, only a fear of death. Polygamous marriage. Quarrels arising within the tribe are settled by means of duels fought with wooden swords and shields. No slaves; no culture of any kind; no pottery; no dress, save an apron sometimes worn by women.'"

With regard to Lumholtz's views concerning Aboriginal polygamy, it is probable that what he means is a group sexuality custom and not a system of many marriages, as Engels relates through his own studies, "Group marriage, which in the case of Australia is still class marriage, the state of marriage of a whole class of men, often scattered over the whole breadth of the continent, with an equally widely distributed class of women...the law according to which an Australian Negro, even when a stranger thousands of miles away from his home, among people whose language he does not understand, nevertheless, quite often, in roaming from camp to camp, from tribe to tribe, finds women who guilelessly, without resistance, give themselves to him; and according to which he who has several wives cedes one of them to his guest for the night. Where the European can see only immorality and lawlessness, strict law actually reigns".

Grinker et al. also explain the current black predisposition towards polygyny in African customs today. Most likely derived from former group marriage (or group sexuality) customs among tribes and classes, polyandry "in which a woman has more than one husband...is [now] uncommon in Africa, having been outlawed in Nigeria and elsewhere during colonization," which in turn caused the growth of polygyny throughout Africa to expand without the counterbalance of polyandry. The European effectively prohibited the more traditionally black forms of marriage and forced on black people the European forms of marriage. They condemned our sacred forms of sexuality as heathen and immoral and made our ideal form of sexuality that of the slave-master/colonizer. Polygamy by this time had been long extinct in Europe, while among the blacks of Africa and Australia group sexuality still existed up until colonization.

Engels explains the Western marital devolution as such, "the transition [from group sexuality] to monogamy..., implied the violation of a primeval religious injunction (that is, in fact, the violation of the ancient traditional right of...other men to the same woman), a violation which had to be atoned for, or the toleration of which had to be purchased, by surrendering the woman for a limited period of time." But "If, however, we apply this measure to...history, to that of even the most developed peoples of the present day, we find that there still exists here a colossal disproportion between the proposed aims and the results arrived at, that unforeseen effects predominate, and that the uncontrolled forces are far more powerful than those set into motion according to plan."

Whether group sexuality is the custom of the angels or just free love one thing is for certain: early humanity was made in the image of the angels and so followed the custom of the angels. Whereas most Christians believe the angels to all be celibate the onus is on them to prove that, as, all single-gendered species – that is, species in which male or female only have the sexual properties of one gender – copulate with the opposite gender to reproduce. The Kemetic did not share their enthusiasm for angelic celibacy accepting that the divine not only had sex but had offspring too. Based on this understanding it becomes imperative that we consider the early customs of early humanity to determine their cultural development into what would today be called human culture.

According to the current anthropological doctrine concerning the development of original people it is understood that the hominid called Australopithecus africanus was able to evolve into the genus *Homo* by several hormonal transitions. Australopithecus afarensis and africanus being the oldest fossil remains found of early hominidae in Kush and Mwenemutapa (southern Africa) are apparently not too much different from the other primates but for the ability to walk erect, build tools and certain sexual dimorphisms existing between male and female stature. At this time the cranial fossils of the early Homo genus also show not too dissimilar features from the Australopithecus genus. Then, around 1,800,000 BCE that all changed with the coming of the Homo erectus.

These Nilotic black people were bigger brained hominidae, resulting in their having larger heads. This achieved greater sentience and intelligence for these original black people, allowing the now new species to overtake their ancestors at the top of the primate order. Engels furthers this given by explaining the psycho-biological effects more clearly, saying "Hand in hand with the development of the brain went the development of its most immediate instruments – the senses." Hence, early humanity's biological development was intertwined with their sensory and indeed their sensual development.

If we take this concept a bit further, as indeed the interconnection of nature of necessity does, the heightened sensuality of these hominid beings produced their bigger brains, which in turn produced more obvious bodily changes within their species. In order to adjust to the significant bodily change of bigger headed babies, the female body had to up the oestrogen and progesterone to develop wider hips, fatter butt cheeks, larger breasts, softer and more curvaceous frames and higher sexuality. To balance these female adjustments out the male bodies had to up the androgen and testosterone developing bigger muscles, larger genitals, firmer pectorals, stockier and much harder frames and stronger militancy.

Here Engels' interpretations of natural development also deserves some remembrance, "Man alone has succeeded in impressing his stamp on nature, not only by shifting plant and animal species from one place to another, but also by so altering the aspect and climate of his dwelling-place, and even the plants and animals themselves, that the consequences of his activity can disappear only with the general extinction of the terrestrial globe." Engels appreciated this correlation between humanity and nature throughout his studies of the natural sciences, making clear to the readership of his time; "There is a whole series of processes in chemistry which, given an adequate supply of raw material, constantly reproduce their own conditions, and do so in such a way that a definite body is the carrier of the process. This is the case in the manufacture of sulphuric acid by the burning of sulphur."

It is also the case with regards to the organic beings in nature, as Engels continues, "The most simple type found in the whole of organic nature is the cell; and it certainly is the basis of the higher organisms. On the other hand, among the lowest organisms there are many which are far below the cell – the protamoeba, a simple albuminous particle without any differentiation whatever, and a whole series of other monera and all bladder seaweeds (Siphoneae). All of these are linked with the higher organisms only by the fact that their essential component is albumen", and effectively, "an albuminous body absorbs other appropriate substances from its environment and assimilates them, while other, older parts of the body disintegrate and are excreted. Other, non-living, bodies also change, disintegrate or enter into combinations in the natural course of events; but in doing this they cease to be what they were. A weather-worn rock is no longer a rock; metal which oxidizes turns into rust. But what with non-living bodies is the cause of destruction, with albumen is *the fundamental condition of existence*."

But whereas albumen is an organism that is the key component for all white substances and therefore repels light; melanin is an organism that is the key component for all black substances that like all black substances absorbs light. Therefore the darker a body the more colour it can see and even consume, the more sound it can hear and the deeper sensation it can feel. Light is no more than electromagnetic energy waves, but a body is also no more than positive and negative energy waves in balance. All races possess melanin and albumen, but whereas black people contain a higher percentage of melanin white people contain a higher percentage of albumen.

In actual fact, the idea that we are all born equal is respectable politically, but is biologically flawed. All races are in fact different. Not to say that one race is better than the others, just that we all contain a veritable distinction. We blacks *are* more emotional, sensual and spiritual because there is more melanin in the pineal gland of our brain absorbing the light of the sun. At night these light rays convert the tryptophan aminos into melatonin, which produces dream and vision states. During the day it converts them into serotonin, which makes us more emotional, sensual, spiritual, and more susceptible to mental so-called abnormalities. (The fact is that the standard of mental normality is white people, whose pineal gland calcifies by the age thirteen.)

To give further explanation to this phenomenon Engels says, "If therefore tree-frogs and leaf-eating insects are green, desert animals sandy-yellow, and animals of the polar regions mainly snow-white in colour, they have certainly not adopted these colours on purpose or in conformity with any ideas; on the contrary, the colours can only be explained on the basis of physical forces and chemical agents. And yet it cannot be denied that these animals, because of those colours, are purposively adapted to the environment in which they live, in that they have become far less visible to their enemies. In just the same way the organs with which certain plants seize and devour insects alighting on them are adapted to this action, and even purposively adapted."

A consideration of these biological distinctions within the evolution of early humanity has been, and still is, the subject of great debate, but to Engels the case is simple: "the first to develop, as it is permissible to assume from the whole analogy of the palaeontological record, were innumerable species of non-cellular and cellular Protista...of which some were gradually differentiated into the first plants and others into the first animals. And from the first animals were developed, essentially by further differentiation, the numerous classes, orders, families, genera, and species of animals; and finally vertebrates, the form in which the nervous system attains its fullest development; and among these again finally that vertebrate in which nature attains consciousness of itself – man." Yet the classification of humanity is not fully defined until we consider their social element in mutual aid and the avoiding of competition.

What Kropotkin says concerning mutual aid is that, "In the great struggle for life – for the greatest possible fullness and intensity of life with the least waste of energy – natural selection continually seeks out the ways precisely for avoiding competition as much as possible. The ants combine in nests and nations; they pile up their stores, they rear their cattle – and thus avoid competition; and natural selection picks out of the ants' family the species which know best how to avoid competition, with its unavoidably deleterious consequences. Most of our birds slowly move southwards as the winter comes, or gather in numberless societies and undertake long journeys – and thus avoid competition. Many rodents fall asleep when the time comes that competition should set in; while other rodents store food for the winter, and gather in large villages for obtaining the necessary protection when at work. The reindeer, when the lichens are dry in the interior of the continent, migrate towards the sea. Buffaloes cross an immense continent in order to find plenty of food. And the beavers, when they grow numerous on a river, divide into two parties, and go, the old ones down the river, and the young ones up the river – and avoid competition. And when animals can neither fall asleep, nor migrate, nor lay in stores, nor themselves grow their food like the ants, they do what the titmouse does, and what Wallace (*Darwinism*, ch.v) has so charmingly described: they resort to new kinds of food – and thus, again, avoid competition."

For the best example of what Kropotkin means his description of the ants is perfectly fitting:

> *"If we take an ants' nest, we...see that every description of work – rearing of progeny, foraging, building, rearing of aphides, and so on – is performed according to the principles of voluntary mutual aid":* "In that immense division of the animal kingdom which embodies more than one thousand species, and is so numerous that the Brazilians pretend that Brazil belongs to the ants, not to men, competition amidst the members of the same nest, or the colony of nests, does not exist" at all, even to the point where "If an ant which has its crop full has been selfish enough to refuse feeding a comrade, it will be treated as an enemy, or even worse. If the refusal has been made while its kinsfolk were fighting with some other species, they will fall back upon the greedy individual with greater vehemence than even upon the enemies themselves. And if an ant has not refused to feed another ant belonging to an enemy species, it will be treated by the kinsfolk of the latter as a friend. All this is confirmed by most accurate observation and decisive experiments."*

> *"And yet the ants, in their thousands, are not much destroyed by the birds, not even by the ant-eaters, and they are dreaded by most stronger insects. When [François] Forel emptied a bagful of ants in a meadow, he saw that 'the crickets ran away, abandoning their holes to be sacked by the ants; the grasshoppers and the crickets fled in all directions; the spiders and the beetles abandoned their prey in order not to become prey themselves;' even the nests of the wasps were taken by the ants, after a battle during which many ants perished for the safety of the commonwealth. Even the swiftest insects cannot escape, and Forel often saw butterflies, gnats, flies, and so on, surprised and killed by the ants. Their force is in mutual support and mutual confidence."*

Basically, mutual support and avoidance of competition are here shown to be prerequisites for the continuance of species or breeds within the animal world. It is this social combining and associating that allows time in the animal world to be spent productively and it is this avoidance of competition that keeps them from social breakdown. Again, with social disorder curbed by the non-existence of competition or jealousy, the animal world can find and maintain a high level of balance and equality within its surrounding habitat regardless of its location. They can also find and build advanced natural societies from the free associations they develop through interaction. In fact, Kropotkin says:

> *"life in societies enables the feeblest insects, the feeblest birds, and the feeblest mammals to resist, or to protect themselves from, the most terrible birds and beasts of prey; it permits longevity; it enables the species to rear its progeny with the least waste of energy and to maintain its numbers albeit a very slow birth-rate; it enables the gregarious animals to migrate in search of new abodes. Therefore, while fully admitting that force, swiftness, protective colours, cunningness, and endurance to hunger and cold, which are mentioned by Darwin and Wallace, are so many qualities making the individual, or the species, the fittest under certain circumstances, we maintain that under any circumstances sociability is the greatest advantage in the struggle for life. Those species which willingly or unwillingly abandon it are doomed to decay; while those animals which know best how to combine, have the greatest chances of survival and of further evolution."*

This adaptation and sociability within the animal world coincides with what is written in the Bible of these events, "And out of the ground the Lord God formed every beast of the field, and every fowl of the air; and brought them unto Adam to see what he would call them: and whatsoever Adam called every living creature, that was the name thereof. And Adam gave names to all cattle, and to the fowl of the air, and to every beast of the field; but for Adam there was not found an help meet for him." (Gen 2: 19,20.) At which point another appropriate lesson comes to us from Kropotkin concerning mammalia: "the first thing which strikes us is the overwhelming numerical predominance of social species over those few carnivores which do not associate. The plateaus, the alpine tracts, and the Steppes of the Old and New World are stocked with herds of deer, antelopes, gazelles, fallow deer, buffaloes, wild goats and sheep, all of which are sociable animals. When the Europeans came to settle in America, they found it so densely peopled with buffaloes, that pioneers had to stop their advance when a column of migrating buffaloes came to cross the route they followed; the march passed of the dense column lasting sometimes for two and three days."

Again, we must appreciate the communal lives these animals live under and have lived under for millennia. When and if they were bought before Adam by God they would have already perfected and found their place in nature; and understood what it was they were able and supposed to do. And as Kropotkin shows, "Life in societies is again the rule with the large family of horses, which includes the wild horses and donkeys of Asia, the zebras, the mustangs, the *cimarrones* of the Pampas, and the half-wild horses of Mongolia and Siberia. They all live in numerous associations made up of many studs, each of which consists of a number of mares under the leadership of a male. These numberless inhabitants of the Old and the New World, badly organized on the whole for resisting both their numerous enemies and the adverse conditions of climate, would soon have disappeared from the surface of the earth were it not for their sociable spirit."

Even so, as he continues, "Many striking illustrations of social life could be taken from the life of the reindeer, and especially of that large division of ruminants which might include the roebucks, the fallow deer, the antelopes, the gazelles, the ibex, and, in fact, the whole of the three numerous families of the Antelopides, the Caprides, and the Ovides. Their watchfulness over the safety of their herds against attacks of carnivores; the anxiety displayed by all individuals in a herd of chamois as long as all of them have not cleared a difficult passage over rocky cliffs; the adoption of orphans; the despair of the gazelle whose mate, or even comrade of the same sex, has been killed; the plays of the youngsters, and many other features, could be mentioned."

To further explain the sociability of animal life Kropotkin goes on to say, "Let me only remark that with the beavers, the musk-rats, and some other rodents, we already find the feature which will also be distinctive of human communities – that is work in common." In fact, "Almost all free grass-eating animals and many rodents in Asia and America being in very much the same conditions, we can safely say that their numbers are *not* kept down by competition; that at no time of the year can they struggle for food, and that if they never reach anything approaching to over-population, the cause is in the climate, not in competition."

Kropotkin also shows how the same is true of the birds, which according to the above quoted also passed before Adam. "Hunting and feeding in common is so much the habit in the feathered world that more quotations hardly would be needful: it must be considered as an established fact. As to the force derived from such associations, it is self-evident." "In fact, it would be much easier to describe the species which live isolated than to simply name those species which join the autumnal societies of young birds – not for hunting or nesting purposes, but simply to enjoy life in society and to spend their time in plays and sports, after having given a few hours every day to find their daily food." But for an obvious proof of the sociability that exists in these bird societies, "we have that immense display of mutual aid among [them] – their migrations – which I dare not even enter upon in this place. Sufficient to say that birds which have lived for months in small bands scattered over a wide territory secure for each separate individual the advantages of better food or shelter which are to be found in another district – they always wait for each other, and gather in flocks, before they move north or south, in accordance with the season."

But of all these varieties of "sociable bird, the parrot, stands, as known, at the very top of the whole feathered world for the development of its intelligence." Indeed, "There can be no doubt that it is the practice of life in society which enables the parrots to attain that very high level of almost human intelligence and almost human feelings which we know in them. Their high intelligence has induced the best naturalists to describe some species, namely the grey parrot, as the 'birdman.' As to their mutual attachment it is known that when a parrot has been killed by a hunter, the others fly over the corpse of their comrade with shrieks of complaints and 'themselves fall the victims of their friendship,' as [John] Audubon said...Very few birds of prey or mammals dare attack any but the smaller species of parrots, and Brehm is absolutely right in saying of the parrots, as he also says of the cranes and the sociable monkeys, that they hardly have any enemies besides men; and he adds: 'It is most probable that the larger parrots succumb chiefly to old age rather than die from the claws of any enemies.' Only man, owing to his still more superior intelligence and weapons, also derived from association, succeeds in partially destroying them."

Obviously, "No one will deny that there is, within each species, a certain amount of real competition for food – at least, at certain periods. But the question is, whether competition is carried on to the extent admitted by Darwin, or even by Wallace; and whether this competition has played, in the evolution of the animal kingdom, the part assigned to it." To do this he shows how it could quite easily be seen that "if the evolution of the animal world were based exclusively, or even chiefly, upon the survival of the fittest during periods of calamities; if natural selection were limited in its action to periods of exceptional drought, or sudden changes of temperature, or inundations, retrogression would be the rule in the animal world. Those who survive a famine, or a severe epidemic of cholera, or small-pox, or diphtheria, such as we see them in primitive countries, are neither the strongest, nor the healthiest, nor the most intelligent. No progress could be based on those survival – the less so as all survivors usually come out of the ordeal with an impaired health,... and subsequently shows a quite abnormal mortality. All that natural selection can do in times of calamities is to spare the individuals endowed with the greatest endurance for privations of all kinds."

Certainly, as we can deduce, the more sociable and endowed with co-operative and interdependence tendencies a group or species is, the more likely it is to survive, grow, develop and ultimately to evolve. "That is what Nature teaches us; and that is what all those animals which have attained the highest position in their respective classes have done. That is also what man – the most primitive man – has been doing; and that is why man has reached the position upon which we stand now".

The so-called primitive men (or original people) of which Kropotkin speaks, actually started life as the Homo erectus, the most advanced species of the Homo genus at the time. Engels takes us on a journey into the most evidential reasons for their development into the Homo sapiens sapiens and the proper Homo sapiens they became. By Engels' nineteenth century understanding of anthropology, the science itself still being in its infancy; he conceived that what would otherwise be the earliest breeds of hominidae inhabited certain tropical or semi-barren regions of Asia (which we have now come to find in actual fact was East Africa in the Great Lakes region and along the Nile Valley). "Fruits, nuts and roots served him as food; the formation of articulate speech was the main achievement of this period."

Indeed, "the development of labour necessarily helped to bring the members of society closer together by increasing cases of mutual support and joint activity, and by making clear the advantage of this joint activity to each individual. In short, men in the making arrived at the point where they had something to say to each other." But again, "Just as the gradual development of speech is inevitably accompanied by a corresponding refinement of the organ of hearing, so the development of the brain as a whole is accompanied by a refinement of all the senses." Thus our mental development was and is tied in to our sensory and indeed our sensual development.

All this would obviously correspond to the biblical account of Adam, created in the image of the angels and given dominion over the world; for here Adam, which is ancient Hebrew for original man, that is, the original humanity; was the Homo erectus black man able to arise from among his hominid forebears to take his seat as ruler upon the earth and over its environment. In the account of Genesis God says to Adam, "Be fruitful, and multiply, and replenish the earth, and subdue it: and have dominion over the fish of the sea, and over the fowl of the air, and over every living thing that moveth upon the earth. And God said, Behold, I have given you every herb bearing seed, which is upon the face of all the earth, and every tree, in the which is the fruit of a tree yielding seed; to you it shall be for meat."

However, the mental and sensual accomplishments of Adam were from a social, that is, group perspective. Moreover, to provide Engels' fuller explanation, "Group marriage, the form in which whole groups of men and whole groups of women belong to one another... [left] but little scope for jealousy", and most likely "arose at a time when...intercourse between parents and children *had already been* proscribed by custom when the classes arose," which Kropotkin also confirms, stating "Societies, bands, or tribes – not families – were...the primitive form of organization of mankind and its earliest ancestors." Or as he continued, "The first human societies simply were a further development of those societies which constitute the very essence of life of the higher animals."

So the basic reality of the black people as we developed from a non-sapiens to a sapiens people was that need and desire for social development – and in particular as sexual beings. Here the words read earlier from Genesis prove particularly fitting: "And the Lord God said, It is not good that the man should be alone; I will make him an help meet for him." And this help which he made would be to him a queen among princesses, the beautiful black woman: the receiver, the bearer, the mother of civilization, goddess divine, the Nature that gives birth to worlds.

At the same time, the black woman too has deep within her soul a drive toward unashamed sexuality that makes her divine. Interestingly enough, the younger generation of black women who inherit this soul, against all odds, and against the wishes of the older generation, usually find newer and more explicit, even shocking ways to manifest it; which is also – contrary to their current testimony and reality – exactly what the older generation also did in their youth, though obviously through different ways and under different circumstances. On top of that, the fact that our white counterparts have very little understanding of our sexual liberality and forthrightness they told our women that these beautiful expressions of their sexuality were an immoral and immodest expression of their ignorance, that they were an embarrassment to women everywhere, and that they were being used, bullied and exploited by our brothers.

So now, at present the actual reality of most of our black sisters is a far cry from their sensual nature. Having lost themselves and a knowledge of themselves and of their origins in the world, they have become like the proverbial Eve, seduced by a desire to be what she already was by nature, a Goddess, she became a fool and fell from the beauty and grace given to her and her husband by the angels, who formed them in their image. Again, her partner Adam was no better, far from protecting her and fighting against the falsehood of the lies, he joined in the lie and became as lost as she was. He did not rebuke her, judge her, or discipline her; and he allowed a snake to worm its way into her heart and thinking.

Here the tragedy of Adam and Eve carries great similarities to the Kemetic apocalypse of Geb and Nut. An apocalypse which tells us how the two lovers, who make love continually and everywhere, were separated when Ra Atum, unwilling to allow one as irresistible as Nut to remain in the hands of one so vain as Geb, sends his son Shu to divide them. Then, sometime after he ascended again to Pet, the realm of the heavens; he begins a ritualistic process of being swallowed by Nut every night and being birthed by her every morning; basically meant to be symbolic of the daily rise of a man at these his most libidinally suggestible times. Finally, when Geb can take no more, he rebels against his father's unjust punishment and seizes the crown from his head, causing Shu to retreat into Pet. Unable to wear the stolen crown Geb then places on his head the wig of Ra Atum and so is able to wear the crown and rule over the earth.

This story, mainly spoken to encourage the people towards Ra Atum, that is, all-knowledge of self-creation, shows Geb's own internal weakness at the time was his lack of self-knowledge, which caused him to be separated by his father Shu from his beloved Nut. The correlation between the two stories is considerable: Geb, which means land, ground, earth and solidity corresponds substantially to Adam, whose Hebrew root is *Admah*, meaning, land, ground and soil; while at the same time Nut, which means sky, Nature and lucidity corresponds to Eve, whose Hebrew root is *Khavah*, meaning life, Nature and motion. Hence, Adam and Eve's falling coincides with Geb and Nut's separation, in which knowledge of self was the key issue. The terrible tragedy of these original people (black people); was due to the false moralistic traditions that damaged the innocence of their former cultures, where it is said of them that "they were both naked, the man and his wife, and were not ashamed."(Gen 2: 25.)

But godhood, which was personified through knowledge of self or Ra Atum, allowed Nut to see the beauty of her own nakedness and sexuality and Ra Atum to experience the pleasures of his morning and nightly suggestibility, which Geb only experiences again when he gains the wig of Ra Atum and becomes *Peraa*. So, every morning, no matter how bad the night before was, the goddess Nut births god, while every night, no matter how bad the day has been, the goddess Nut swallows god.

But within this Kemetic story of early humanity there is also a marked difference from that of their Hebrew descendants: when Nut and Geb were together they had a liberal sexual relationship, which produced four (and in some stories five) children: Ausar and

Setek, Auset and Nebthet and sometimes Horu. Of the four Auset was given to Ausar and Nebthet was given to Setek. Being children of the soil and sky, Ausar and Auset, Setek and Nebthet were all black. The throne of Kemet passed from father to son in those times so Ausar received the throne from his father Geb. Ausar, the fourth Peraa of Kemet, taught the men to irrigate lands, cultivate fields, domesticate animals, worship deities, obey laws and practice sanitary rituals; while Auset taught the women to work magic, understand mysticism, appreciate holism, learn sciences, become beautiful, practice healings, and consume the right herbs.

Again, considering the fantasy element of this situation does an injustice to the intellect of the people of Kemet, known for their knowledge of mathematics, science and architecture. So from a more symbolic perspective this apocalypse of Ausar and Auset takes us back into the story of the early hominidae, and in particular the Homo erectus. The Homo erectus created laws and rituals which were mastered in ancient Kush. They also mastered the art of cultivation and domestication. They then migrated out of Kush to other parts of the world: to Arabia, Kemet, Melanesia and China spreading civilization as they travelled. This bears remarkable similarity to the apocalypse of Ausar where he travels the earth spreading civilization wherever he goes.

However, these original people had no anticipation of the dissimulation to come about from that old snake in the grass. "Now the serpent was more subtle than any beast of the field which the Lord God had made." (Gen 3:1.) This serpent, taking every advantage, would go on to bring about Adam's complete demise even as Setek brought about the demise of his brother Ausar in the ancient Kemetic version: first throwing him into a box built only for him, then, after he was finally found by Auset, chopping up his body and scattering it around the world. Even so, the black man, like Ausar: whether in the box built just for him, scattered from hood to hood, or taking over Dwat to become *Peraa* and god of the Dwat; is still in a state of near shock and pain over his brother's betrayal; while his black woman today stands like an Auset without her Ausar: lost, alone, and driven to near madness.

But as mentioned in the apocalypse of Geb and Nut: it was the demonizing of our African exhibitionism and seductionism by moralistic opinions, turning them into something evil, sinister, ignorant and animal that left our poor black family dehumanized and semidetached from their true nature and natural self-identities; hence leaving us open to a mass of unnatural and unhealthy outside opinions as to our reality.

In fact, the poisoned fruit in the garden was more likely a fruit of trick knowledge, which corrupted their minds leading them to follow unreal and unnatural ideas. The black man and black woman both ate of this fruit and found themselves lost and naked in a world in which they were no longer free to be naked. And as those who we looked to to restore our freedom and give us a knowledge of ourselves were usually those who had no knowledge of us as black people our black women were now left with a false consciousness: loving sex and their own sexuality while feeling and believing they are wrong or immoral for it. Or wanting to be loved and seen as sexy while fearing being seen as vain or base, or as a user, manipulator or the disreputable "harlot," for these desires.

Nevertheless she still has hope. Even as Auset in the Asarian apocalypse was eventually able to restore Ausar to life again through her feminine charms, sensuous spells, and seductive faithfulness; so the black woman as an Auset contains within herself and a love for herself the power to restore her Ausar to life and sanity. Not to become like Setek or those snakes that were with him, but to become the god of his own domain through regaining a true knowledge of himself and dispelling the trick knowledge that corrupted him. It is through our Auset, that we see self as strong, confident and psychologically stable, so that through their manifestation of beneficence and mercy to us, we too may become manifestations of beneficence and mercy to them, till we both return to that paradise we fell from in the beginning, or till we turn this hell on earth into an even better paradise.

For which cause it is best and necessary for the black woman to look at God not as a Judge, nor as a Ruler, nor even as a form of Justice; but as a Lover; one who, though not being a pervert, can be seduced and one who loves to seduce her with the pleasures, beauties and benefits he showers on her. This is not the God called Reason; this is the God called Romance. This is the God who blesses his children for their obedience and punishes his children for their disobedience. He never punishes us for our mistakes, but he does discipline us for our going astray. This is a loving father figure God who is filled with compassion. However, though to view God simply as a loving Father carries many inspiring images of his grace, if our women were to view God as a loving husband it would allow them to find a deeper and closer insight into the holiness of his Spirit, carrying with it beautiful images of his own seductionism.

Obviously, we brothers should also learn to appreciate the godhood within our sisters: that they, through his Spirit, are Goddesses; even as we, through his Spirit, have become Gods. They are not bitches or hoes, but temples of the living God and should be reverenced as temples of God no matter how promiscuous they are. We should, therefore, view any service or benefice we do to them or for them as an act inspired by the one God to she in whom he has chosen to dwell. Her black body and her black skin are the house of very God, thus she, to us, should be a sacred shrine of honour; a living monument to God, and therefore a Goddess on the earth. And if she is a Goddess then we should protect her, stand up for her and respect her. The same with our women, they should view us as the Lord God himself, and whatever good they do to us or for us as being done to God and for God. We should therefore be considered and treated as divine by her. Not as fools, idiots, slobs, embarrassments, wastes of space, or walking dildos, but as God in the flesh, one in whom the Spirit of her Benefactor and Messiah dwells. And if we all have Christ within us, then what she does for him is being done for Christ and what he does for her is again done for Christ.

All this is through the divine nature of unconditional love, by which we can see that though the serpent seduced the black woman out of Eden, God is able to seduce her back into Eden, for he said, "behold, *I will allure her*, and bring her vineyards from thence, and the valley of Achor [loosely translated: valley of tribulation] for a door of hope: and she shall sing there, as in the days of her youth" (Hos 2: 14, 15; emphasis mine). Now the word used here for allure is the Hebrew *pathah*, which means to open, to entice or to seduce; so that we can now see clearly a new pneumatology based on seductionism. We can also find that through our seductionism, which includes light exhibitionism, we godbodies are able to build up the theocracy, assuming the full expression of the Godhead. But as a seductionist is any man or woman who gets a rush from driving people mad with sexual lust, or who gets sexual pleasure from giving other people sexual pleasure; it seems that in order to build up the theocracy we will have to know how to seduce the black woman.

To help us to arrive at a more heightened state of sexuality thus making us more seductive to the black woman the romance between King Solomon of Israel and Queen Makeda of Sheba in the Song of Songs presents us with a most beautiful means of attaining to an Afrosensual resurrection. It is undeniable throughout the pages of this Scriptural masterpiece the amount of sexual innuendos exchanged between Solomon and Makeda; and as it is still holy Scripture, the eroticism and seductionism of today's black woman is justified.

Again, within this tale Solomon, in the holy Spirit, says to Makeda:

> *"How beautiful are thy feet with shoes, O prince's daughter! the joints of thy thighs are like jewels, the work of the hands of a cunning workman. Thy naval is like a round goblet, which wanteth not liquor: thy belly is like an heap of wheat set about with lilies. Thy two breasts are*

like two young roes that are twin. Thy neck is as a tower of ivory; thine eyes like the fishpools of Heshbon, by the gate of Bath-rabbim: thy nose is as the tower of Lebanon which looketh toward Damascus. Thine head upon thee is like Carmel, and the hair of thine head like purple; the king is held in the galleries. How fair and how pleasant art thou, O love, for delights!

"This thy stature is like to a palm tree, and thy breasts to clusters of grapes. I said, I will go up to the palm tree, I will take hold of the boughs thereof: now also thy breasts shall be as clusters of the vine, and the smell of thy nose like apples;" "Thy lips, O my spouse, drop as the honeycomb: honey and milk are under thy tongue; and the smell of thy garments is like the smell of Lebanon. A garden inclosed is my sister, my spouse; a spring shut up, a fountain sealed" (Song 7:1-8; 4:11,12).

To which Makeda responds:

"I am black, but comely, O ye daughters of Jerusalem, as the tents of Kedar, as the curtains of Solomon. Look not upon me because I am black," "I sleep, but my heart waketh: it is the voice of my beloved that knocketh, saying, Open to me, my sister, my love, my dove, my undefiled: for my head is filled with dew, and my locks with the drops of the night. I have put off my coat; how shall I put it on? I have washed my feet; how shall I defile them? My beloved put in his hand by the hole of the door, and my bowels were moved for him. I rose up to open to my beloved: and my hands dropped with myrrh, and my fingers with sweet smelling myrrh, upon the handles of the lock." "Awake, O north wind; and come, thou south; blow upon my garden, that the spices thereof may flow out. Let my beloved come into his garden, and eat his pleasant fruits." Solomon, "I am come into my garden my sister, my spouse: I have gathered my myrrh with my spices: I have drunk my wine

with my milk: eat, O friends; drink, yea, drink abundantly"
(Song 1:5,6; 5:1-5; 4:16).

The same could also be said of Christ and his Church, which the apostle John saw, "coming down from God out of heaven, prepared as a bride adorned for her husband." Again, the word used here – and throughout the New Testament – for bride is the word *nymphe*, which might as well have been the word 'nympho,' as, though her body is said to be of the colour of jasper, which is mahogany, she is adorned in clothing of "pure gold, as it were transparent glass" (Rev 21: 11, 21); which coincides completely with the psalms, where it says, "Kings' daughters were among thy honourable women: upon thy right hand did stand the queen in gold of Ophir" (Ps 45:9). And when one remembers that the Hebrew word for holy is also their word for harlot we can also see the relation this Scripture has with what the Messiah exclaimed when he said, "Verily I say unto you, That the publicans and the harlots go into the kingdom of God before you. For John came unto you in the way of righteousness, and ye believed him not: but the publicans and the harlots believed him" (Mt 21: 31,32). Basically, the female street lifers, who have the right to be seductionists just as much as their male counterparts, through knowledge of self can become the *nymphe* of Christ.

From all this it becomes clear that to the black soul sexuality was something highly valued, while monogamy was not as respected by our Asarian ancestors – all initiated Ausars were considered married to all initiated Ausets, while all initiated Ausets were considered married to all initiated Ausars. Again, by our faithfulness to this Afrosensuality, we Ausars and Ausets are able to find that eternal Eden of the black theocracy, where love, as romance: which is agapic, empathic and erotic, permeates the atmosphere. Furthermore, we Ausars and Ausets reach a higher elevation through walking in the freedom of seductionism, so that now we can also see a new theodicy for the Black Church to consider in truth.

Again, like within the kaula school of Tantra, through becoming one with either an Ausar or an Auset an initiate would be a part of a kind of polyamorous group sexuality. (And for the record, growing up in Brooklyn I also experienced this kind of polyamorous group sexuality in the street life, though it was secretive. Black men let their good friends sleep with their girlfriend and her good friends while black women let their good friends sleep with their boyfriend and his good friends: we called it running a train, and both men and women did it. This practice was very well respected back then as everything that happened was all in the family. What happened to those days of "It ain't no fun if my homie can't have none"? White people began calling it gang rape and our black women began to feel ashamed of their actions and blamed the men. The truth is, it is neither sin nor shame to have multiple sex partners, as the ancients did it all the time. The godbodies used to do this time honoured practice all the time too, but now they have allowed white propaganda to convince them that this sacred African tradition is in fact evil. We should actually be more concerned about our ancestors' opinions than white people's, but I digress.)

As a movement we godbodies should focus on considering the sacredness of the body our ancestors used to respect; which modern minds have now vulgarized and made embarrassing by their moralistic corruptions, and not in accordance with the black soul. The body (even the astral body of angelic beings) was always held as a holy temple, a thing of beauty, not to be gawked at or lusted over, but to be enjoyed and appreciated along with all the beauties of God's creation. The sacredness of the body is what causes we black brothers and our black sisters to be in awe of its naked presence; as to us its beauty is something to be awed. Tyldesley also said on the subject, that the "overtly sexual images [of ancient Egypt] contributed to a general misinterpretation – fuelled by the apparently damning evidence of incest, polygamy, transparent dresses, sensual poetry and erotic papyri, and the complete absence of any wedding ceremony – of the Egyptians as a louche, even lewd, people. Yet there is no evidence to suggest that the Egyptians led promiscuous lives and, indeed, personal writings recovered from the New Kingdom workmen's village of Deir el-Medina confirm that society expected individuals to adhere to a firm moral code." Nevertheless, black sensuality and sexuality can be traced back to these early origins, and also our early group sexuality.

Considering again the Asarian apocalypse we come to the place of his sensual resurrection; where Auset, after gathering together the scattered pieces of Ausar's body and mummifying them with spices and oils and strips of fine spun linen; is able to reanimate him by unifying his *khat* with his *ba* and *ka*. Then she gets impregnated by him and conceives a man child, who was to rule all nations with a rod of iron.

The ancestors anticipating this reality for the black man and black woman designed a psychological system suited to the black soul and the attaining of its sensual resurrection. Here the being is divided into three, or more, technically four, parts: The *khat*, which is the lower self, representing the flesh or physiological body. The *ka*, which is the higher self, representing the soul or astral body. The *ba* or lower mind, representing what Freud called the id or instinctual mind; which physiologically resides in the brain. The *akh* or higher mind, representing those ethical and cultural mores we acquire in life; which physiologically resides in the heart or what the Kemetic people called the *ab*. As mentioned earlier, according to the Heliopolitan view the unifying of the three (or four) attributes allowed one to attain to divinity. (As the heart was the only thing preserved in the *khat* during the process of mummification it was only the *khat*, the *ba* and the *ka* that needed reunion after death.)

Auset, by now subsumed in the diabolical drama, represents the black woman. It is she who reunifies the body and soul of Ausar and allows him to reanimate, thus orchestrating Ausar's empowerment and resurrection. By the powers she gives him through her magic he then goes on to overcome the Dwat and become god and Pharaoh of the Dwat, taking his seat upon the square of morality. By this square he would also judge all those who came before him: any who were found perfect would enter his paradise, any who were not would suffer the tortures of chaos, or, from the time of the New Kingdom, Ammit – a monstrous combination of crocodile, lion/leopard and hippopotamus – would swallow their heart: the seat of the *akh* or the moral conscience. (Contrary to the view of most Egyptologists that the intelligent Egyptians – the Kemetic people – were ignorant of brain matter thought, this book states that they not only knew that thoughts took place in the brain, but that they also understood, even back then, that the heart produces more electricity than the brain and thereby was more sensitive, and sensual, than even the thought producing brain; making it the most likely seat of the conscience.)

This square of morality, to those in the godbody, is articulated in the Build Allah Square, a fighting ring in which we fight it out one-on-one with anybody we have a personal problem with, or six-on-one with anyone who speaks knowledge without showing and proving what they say. By so doing we godbodies and street lifers use our square to show and prove our devotion and morality, but not to any person in particular but to our God – who, while being Intelligence, is manifested in I Self Lord And Master. This square being that fighting ring in which we unleash our wrath and aggression on our brothers and afterward, win or lose, show them love and brotherly forgiveness, forgetting whatever it was we had against them; allows us to stay real with each other instead of hypocritically holding a grudge against somebody and yet smiling in their face; it is our repentance, penance and trial court at the same time.

Kropotkin confirms that the ancients used to also practice these kinds of traditions by stating of the nineteenth century tribal people, "feuds are not uncommon – not in consequence of 'overstocking of the area,' or 'keen competition,' and like inventions of a mercantile century, but chiefly in consequence of superstition." In fact, according to all research early Homo sapiens people were a blood-vengeance people, keeping to the tradition of "eye for eye" justice long before

Moses' celebrated exposition of it. Kropotkin said, "All savages are under the impression that blood shed must be revenged by blood. If any one has been killed, the murderer must die; if any one has been wounded, the aggressor's blood must be shed....Now, when both the offender and the offended belong to the same tribe, the tribe and the offended person settle the affair. But when the offender belongs to another tribe, and that tribe, for one reason or another, refuses a compensation, then the offended tribe decides to take the revenge itself." Again, even "'head-hunting' takes quite another aspect when we learn that the supposed 'head-hunter' is not actuated at all by personal passion. He acts under what he considers as a moral obligation towards his tribe."

But Ausar, as noted, was the Kemetic god of vegetation and was himself murdered by Setek, who was the Kemetic god of desert; hence blood-vengeance was required. This is where Horu becomes all important to the Kemetic traditions. The people of Kemet, being very educated and intelligent, learned history and anthropology from ancient Kush, south of which is where were discovered the fossils of Australopithecus afarensis. The traditional story is obviously lost but we can gain a general idea based on the Kemetic tale of Horu and Setek.

In considering the development of Homo erectus, Engels puts his physiological change from Homo erectus to Homo sapiens sapiens (otherwise known as Cro-Magnon man) down to their slow change in diet. In sketching out his theory in his *Transition from Ape to Man*, Engels says, "A meat diet contained in an almost ready state the most essential ingredients required by the organism for its metabolism. By shortening the time required for digestion, it also shortened the other vegetative bodily processes that correspond to those of plant life". Thus, according to Engels, as the early hominidae began to change their diet they began to change their own metabolism also, which as we know has actually been proven.

However, Engels goes further within his theory to show how, "Just as becoming accustomed to a vegetable diet side by side with meat converted wild cats and dogs into the servants of man, so also adaptation to a meat diet, side by side with a vegetable diet, greatly contributed towards giving bodily strength and independence to man in the making." This would have also contributed to the hormonal shifting of the proto-Homo sapiens, allowing for the upping of various hormones that they otherwise had in limited supply: such as, progesterone, testosterone, endorphins and enkephalins. These hormonal changes would come to have a direct effect on the endocrine systems of both genders around about this time allowing for humanity's sensual reshaping also.

The hypothalamus part of the brain, which interacts with the endocrine system and the pituitary complex; is where all our spontaneous, dietary, sexual, emotional, thermal, violent and growth activity is coordinated. It is also that part of the brain that produces and modulates the hormones best suited to the development of these activities. So here Engels shows us how, "the body benefited from the law of correlation of growth, as Darwin called it. This law states that the specialised forms of separate parts of an organic being are always bound up with certain forms of other parts that apparently have no connection with them." But these hormonal adjustments were merely a part of our premature development into the Homo sapiens people we are today.

Around the time the ancient Homo erectus died out or were replaced by the Homo sapiens sapiens the whole situation must have appeared like a killing off. For this cause vengeance was sought for by God, by Nature or by some supernatural force. Even so, the environmental adjustments occurring in the world about this time triggered an ecological consequence that would shake everything: the last ice age. Kropotkin sheds a little more light on this situation, saying "Now it must be borne in mind that the glacial age did not come to an end at once over the whole surface of the earth. It still continues in Greenland. Therefore, at a time when the littoral regions of the Indian Ocean, the Mediterranean, or the Gulf of Mexico already enjoyed a warmer climate, and became the seats of higher civilizations...territories in middle Europe, Siberia, and Northern

America...remained in early post-glacial conditions". "Later on, when desiccation rendered these territories more suitable for agriculture, they were [soon] peopled with more civilized immigrants; and while part of their previous inhabitants were assimilated by the new settlers, another part migrated further, and settled where we find them. The territories they inhabit now are still, or recently were, sub-glacial, as to their physical features; their arts and implements are those of the Neolithic age...their modes of life and social institutions bear [still] a striking likeness. So we cannot but consider them as fragments of the early post-glacial population of the now civilized area."

The hope that Ausar – whose name in the language of Kemet is the masculine of blackness, and who represented the agricultural form of the Homo erectus – would have found an afterlife in which his agricultural lifestyle and mentality would be, not only the norm but also the mandatory and customary practice, would have been present in ancient Kush as a result of his demise. This afterlife of simplicity and peaceful coexistence being no longer available to these still developing hominidae, was, in their view, the realm of the divine black, a now unreachable past that can no longer be attained but by moral uprightness. But according to the tradition, to gain for us, and himself, this eternity he first had to conquer that great serpent of darkness and chaos: Apop, and thus take control of the Dwat taking his seat on the square. And sure enough Ausar would eventually charm Apop and take over the entire Dwat, coinciding with his title as god of the Dwat.

The agricultural ideal that Ausar represented, the nostalgia he brought to the minds of his descendants and successors, caused him to have that high place within the social and intellectual soul of the ancient world. Again, the tragedy of his demise at the hands of his fellow hominidae made it all the more tragic. This obviously played a big part in why, as Kropotkin said, "All savages [were] under the impression that blood shed must be revenged by blood. If any one has been killed, the murderer must die; if any one has been wounded, the aggressor's blood must be shed. There is no exception to the rule, not even for animals; so the hunter's blood is shed on his return to the village when he has shed the blood of an animal."

The square of morality, upon which Ausar would sit in his judgment hall, thus also became a representative of that by which one has to prove one's heart pure and free from all vanities and unnecessary attachments to this life and world. The violent testing practiced by us godbodies coincides with this scalar testing of the Kemetic; by which the heart was weighed with that of a feather, the feather of Maat, to see if they were worthy of *Sekhet* (or paradise).

To the Kemetic when someone died they would stand before the ancestors, who were all personified in Ausar, who judged them according to the inaccurately named *42 Negative Confessions* to see if they were worthy of initiation into *Sekhet*. The soul of the righteous dead would thus be judged as right and exact (equal to Maat) having completed this process. It was also very closely related to the idea of freedom from sin; that is, a sinless life. This also meant the mature practice of seductionism and militarism by the individual, so as to keep them from any social or moral imbalance. All these would effectively produce a hormonal rebalancing within their bodies leading them back to sensual fullness.

And considering that according to modern physics energy cannot be created or destroyed and is so eternal; what God does is organize, mold, build and beautify it. But if energy is so eternal and the soul is energy then the sensuality of the hypothalamic region of the brain, being based primarily on militarism, seductionism and naturalism; becomes a doorway to monism. And seductionism, like a river of life to we Ausars and Ausets, keeps our mind free from sin and unnecessary vanities.

Where development by martiality and development by sexuality are practiced all social elements come into play allowing the nutrients gained by the body through food consumption to be applied to the body in ways that are most perfect for our ability and appearance; so that hormones like oestrogen, androgen, progesterone, testosterone, endorphins and enkephalins can be distributed through our body in a well-balanced way. Thus, through improving our martial life and martiality and our sex life and sexuality we can develop a more balanced and not one sided view of life; which is not too dissimilar to what occurred with our Asarian ancestors.

According to Engels, "The meat diet...had its greatest effect on the brain, which now received a far richer flow of the materials necessary for its nourishment and development, and which, therefore, could develop more rapidly and perfectly from generation to generation." And of course, "The reaction on labour and speech of the development of the brain and its attendant senses, of the increasing clarity of consciousness...gave both labour and speech an ever-renewed impulse to further development. This development did not reach its conclusion when man finally became distinct from the ape, but on the whole made further powerful progress[;] its degree and direction...has been strongly urged forward, on the one hand, and guided along more definite directions, on the other, by a new element which came into play with the appearance of fully-fledged man, namely, *society*."

The environmental conditions of ancient East Africa allowed for the intellectual capacities of the Homo sapiens to develop further than those of the Homo erectus through the realizing, quite early on, that their survival would be far more achievable through having large groups working in unison than having a few people working alone. This development in human reasoning allowed for the creation of large groups and societies in early human history. Thus, as Kropotkin continues, "Common hunting, common fishing, and common culture of the orchards or the plantations of fruit trees was the rule with the old gentes....In short, communal culture is so habitual with many Aryan, Ural-Altayan, Mongolian, Negro, Red Indian, Malayan, and Melanesian stems that we must consider it as a universal – though not as the only possible – form of primitive agriculture."

This helps us substantially to understand the development of the Homo sapiens people. From these practices came new traditions, which would be formed and passed down via the communal societies of the time from generation to generation. Engels says, "The work of each generation itself became different, more perfect and more diversified. Agriculture was added to hunting and cattle raising; then came spinning, weaving, metalworking, pottery and navigation. Along with trade and industry, art and science finally appeared. Tribes developed into nations and states. Law and politics arose, and with them that fantastic reflection of human things...religion." And though it may be obvious to most that religion, or something comparable to religion, was in existence from the earliest human communities, Engels' general theory of the evolution that occurred in the development of the human societies during the Pleistocene epoch becomes clear.

As to the development of human families, Kropotkin states, "far from being a primitive form of organization, the family is a very late product of human evolution. As far as we can go back in the palæo-ethnology of mankind, we find men living [mainly] in societies – tribes similar to those of the highest mammals; and an extremely slow and long evolution was required to bring these societies to the gentile, or clan organization, which, in its turn, had to undergo another, also very long evolution, before the first germs of family, polygamous or monogamous, could appear." And sure enough, even "when the bonds of common descent had been loosened by migrations on a grand scale,...the development of the separated family within the clan itself had destroyed the old unity of the clan, a new form of union, territorial in its principle – the village community – was called into existence by the social genius of man."

All corresponding to the Asarian apocalypse in that the now pregnant Auset was forced into wandering in the desert during the time that her brother Setek was ruler over the earth. This may also have been a symbolic representation of the historical events of a Kingdom in ancient Kush known as Ta Seti. This kingdom in around about 26,000 BCE – not that long after the extinction of the Homo erectus and while the last ice age was still at full strength – was a somewhat renowned paradise of conquerors in ancient East Africa. The fall of Ta Seti, which itself corresponded with the general ending of the ice age, would prove to have a lot to do with the mass migrations occurring from South to North in those days. As the ancient people began to migrate up the Nile Valley area, and beyond the Mediterranean northward, westward and eastward, they carried with them their agricultural methods. They also developed and built canoes and boats; domesticated animals and cut down vast forests and formerly uninhabitable terrain.

Again, during this time the system of most black and Kushitic tribes was matrilineal and semi-matriarchal. Women were then hailed as goddesses (all deities were predominantly female, the priesthood was also exclusively female and sensual; and the cultural lessons and secrets were held by women in common). If a patriarchal system existed at all during these times it is most likely (based on the Kemetic tradition) to have been in Ta Seti (which means the land of Set (Setek)). And to be a little clearer, the matriarchal systems were usually tribal and scattered; they practiced gypsy and Bedouin style migration and had no hugely centralized authority system, as discussed earlier by Kropotkin. These, though somewhat beautiful and free, were no match for any patriarchal system of war-ready fighters, hunters and chieftains, all energized and ready to conquer. And though the matriarchal systems had warriors and warlords within their structure they were still no match for any patriarchal tribe. It seemed the only way for the female to gain or maintain any form of substance was for her to have a male authority with her.

Here we see the significance of the man-child Horu; he was to rule the two kingdoms with two-fold strength, and to take back the throne of his father Ausar. According to the Asarian apocalypse Setek, knowing Auset was pregnant with Ausar's son, went out searching for her to destroy whatever son she gave birth to. At this time Auset took upon herself the wings of a great eagle that she might fly to the Nile River and hide by the bulrushes. It is there that she was met by Djehuti, the god of wisdom and law, who prophesied that

Horu would grow to avenge his father's murder and to overthrow the kingdom of Setek that was then still in operation. And it would be his coming that was the hope of all the Kushite tribes of the time.

Blood vengeance would soon be sought for by Horu against Setek in revenge for the murder of his father, so that Horu confronted Setek having reached full maturity; at which time a tribunal also ensued. This tribunal being won by Horu gave Horu an open right to the throne of his father, a fulfilling of his own destiny as prophesied by Djehuti, and a form of vengeance for the murder of his father. But this was not good enough for some of the gods, particularly Ra, king of the gods and definition of godhood, who said Horu was too young and premature; he could hardly handle the responsibilities of governing the rebellious and corrupted ways of nature, let alone those of humanity; which caused the heavenly court to then be divided.

Horu was thus forced to fight Setek in a contest in which Setek and Horu both became hippopotami. At this point Auset was able to harpoon Setek and thus draw him close to the pangs of death; where he would have inevitably entered the Dwat to meet his brother and victim Ausar face to face, facing trial and judgment under his authority. Realizing what awaited him should he die Setek cried out to his sister Auset for mercy, who, taking pity on her brother, healed his wound, and he was made whole. This caused Horu to get vexed and cut off his mother's head for helping his father's enemy. For this insult to his sister and to get revenge for his own humiliation Setek then beat up Horu and plucked out his eyes leaving Horu blinded.

Now, as eyes in ancient Kemet carried a very distinctive quality about them – they symbolized righteousness, truth and justice – the symbolism of this act is undeniable. The right eye in the Kemetic language was the *maa* and the left eye the *maat* and they both bore significant meaning to the Kemetic people of the order underlying the physical order of the universe; and Horu being the god of kings bore a mathematical symbolism in his eyes – primarily in the language of the *Metu Neter* (hieroglyphics), as a fractional sequence.

The symbolisms contained in these Kemetic apocalypses – being of the similitude to the symbolisms contained in the Hebrew apocalypses, and where the symbolic language of the Revelations came from – was to tell the story of how the ancient Kushites (and by extension the Kemetics) came to be one people. Here the Horu son, in cutting off the head of his Auset mother proves to be unjust and unrighteous (that is, unworthy of his eyes). The evident conflicts between the black woman and her black son are understandably also quite problematic. Inasmuch as the single-mother Auset is chastised for aiding her brother and widow-maker Setek; the action was not of truth as Auset was Horu's first teacher and his most faithful supporter. The eye in itself symbolized balance, truth and order: the eyes of Horu symbolized the divine order of mathematical integrity. If the divine order was to be unjust then no one would be able to see the truth from falsehood, like Setek plucking out Horu's eyes.

In the story at this point Horu is left wandering, lost, blind and alone. Seeing him virtually powerless the goddess Hethor (Het-Hor, Kemetic for house of Horu, that is, the divine woman) takes pity on the lost and lonely Horu and calls for the god Djehuti to make for him two new eyes, which he makes using her breast-milk. This is part of the reason why Hethor's hieroglyph usually has cow horns covering a sun-disk or the image of a light skinned woman with a crown of cow horns covering a sun-disk. Even so, the man without the nurturing of his woman is lost, blind and lonely. It is she who gives him eyes to see himself as she sees him, as majestic.

However, when Horu had regained his sight and right mind from Djehuti he later returned to the court of the gods, making some of the gods vexed, in particular Ra. To add insult to injury, Babi, the baboon god of sexual potency, then called Ra an old wind-bag whose temples were deserted; causing Ra to lock himself away vowing never to return again, thus turning the universal orders back into darkness and chaos. It is then that Hethor entered into his secret chamber, wearing her usual fine spun linen, and performed a strip-tease sun-dance for him in which she became fully naked before him. The sun-dance ritual she performed broke his spirit and made him forget his wrath.

Now the ritual of the sun-dance and of the strip-tease would also be re-enacted by future generations of African women in their regional exhibitionist traditions; which all sprang from this Kushite and Kemetic source. Those areas that needed rain would have the rain-dance, while those areas that needed the sun would have the sun-dance. And as mentioned earlier, the unashamed brazenness of these strip-tease practices, and of their light exhibitionism, being manifestations of black erotica, are and were performed at special tribal events accompanied by music and exotic dances. The so-called lewdness and sexuality of the dances of most black, Latin and Asiatic women today also mark an unconscious link with this event. Even in his research of the nineteenth century Aborigines of New Guinea, Peter Kropotkin could not help but mention how they all "live under their primitive communism, without any chiefs; and within their villages they have no quarrels worth speaking of. They work in common, just enough to get the food of the day; they rear their children in common; and in the evenings they dress themselves as coquettishly as they can, and dance. Like all savages, they are fond of dancing." And although this kind of gives credence to what Jose Malcioln says, "When prejudiced writers become vicious, it is easy, perhaps gratifying, for them to present Africans [and by extension all black traditional peoples] as backward people or members of naked tribes dancing and living in the jungle"; I feel that Kropotkin only spoke like this to sound scientific, not necessarily to be vicious.

Acknowledging that the thrill and rush of exhibitionism which exists in a large number of we black people has somewhat been lost to a lot of our people who have accepted the modernist doctrine of morality and count piety as something unsexed and unsexual, I feel that we have lost touch with our Afrosensuality. Exhibitionism, which is usually considered the act of exposing the private parts of our body in public for the sake of sexual self-gratification, is basically the getting off on being naked in front of someone else.

With regard to these practices it is clear to see from their apocalypses the significance the Kemetic people gave to sexuality. When Tum arises from the primordial chaos he first creates light and darkness. The light he calls Ra and the darkness Apop. Tum chose the light over the darkness and became Ra Atum; and as Ra he creates Hethor as his lover and daughter and technically his hand. Here Ra Atum begins the process of creation producing first the male sexual deposit (Shu) then the female sexual deposit (Tefnut) to be fertilized. At this point Tyldesley articulates the white misconception of this sexuality, showing how "thousands of years later, scenes of Atum impregnating himself caused many Victorian Egyptologists to blink, while images of the unashamedly ithyphallic gods Geb, Min and occasionally Amen led to such absurdities as strategically placed museum labels designed to conceal the gods' true nature from the eyes of delicate lady visitors."

But it coincides with the Kemetic love for scientific exploration. As the Kemetic people viewed Ra as godhood, knowledge, and as the sun – even as the godbody view the black man as Allah, knowledge, and as the sun – their studies of the self-reproducing species of amoebic, plant and marine life, as well as their knowledge of pollination and its role in the procreation process allowed their creation stories and apocalypses to be more scientifically correct than most were. The Kemetic were thereby able to develop a high regard for the creative and sanctifying powers of sex and sexuality. They understood that sex also plays a huge role in self-creation and in the process of self-knowledge.

It was by her sexuality that Hethor saved the world and ultimately helped her future husband Horu with his case; something also done quite often by many black females around the world. What the ancestors were trying to do here was justify among their descendants, who we are, the right to use sex as a weapon. Therefore the naked body, and especially the naked female body, was always held as something sacred to the ancients; something to be used with honour, respect, and appreciation, as it has within itself the power to save the world and the mental frame of a struggling man. The ancients had no fear of misuse of the body as all the children of Kemet were taught from early childhood about sexuality.

But Auset, by now tired of her son constantly getting rejected, and of the stubbornness of the gods, particularly that of Ra, chose to go to her husband Ausar for help. But when even the messages sent by Ausar seemed to meet the stubborn moanings of the gods, Ausar gathered together the hoards of hell and of the entire Dwat. He also prepared that ancient serpent Apop, who represented the darkness of ignorance, madness, anarchy and chaos; and who even Ra was powerless against, and reminded Ra that he dwelt among innumerable daemons, who feared neither god nor goddess, and that if they were to destroy any of the deities their heart would be bought before his square to be judged even as all hearts were. So that through the militarism of Ausar in the Dwat and the seductionism of Hethor in Pet, Ra came to the conclusion that Horu was the rightful heir to Ausar, as Ausar's testimony took precedent over Setek's kinship position. Horu was thus given authority over all the kings of the earth, that is, over Kush; and chose for Hethor to be his main wife and beloved, as she was the goddess who supported and believed in him from the beginning.

From the etymology of this literary masterpiece the Hebrews took three concepts that would effectively be unified within the Christian traditions: that of *Ashar*, which the Hebrews defined as happiness, righteousness and honesty; that of *Ra*, which the Hebrews redefined in their concept of the Evil One; and that of *Satan*, which was based on what Setek represented to the forces of righteousness in the story. Etymologically the word *satan* does go a little deeper though: in Hebrew the word *sâtan* means to attack or accuse and comes from the root *shotet*, meaning to flog or scourge. But *shotet* also bares some similarities to the word *setek*, which means negativity, but mainly in the sense of violence, harshness, calamity, aridity and barrenness. Basically, the Hebrews saw Ra as a socio-cultural evil and Satan as a kind of natural and supernatural evil. To be sure, neither Ra nor Satan carried any favourable position in the Hebraic jargon or mindset; both were treated with contempt and ambivalence even as they were in the Asarian apocalypse.

This ancient tale of early humanity comes to us via ancient Kemet and is the best portrayal of the events of how humanity evolved into the Homo sapiens people we are today. Here Horu, representing the Shemsu Heru tribes and Setek, representing the tribes of Ta Seti, face off for ultimate supremacy over the world, that is, over ancient Kush. In both cases these early societies were most probably polyamorous: that is, they most likely practiced a kind of free love and group sexuality; so that ideas like competition and jealousy would have been alien to these tribal communities within their territorial jurisdictions. Whereas to the modern mindset and to modern moral standards their systems may seem shocking, in the traditional nations such practices were quite valued, and have only been losing their value as modernism has replaced the ancient and more traditional ideas of the past.

So now, based on the understanding that in the resurrection we shall once again be like the angels, or the *Elohim*, and seeing that early humanity were themselves made in the image of the Elohim; early humanity presents the clue as to how we shall live in the resurrection. Again, in considering the story of human development, it begins in the form of the proto-human: Homo erectus, who first learns "the utilisation of fish (under which heading, we also include crabs, shellfish and other aquatic animals) for food and...the employment of fire. These two are complementary, since fish food becomes fully available only by the use of fire," as Engels informs us. "But all that was not yet labour in the proper sense of the word. Labour begins with the making of tools. And what are the most ancient tools that we find...and of the rawest of contemporary savages? They are hunting and fishing implements, the former at the same time serving as weapons. But hunting and fishing presuppose the transition from an exclusively vegetable diet to the concomitant use of meat, and this is another important step in the process of transition from ape to man."

Indeed, Engels tells us that, "This new food, however, made men independent of climate and locality. By following the rivers and coasts they were able, even in their savage state, to spread over the greater part of the earth's surface....The newly occupied territories as well as the unceasingly active urge for discovery... made available new foodstuffs...and game, which was occasionally added to the diet after the invention of the first weapons – the club and the spear." These early people, Homo erecti, also tracked the stars, studied the celestial cycles and developed traditions based on the electrical currents flowing through the earth. The extent of their calculations is such that even to this day we are unable to accomplish what was accomplished in the ancient times, and this is before Ta Seti. In fact, even ancient Egypt would not have been able to master the arts, sciences, technologies and calculations they mastered without the teachings, guidelines and maps worked out by these early civilizations.

It is undeniable that a change in diet and in scientific discoveries effected these Homo erecti allowing civilization to begin. And these fathers and mothers of civilization definitely had advanced technologies in their time that bastardizes our own modern technologies. "But [as] animals exert a lasting effect on their environment unintentionally and, as far as the animals themselves are concerned, accidentally", whether by fluke or by chance, the tribes of the Homo erectus, by their change of diet and by adopting new scientific practices may have not only superseded their hominid forbears but may also have bought on the ice ages that followed in the Pleistocene epoch. It would be during these glacial periods that the greatest developments in humanity would occur in our transition from the Australopithecus afarensis into proper Homo sapiens people.

This presents us with a definitive relation here to the story in Genesis of Noah and the flood: a flood reported of in all ancient traditions but those of Kemet, reflecting the reality of what happened after the last glacial age on the earth. For the results of the last glacial age, when the ice sheets melted, was mass rain and mass flooding, the forty days and forty nights being symbolic of a more lengthy time period of rains and rising sea-levels. By this time the Ta Setian tribes would have already died off and the Shemsu Heru tribes would have been developing into the matriarchal tribes of pre-Dynastic Kemet. Again, the ark that Noah built is in actual fact more likely to have been symbolic of wooded forestland than a wooded boat or ship. This wooded planting expedition in which he hid all the wildlife of the ancient world, still works even now. For even today wildlife is and can be preserved for future generations from ice ages or other natural disasters by conserving them in forests, woodlands and savannahs. We also see in these stories an opposite view of a state-of-nature to that of Thomas Hobbes. Rather than the random chaos of all against all we have the sociable relatedness of early human and animal societies.

And so, in that the genuine resurrection of the father is in his son; Noah, representing himself a Horu figure, is given a command of the similitude to that given to Adam that proves very fitting at this time, for "God blessed Noah and his sons, and said unto them, Be fruitful and multiply, and replenish the earth. And the fear of you and the dread of you shall be upon every beast of the earth, and upon every fowl of the air, upon all that moveth upon the earth, and upon all the fishes of the sea; into your hand are they delivered. Every moving thing that liveth shall be meat for you; even as the green herb have I given you all things. But flesh with the life thereof, which is the blood thereof, shall ye not eat. And surely your blood or your lives will I require; at the hand of every beast will I require it, and at the hand of man; at the hand of every man's brother will I require the life of man. Whoso sheddeth man's blood, by man shall his blood be shed: for in the image of God made he man." (Gen 9:1-6.)

TOWARDS A BLACK THEOCRACY

The history of the early messianic movement marks a turning point in world history and the beginning of a rival institution to all politico-religious structures then and today present in the world. The messianic communion founded by Peter and James in Jerusalem began as merely a branch of the Judean liberation movement started by John the Baptist in Qumran.

This Jerusalem branch practiced the same rituals and traditions but they were a more urban form and tailored towards urbanized individuals outside of the desert oasis of Qumran. Moreover, whereas the Baptist mainly preached the coming of a messianic redeemer and revolutionary deliverer to overthrow Roman imperialism; the Messiah came preaching to those who followed him, "The kingdom of God cometh not with observation: Neither shall they say, Lo here: or, lo there: for behold, the kingdom of God is within you." What Peter and James did was continue on this vision the Messiah began before his disappearance up the mountain.

Now for the record the Bible says concerning the Messiah, "And he came and dwelt in a city called Nazareth: that it might be fulfilled which was spoken by the prophets, He shall be called a Nazarene" (Mt 2: 23); or to give a more in-depth quotation: "Now therefore beware, I pray thee, and drink not wine nor strong drink, and eat not any unclean thing: For lo, thou shalt conceive, and bear a son; and no rasor shall come on his head: for the child shall be a Nazarite unto God from the womb: and he shall begin to deliver Israel out of the hand of the Philistine"(Jg 13: 4, 5). If the Messiah was a Nazarene from the city of Nazarites, then he would have been like a dread who did not cut his hair, and seeing that he was also said to have been "clothed with a garment down to the foot", and having "feet like unto fine brass" the Messiah's description falls closer to the Afrocentric spiritualist than the European pretty boy – using the God of the Judeans as the figurehead for his movement; a movement mainly consisting of those practices already existing in the community at Qumran:

- Baptism was simply a full-body washing followed by the daily ritual of washing to symbolize both death and resurrection, and spiritual cleansing and purifying, for the renewal of the soul. Thus to them the physical cleansing was a seal and sign to mark their spiritual cleansing.
- Rejection of wealth was the renunciation of the world and the temptation of riches for a place in God's kingdom. Upon entering the brotherhood they were told to distribute their possessions within the brotherhood as they were to have all things common. And nothing was bought or sold among them. Distribution was made according to need at the time of asking. Thus they had all their daily needs satisfied.
- Sexual regulation was a lot more difficult and complex. Though matrimony would not be fully defined till after the Reformation, the messianic movement had been seeking a way to Christianize sexual congress since the second century of its existence. The best means considered for policing sexual behaviours was to teach and promote abstinence, as has been the favourite down the millennia.

  The promotion of celibacy, in continuance to the adultery laws, as a means of sexual purity; though somewhat lazy in orientation, has always been able to find followers and adherents willing to practice it. But also promoted have been other restrictions on sexual expression against the sexual liberties of Rome. These traditions conflicted heavily with Roman sexual ideals, which were a lot freer back then with their theatres and public baths (yet still more austere than sensual Egypt, hence why Mark Antony was so easy to seduce).

- Public confession was an outward display of rejection of the world and its values, and its morals, and its standards; and a recognition of God and his Messiah as the only authorities worth respecting; all ideas very confusing and insulting to Rome.

For this cause public confessions were considered martyrdom, as the faithful faced daily persecution and hostility; not to mention the Roman worship of the Emperor as the living expression of the deity on earth. The messianic devotion to Christ over Caesar and the kingdom of Heaven over the empire of Rome destroyed all Roman religious preconditionings. The threats of the kingdom of heaven and kingship of Christ were not only challenging but explosive.

To confess publicly one's devotion to Jesus as Messiah and self as a sinner was as brave an act as it was ridiculous. The Roman world could accept neither idea as conducive to intelligence or sanity; and definitely could not accept them as religious or acts of piety.

- Devotional pursuits and exiles were usually expressed in times of solitude, personal suffering and patient obedience; which also produced within the mind and heart a longing and searching for God and godliness. In these instances the loneliness of the situation forces one into closer union with God having left behind all worldly sensibilities. And so nothing but the divine exists to the pursuing or exiled individual.

Even so, times of solitude, personal suffering, and tests of fruitless obedience can and usually do produce within the mind and heart of the pursuer a desire and need for God. Furthermore, it is not the attaining that counts but the pursuit; and not to gain from the pursuit, just to pursue God for the sake of pursuing God – to pursue him because he is real, and can be found inside every one of us. And even though the ultimate purpose behind these periods of isolation and pursuit was to find God and self; self, when found, was to be made subservient to God by the end of the pursuit.

Without finding the self and loving what you have found, the finding of God would ultimately have proven pointless and most dangerous. This in no ways negates the unity of God or submission of Satan to God; all the gospels show daemons trembling before the Messiah, and obeying in complete submission the commands he gave them. This does, however, show the ignorance of modern people, who believe they can find God without finding self first.

Ultimately, to the early messianic movement, for someone to come to God without first having knowledge of self as sinner was basically coming to God as a hypocrite and not as the sinner you are. But this self-knowledge never meant to the early messianic movement weakness, guilt or unworthiness, nor did it mean self-interest, self-concern or outright selfishness; it meant self-realization, being true to self and honest to self. It was the coming to the ultimate self-discovery: that though sinners we can still attain the divine, being children of the one true God. And by this revelation we also find that knowledge of self is in actual fact knowledge of God, as by walking in his love we manifest divinity.

But the Messiah also made very clear to his disciples, "thou shalt not be as the hypocrites are" "But seek ye first the kingdom of God, and his righteousness" (Mt 6: 5, 33); so that to these already existing Qumran traditions the messianic movement added acts of penance and Agape Feasts:

- Acts of penance were to make or show oneself worthy of the kingdom of God, and were performed in remorse for having broken, after initial baptism, any one of God's laws as prescribed in the Ten Commandments. As the breaking of any of these was considered worthy of excommunication from the messianic brotherhoods in the world here and in the world hereafter; the act and proof of repentance was of necessity performed openly by the penitent.

The first act of repentance would be the confession of guilt before the assembly, at which time the entire assembly and the assembly leader, the bishop, would decide based on the gravity and reason of the sin what manner of punishment they required. This usually consisted of fastings, prayers, abstinences, or beatings until the sin was atoned for; after which point they would be accepted again back into the eternal kingdom of God for having suffered their penalty.

- Agape Feasts were the truly blessed coming together of the brotherhood celebrated on the Lord's Day every week to give thanks to God for the death and resurrection of the Messiah. It was also a declaration of their undying devotion to and union with the Messiah both in the world here and in the world hereafter as one body, to the eternal glory of God the Father; and an expression of allegiance to the Messiah's dictatorial authority until we are righteous enough to submit to God's authority. Thus severing all ties to this world and social order in anticipation for a newer and better world and social order.

But still, perhaps the most important and yet complicated teachings within the messianic schools were their doctrines on the incarnation, crucifixion and resurrection of the Messiah. These three fundamental doctrines and teachings of the messianic movement were the most difficult to understand and explain. Such that even the most studious masters of the ancient times had immense difficulty reporting and explaining them in their own day. Their best solution was to steal from Heliopolis the trinity concept of a long-suffering God. The dialectic of Ausar, Auset and Horu (like man, woman and child) was transformed into the trinity of Father, Son and Holy Mother. Even the

Immaculate Conception was stolen from Heliopolis, where the Auset was said to be immaculate when she was completely pure, and only had sex with men who had already become one with Ausar.

In the early days of the messianic movement the argument was relatively different from what it is today. In their day the idea of God being born or incarnated was not such a big deal or too difficult to come to terms with. The stone of contention was a God who suffers and dies a criminal's death. This idea to ancient Rome displayed weakness, incompetence and insanity. Any god who suffers must suffer due to some personal defect. The gods, by a Platonian standard, were to be perfect; for the most High God to not only suffer but to even die as a criminal was one of the greatest expressions of weakness, defect and fault to them. The messianic God, *to them*, was the epitome of madness, a lying deity unworthy of the title. But the idea of self-sacrificing (yet undying) love was a paradoxical conundrum to the entire ancient world too.

Still, in spite of these difficulties the messianic movement was able to assimilate many different interpretations within its own world vision. The most influential culture within this messianic vision was obviously the Judean. The traditions within the early messianic movement were taken and reinterpreted from pre-existing Judaic traditions of law, blessing/curse, sacrifice, covenant and purification. Another heavy and vital influence was Greece. The assimilation of the Greek cultural interpretations of reason, logic, philosophy and politics allowed for the teaching and adopting of messianic ideas and practices to be continued. Thus the ancient Greek schools and townships were converted into messianic churches and communities.

The Messiah's message of an interdependent ethic was the basis of these communities, as he taught them, saying "Give to him that asketh thee, and from him that would borrow of thee turn not thou away." "But love ye your enemies, and do good, and lend, hoping for nothing again; and your reward shall be great, and ye shall be the children of the Highest: for he is kind unto the unthankful and to the evil." Even so, his disciples applied this doctrine: "And all that believed were together, and had all things common; And sold their possessions and goods, and parted them to all men, as every man had need" (Acts 2: 44, 45).

As these early communal parishes all believed in working out "your own salvation with fear and trembling"; to them Christ's goodness meant nothing for that of his followers, and Adam's sin meant nothing for that of his children. You had to be good to inherit the blessing and be evil to inherit the curse. My goodness would not mean my son would be entitled to my achievements and my sinfulness would not mean my son would be liable for my punishments. Though I could teach my son to be good by example, I could not make him a good person. Examples of right and exact living were therefore of greatest importance to the early messianic movement.

This messianic movement has grown a lot since these earlier days. At this time the two largest manifestations of Christianity are Roman Catholicism and Charismatic Pentecostalism. To understand the issues facing the theocratic movement we must understand the place of this Pentecostalism as the six major topics of modern Christianity can be related to the Charismatic Pentecostal movement. These topics are as follows: fundamentalism, spirituality, prosperity theology, faith and deliverance, praise and worship and dispensationalism.

The transition from Puritan Protestantism to Charismatic Pentecostalism is a relatively tumultuous one filled with wars, revolutions, revivals, emancipations, Great Awakenings and the rise of modern industry. Started at two significant times in two significant places: Topeka, Kansas in 1901 and Azusa Street, Los Angeles in 1906, the movement has adopted two very different forms and styles.

Those that traditionally call themselves Pentecostal tend to be more rustic, more earthy, more otherworldly. This batch, taking their cue from the black William Seymour, founder of the Azusa Street revival; tend to give more place to the spiritual. They have an Afrocentric pneumatology and demonology, they can be prone to singing and making long prayers and are likely to fall into visions and dreams and words of prophecy. Trusting more in being "led by the Spirit," they do not have a seriously rigorous structure but like to leave everything open for the Spirit's guidance. Exorcisms are frequent as are warfares in the spirit. Having been raised in a Pentecostal family I know the genuineness of their fervour and determination; they cannot bear losing anything to Satan. They also have a tendency of being anti-modern and have an air of the house church movement and localization about them.

The second group is the Charismatics. This group tend to take their cue from the white Charles Parham and the movement he started in Topeka, Kansas. They have an Americanized missiology and ecclesiology, they are more concerned with the atmosphere of a song than its words – does it bring the Spirit. They focus a lot on faith, healings and signs. Trusting more in the Charismata of the Spirit and the charisma of the leader they tend to be more all-American in style. These also are more likely to have "prosperity preachers" and "miracle workers" than the regular Pentecostals, and as charisma matters they tend to boast mega-churches with big name leaders. They are also usually quite exuberant about modernism and globalization, adopting newer and newer technologies for spreading the gospel around the world. Having myself left or grown out of the Charismatic movement I can say that they are not necessarily the bloodsuckers of the poor most godbodies acknowledge them as, they are just misled. I can vouch that in most cases their faith is not artificial and their integrity is true. But they have not taught us the truth about our history. All they seem to have taught us is to idolize the West and a historically inaccurate white Jesus.

Though these definitions are not static, or absolute; and though some interchange and cross-identification exists between both camps, this does give a general understanding of the preceding movements. However, both had the fundamental failure of believing that the seal of the Holy Spirit comes with the evidence of speaking in tongues. What they have not seemed to have appreciated is that a demoniac spirit could just as easily have beguiled the people, causing them to speak in those tongues. Conversely, when the Messiah spoke of the holy spirit in his messianic movement he most likely used the Aramaic word *qaddish*, which means both classy and sexy. In this the theocratic movement proves a lot more Scriptural in its definition of holiness as, being classy and refined can make any people genuinely holy – even as most Muslims exemplify holiness in their jellabiyas and abayas, through the high class demeanour they were bought up into. Indeed, the theocratic movement – itself evolving from a section of Islam – has high class and refinement too, but having adopted a few Pentecostal supplements it also contains elements of the anti-modern and a prophetic edge about it. While still, in similitude to the Charismatics it is riddled with a this-worldly message and hope.

But we who acknowledge God to be self and kind enter into this theocracy through individually experienced tribulation and a cultural enrapturement. This glorious vision thus manifests in our eternal nature and spiritual reality to make us all divine. Unfortunately our physical current is a lot more complicated, here we all: Catholic and Protestant, Shia and Sunni, Christian and Muslim, carry many hostilities towards our fellow brothers and sisters, who are and will be joint-heirs with us to the godhood ready to be revealed. As one who personally seeks racial and religious harmony I feel all these unnecessary wars and conflicts are a plague on the universal body of God; for which cause I warn the reader that even as God was able during the times of the ancients to destroy the temple that carried his name, so he is able at this time to destroy the temple of the body of Christ. Even to this day they all profane his name among the Gentiles, of which many have now become post-Aristotelian scientists and atheists for their misrepresentation; but I will say, *hashal Ilah*.

The scientific community have been held together by a mutual appreciation for the laws of the material world, which were from yonder times compiled into a standard set of physical principles. These principles would then become for us the basis for our classical physics. Again, according to Cheikh Anta Diop, "classical physics is founded on three principles that quantum physics has proven wrong: determinism, objectivity, and completeness." But it could be said the classical science of mechanical physics has also been shifted by Charles Darwin's evolutionary theory; the process by which physical entities progress is no longer thought to be through repetitious cycles and ellipses of curvilinear motion, but through the evolutionary processes of non-linear transitions. Engels says on the subject: "Of the Darwinian doctrine I accept the *theory of evolution*, but Darwin's method of proof (struggle for life, natural selection) I consider only a first, provisional, imperfect expression of a newly discovered fact. Until Darwin's time the very people who now see everywhere only *struggle* for existence... emphasised precisely *co-operation* in organic nature, the fact that the vegetable kingdom supplies oxygen and nutriment to the animal kingdom and conversely the animal kingdom supplies plants with carbonic and manure...Both conceptions are justified within certain limits, but the one is as one-sided and narrow-minded as the other. The interaction of bodies in nature – inanimate as well as animate – includes both harmony and collision, struggle and co-operation."

But in these situations "only one member of an integral, highly complex organism...benefited also the whole body it served." For "the body benefited from the law of correlation of growth, as Darwin called it. This law states that the specialised forms of separate parts of an organic being are always bound up with certain forms of other parts that apparently have no connection with them." So we can see that the laws and rituals of nature and physics need not be discovered or mastered as such, merely appreciated; while, at the same time, its progress should be considered and reviewed so as to make sure self is not being sacrificed in vain or for a vanity.

But we must still remember, according to Engels, natural forces are just like social forces, once we can grasp them we can gain a level of power over them. Deducing from this that even if we ignore the realities of natural reproduction and of its forces upon our lives, these self-same forces will still be "at work in spite of us, in opposition to us, so long they [will] master us," and maintain mastery over us. But rather than turning these forces "from master-demons into willing servants", we should seek instead to turn them into friendly allies. Thus there will be neither masters nor slaves, governors nor governed, oppressors nor oppressed but all will be one and in true brotherhood. Again, "The animal destroys the vegetation of a locality without realising what it is doing. Man destroys it in order to sow field crops on the soil thus released, or plant trees or vines..." And "Just as man learned to consume everything edible, he also learned to live in any climate. He spread over the whole of the habitable world, being the only animal fully able to do so of its own accord."

But even as Darwin's evolutionary theory shook classical Newtonian physics from cyclical mechanical determinism even so, Diop's theory of parapsychology has the potential to shake modern quantum physics. This theory is based mainly on ideas of hypnosis, telepathy, thought transmission, clairvoyance and astral travel, which stands within the framework of what is called extra-sensory perception (ESP) one of the main topics within parapsychology. The general understanding is that the five basic senses: those of touch, taste, smell, sound and sight are based on energy waves stimulating a sense receptor. But on top of the five basic receptors of skin, tongue, nose, ears and eyes are the sixth and seventh receptors of the pineal gland and the erotogenous zones: The pineal gland containing access to clairvoyance, clairaudience, clairalience, clairgustance, clairsentience, panopathy and telekinesis; the erotogenous zones access to sensual pleasure.

Diop felt that only one of these: clairvoyant premonition "would be too much for today's science; all its bases would be ruined, as would those of philosophy." For in that one could foresee and foretell a future event before its actual manifestation into the physical "it would certainly mean the revelation of a natural, objective order, independent of us. This then would [also] mean the death of the whole notion of metaphysical freedom." And again, "If it were, really so, modern physics would require us to admit the idea that nature is subject to nonlocal causality or even 'the undivided unity of the universe in its entirety,' as Bohm prefers to call it." This interconnectedness I have found is not necessarily a deterministic causality as much as a theocentric monism. And as cyclic and elliptic mechanisms are no longer a veritable conclusion of reality, so the interconnection must be based on transformation and transition towards unity; that is oneness.

Engels gives the explanation of these things in his debates with Dühring, "The old Greek philosophers were all born natural dialecticians, and Aristotle, the most encyclopaedic intellect of them, had already analysed the most essential forms of dialectic thought. The newer philosophy, on the other hand, although in it also dialectics had brilliant exponents...had, especially through English influence, become more and more rigidly fixed in the so-called metaphysical mode of reasoning".

Engels furthers his point concerning the development of Western philosophy, stating "In this connection Darwin must be named before all others. He dealt the metaphysical conception of Nature the heaviest blow by his proof that all organic beings, plants, animals, and man himself, are the products of a process of evolution going on through millions of years." "And, in fact, with every day that passes we are acquiring a better understanding of these laws and getting to perceive both the more immediate and the more remote consequences of our interference with the traditional course of nature."

In a natural disposition, the stimulation of our pineal gland by the breath which passes through our bodies in meditation activates our reactive mentality so as to cause us to answer the ideas stimulated in our mind. Our responses at these times are usually from a disinterested observatory position in that we receive and believe none of the thoughts passing through our mind but instead consider them and let them go. They are no laws or truths they are merely ideas and images. There is no substance to any of the images that pass through our mind at any given moment as all can be doubted, but there is substance to our being and our interconnection to the Supreme Being.

To fully purify our souls we must first know ourselves. This journey of self-exploration is and should be a direct result of *building* and meditation. Building is the term given for sharing and discussing information. Godbodies Build and Destroy through show and prove. The godbody hold secret ciphers, where we meet with other Gods and Earths (male and female godbodies) to talk about history, current events, community activities, the Scriptures; to share science, and to prophesy future events: 360° of knowledge, wisdom and understanding. But each lesson shared must be backed up by proof. If it cannot be proven then it gets destroyed by the wise God or Earth.

As for meditation, it is the centre of a godbody's life. Meditation should not be feared as though a ritual of Satanism, but embraced, even as it says in the Scriptures: "My soul shall be satisfied as with marrow and fatness; and my mouth shall praise thee with joyful lips: When I remember thee upon my bed, and meditate on thee in the night watches." And again, "My hands also will I lift up unto thy commandments, which I have loved: and I will meditate in thy statutes" (Ps 63: 5, 6; 119: 48). The stimulation of the pineal gland in "the night watches" is a spiritual act. When we learn to allow our breath, which contains interactive energies, to pass in and out of our natural bodies it stimulates the various energies in our brain bringing to our vision some healthy some unhealthy images from the astral plane. The third eye then captures these images like a camera and transmits them to self. To a godbody, when this third eye is mastered so as to capture images of past, present and future on command it becomes the All-Eye Seeing able to bring to our remembrance stored or eventual images.

But the visions that flow through our mind at any given time, though self, merely represent an intersubjective truth. Though they may have a form of truth to them what they show are really nothing more than forms and ideas distributed from the astral plane representing an unreality; we can easily let them go understanding their unreality and surreality. They are not hidden truths of the universe. They are merely vanities or fantasies stored in our mind that come either from desire or fear.

Visions and dreams occur when the third eye sees beyond the physical plane and into the astral plane of the Dwat or of Pet. The Dwat is the astral realm beyond time-space that I, for the sake of this purpose, will call imaginal-space. Pet is the astral realm beyond imaginal-space that I have chosen to call phase-space. The Dwat represents a distorted imaginality of non-real phantasm while Pet represents a distorted causality of the past, present and future. When the third eye of the self has begun its journey into the astral plane it interacts with ideas, individuals and settings that are familiar to it. The settings, ideas and individuals in the vision or dream are called by Freud condensed and distorted. To find the true meaning of what self sees in a vision or dream we must consider the socio-cultural significance these images represent to the self. So the interpretation of an astral journey is subjective. However, sometimes the distortions and condensations experienced in the astral represent something gained by self via education or interaction, and hold no real significance to self but via that communication, hence all astral journeys are intersubjective.

As astral journeys mainly take place in the Dwat they are, for all intents and purposes referred to as visualizations. When a visualization is made the first thing the self must do is decide whether or not they agree with the vision being made. If so they should think the word "Amin," if not they should think the words *"hashal Ilah,"* (God forbid) and let it go. The second thing self must do is learn its distortions: what is being represented and misrepresented about self in the vision. Finally, what are the layers of condensation and what do they represent and misrepresent.

To hold on to an astral experience once it has been rejected is to be possessed by that astral experience and the vanity of it, in which case you are a prisoner to that vanity which has now locked up your mind and locked itself in your mind. Once you discover it, allow it to reach maturity and then release it, it no longer represents an obsession for you, nor an inhibition for you. Thus, the acknowledging and confessing of our "sins," vanities and astral experiences, casts out the vanities from our minds and releases them from our hearts so as to keep them from becoming to us an obsession to plague us. In these mental exorcisms the saying of the Messiah proves fitting,

> *"When the unclean spirit is gone out of a man, he walketh through dry places, seeking rest, and findeth none. Then he saith, I will return into my house from whence I came out; and when he is come, he findeth it empty, swept, and garnished. Then goeth he, and taketh with himself seven other spirits more wicked than himself, and they enter in and dwell there: and the last state of that man is worse than the first." "Or else how can one enter into a strong man's house, and spoil his goods, except he first bind the strong man? And then he will spoil his house." (Mt 12: 43-45, 29.)*

The mind should also be free from a desire to glory in astral visions and open to a desire to simply find self and the destiny of self. Again, not in a selfish or self-seeking way but in an informative and observatory way. Not attached to self and the desires of self but completely detached or disinterested in self. Nevertheless, the best way to go about finding the self is through meditation. Within the practice of meditation is the ingestion of Shu (Kemetic for air, breath and gasidity), which allows us to attain a higher elevation into Shu, or perhaps even into Ra or Ausar, even if only for the duration of our meditation. As the self becomes one with Shu, or with Ra or Ausar, it no longer sees the world or the universe in the same light. In fact, the seeking and finding of self should begin the process of one manifesting the Self and living at a higher vibration.

It is the destiny of humanity to identify self in all things, in everything. Through the identification of self in all things we can find our own connection to the universe. This connection abolishes the Manichaeism of Pentecostalism and allows us to see that a person is their own opposite and their opposite is their self. Here the subtleties of the astral are appreciated as dwelling entirely within the world beyond the physical and non-physical. In actual fact, considering the mathematics of the Cantor Set all things outside our bodies are limitless through expansion and extension, and all things inside our bodies are limitless through reduction and minimization. There are no real atoms – in the sense of indivisibles – just an infinitude of self-similar waves. And as all things contain energy, all things vibrate and transmit messages and feedback, i.e. communicate, to all other things. This interconnection of all things shows that life is in more than simply carbon. Life is in energy, which connects all things together.

When we show respect or love to another entity outside of our natural body we are in actual fact showing love to self, when we kiss something outside of our body we are in actual fact kissing self, when we bow to something outside of our body we are in actual fact bowing to self; but when we hurt something outside of our body we are in actual fact hurting self. Thus the finding or acknowledging of the self-reality of God and meditating on his many benefits is not done outside of self by a separate self who seeks enlightenment; it is in actual fact the Self in one of its many manifestations. Moreover, knowledge of self and knowledge of God become one as the monistic reality of the universe becomes understood by one of its many parts, thus keeping itself from disintegration and multiple-mindedness, i.e. loss of self-knowledge through fear of disconnection, that is, rejection.

So setting aside a short time once a day or even once a week to meditate on self is all that is necessary. And not in the hope of gaining anything special or wonderful but simply to find self. Not to gain any powers, freedoms or enlightenment, but to simply observe the reality, nature and potentialities of self; basically, to gain knowledge of self. This is meditation void of selfish ideas, desires and vanities and focused on self-discovery and self-creation. In itself, however, meditation is supposed to be boring, unhelpful and a hindrance. But to the mind free of all selfish motives it is self-fulfilling and salvation. It is calm, ordinary and painful: Nothing special, nothing fantastic, nothing over-the-top; just simply a time to observe self and the astral realm and thereby come to a greater understanding of our place in the universe.

As the fine art of observing self in the astral visions that pass through the mind is refined we will understand more the interconnection of ourselves to God and see the three spaces opened up in newer and different ways. With this the finding of self in all things dissolves our desire to be gratified, indulged or glorified, and enmeshes us in the eagerness merely to manifest and expose self to all things. With this self-exposition comes a desire also to expose self to the self in others that they might have or feel the freedom to expose self back to the self in you. With this freedom of self-exposition also comes peace of mind, as you have not been exposed but have willingly surrendered and exposed yourself.

It is when you become so immersed in meditative living that it just becomes so ordinary, unimportant, ritualistic and instinctive that you have reached a place of pneumatological soundness and balance. Meditation should thus become a means of finding and actualizing self and realigning with that part of self that exists in those outside of self. It should also be a practice that consolidates the various activities of the day to give them meaning and unites them to God, to self, and to your hopes and objectives. For this cause we must do our utmost to keep from falling into complexities and excessively deep or difficult objectives and strive for simplicity and peace. This objective in self and in our lives will be of the greatest value to those who study the Scriptures.

Based on our natural predisposition our bodies interact with forces that transform them by stages of evolution or devolution into the place where they belong and the destiny they are to acquire. The black body, by means of melanin, becomes a temple that captures these forces and allows them to stir within the black body energy waves that stimulate thought. When the thoughts we think are agapic/empathic then they are intersubjective. With these intersubjective thoughts now flowing through our mind we draw closer and closer to Ausar and Auset.

The obvious difficulty at this point becomes manifesting this Ausar nature to worldly and selfish people; people who would no doubt rob, kill and humiliate us. The Messiah provides the path to this, but we must see it in context. The Messiah said, "For there shall arise false Christs, and false prophets, and shall shew great signs and wonders; insomuch that, if it were possible, they shall deceive the very elect." (Mt 24: 24.) And what Christ could be more false than the European Jesus being displayed around the world? Through that Jesus they have tortured, raped, abused, murdered, stolen and humiliated. And this is the most worshiped God of black people; who in defence of him love to say that it does not matter what colour Jesus was. But what does Jesus himself say, "I know the blasphemy of them which say they are Jews, and are not, but are the synagogue of Satan." (Rev 2: 9.) If the true race of the Jews mattered so much to the Messiah himself that he called the imposters blasphemous then what are we to say?

The apostle John goes even further: "Beloved, believe not every *spirit*, but try the *spirits* whether they are of God: because many false prophets are gone out into the world. Hereby know ye the Spirit of God: Every *spirit* that confesseth that Jesus Christ is come in the *flesh* is of God: And every *spirit* that confesseth not that Jesus Christ is come in the *flesh* is not of God: and this is that *spirit of antichrist*, whereof you have heard that it should come; and even now already is it in the world" (1Jn 4: 1-3; emphasis mine). These colourless Jesuses come from a *spirit* that denies the flesh of Jesus, on the one hand. These white and European looking Jesuses come from a *spirit* that denies the *true* flesh of Jesus, on the other hand. Again, as the apostle Paul said, "For if he that cometh preacheth *another Jesus*, whom we have not preached, or if ye receive *another spirit*, which ye have not received, or another gospel, which ye have not accepted, ye might well bear with him" (emphasis mine). Basically, those who worship the colourless Jesus and the white Jesus have no place to hide. They are worshiping the antichrist and have received his mark on their foreheads or on their hands.

To end the speculation, the theocratic movement is an elevation from the 5 Percent Nation, but it still recognizes that the vast majority of black people, mainly Pentecostals, mainly "born again" believers; worship the white Jesus and the white god; which has held us back as a people for a long time, because psychologically we are worshiping two white men who in actual fact have both been very racist towards our people historically. If we worship two racist white men and call them the true and living God, and then say all the other gods are weak compared to them, we are effectively saying that we as a race are weak compared to white people, who, in turn, have every right to look down on us, abuse us, humiliate us, persecute us and be racist towards us as a people because they are God to us. The truth, however, is that the real Jesus was most likely an Afrocentric dread who wore fine spun jellabiyas that went down to his bronze feet. The white Jesus is an illusion, a false god that is delusively worshiped by black people around the world.

In actual fact, everything about modern Christianity is a lie: their idea of the Jews, their idea of the holy spirit, their idea of Jesus and their idea of God. Even those black Christians who allow for God and the Messiah to be Jewish – albeit with the image of Ashkenazi Jews as their standard – have allowed themselves to be possessed by the European God and Christ as that is the image most represented of them. But I charge the European God and Christ with being racist towards black and ethnic people: in his name white people have justified Crusades, Inquisitions, conquests, slavery, expatriation, colonization, segregation, criminalization, genocide and white supremacy. To be fair, he has done more to oppress non-white people than save us; and to add insult to injury, when black Pentecostals think of the love that saved them from their sins (and what sinners we are) they usually think of a white man dying for all the ethnic people of the world, and so can never bring themselves to judge white people for any of the wrongs they have done and still continue to do in the world.

That is not to say that they are not interconnected to us at all; that is just to say that the standard set by this false Christ has left the world in subjection to an evil presence. The white image of the Messiah was already deeply embedded into the white psyche from around the time of the Renaissance. Prior to that the favoured image of the Middle Ages was of the black Madonna and child, or of a black looking Messiah. This was rejected during the Renaissance as Europe was fighting against the Muslim Moors, North Africans and Turks, and to have an image of their Messiah that matched the image of their Muslim enemies would have weakened morale. By 1517 when the Reformation began and by 1555 when slaves were first taken to the Caribbean the false god and false Christ had become such subconscious aspects of Christianity that black people had no idea that Europe had just forced on them a corrupted and whitewashed version of their own messenger. Furthermore, the white Jesus antichrist (the mark of the Beast being how he spreads his kingdom) has now corrupted the whole world with its evil presence poignantly causing people to do more evil believing they will always be forgiven.

To exorcise this evil presence from the planet we need our people to enthrone our true Messiah in our hearts until we become the living embodiment of the deity, it is only then that we will truly be free in the way God has desired for us to be free. The prophet Ezekiel said, along these lines:

> *"A new heart also will I give you, and a new spirit will I put within you; and I will take away the stony heart out of your flesh, and I will give you an heart of flesh. And I will put my spirit within you, and cause you to walk in my statutes, and ye shall keep my judgments, and do them. And ye shall dwell in the land that I gave to your fathers; and ye shall be my people, and I will be your God. I will also save you from all your uncleannesses: and I will call for the corn, and will increase it, and lay no famine upon you. And I will multiply the fruit of the tree, and the increase of the field, that ye shall receive no more reproach of famine among the heathen."*

Right now it could be asked among these so-called heathen: what has happened to black people? There was a time when we had scientists, inventors, physicists, mathematicians, philosophers, artists, masters of industry, masters of finance, business people, etc. And I am not speaking here about Kemet or Kush, I speak here of nineteenth century and early twentieth century America and the Caribbean. Now all we have is experts in exclusivist industries like sports and entertainment – the Ghetto Dream – and experts in waste areas. Being from the ghetto is not the cause of this situation as the nineteenth century and early twentieth century blacks of America and the Caribbean reached their heights despite the fact that they were segregated and extremely poor.

So what is the problem now? The problem is Pentecostalism and its endorsement of a lie. What is that lie? Martin Luther's call of *Sola Fidae* (by faith alone). This slogan has caused a large amount of blacks to believe they can wish their way to success, or that if they believe hard enough and add it to their tithes they will win the lottery or get that promotion, etc. They say insanity is not in doing the wrong thing but in doing the same thing over and over and expecting a different result. Thus many of our black people end up wasting their lives away and with nothing to show for it but faith alone. Yet what does the Bible say, "What doth it profit, my brethren, though a man say he hath faith, and have not works? can faith save him? If a brother or sister be naked, and destitute of daily food, And one of you say unto them, Depart in peace, be you warmed and filled; notwithstanding ye give them not those things which are needful to the body; what doth it profit? Even so faith, if it hath not works, is dead, being alone" (Jm 2: 14-17).

We have become experts in faith alone or in faith added to tithes but we have lost our respect for works, which are needful for salvation and success. If you are saved show me by your works, what can you do? How much responsibility do you have? If you are an expert in faith alone you will die with faith alone. Instead, show me your faith by what you do – again I am not here speaking of tithes. When you add faith to tithes you are guaranteeing yourself a lifetime of giving and very little gaining. Your progress will come when you master the right things; that is not to say master only business, or only finance, or only physics, science, mathematics, etc. What you need to do is stay in a particular field for at least ten years learning not only the field itself but also the areas in that field that lead to public recognition. Put that hard work in with regard to your field and also with regard to those areas that will get you recognition in your field and you will soon be successful. Works remain ineffective until acknowledged by those outside of your peer group, by gaining recognition you ensure that your works make a difference.

For this cause God said through his prophet Joel, "Multitudes, multitudes in the valley of decision: for the day of the Lord is near in the valley of decision." "Let the heathen be wakened, and come up to the valley of Jehoshaphat: for there will I sit to judge all the heathen round about." And what is the decision to be made by the heathen if not the most ultimate decision? Will you allow the true and living God to overthrow all the false teachings and false gods in your heart thus allowing you to become yourself the divine manifestation? Are you willing to put the work in to become your own saviour and to stop trusting in fantasies and delusions to save you?

Again, his Holy Spirit is in actuality a manifestation of class and refinement; not an inhibition or a disorganization of words and actions. Our self-expression should be a manifestation of our divinity as it is – a classy and sexy mind and not a possessed mind. In its manifestation it abolishes and destroys all pre-conceived ideas, thoughts and notions, and impresses itself upon the individual.

To inhibit or adjust our self-expression to suit our surrounding environment only oppresses the self and its manifestation with unnecessary vanities. However, to adjust your surrounding environment to your self-expression liberates the two to allow both you and your surrounding environment to find peace and balance amid the chaos of life. To be sure, it will not happen overnight and it will not come without a fight, but to the soul that is determined to be free it is purity and strength.

Moreover is fulfilled that which was spoken by the prophet Jeremiah, "Behold, the days come, saith the Lord, that I will make a new covenant with the house of Israel, and with the house of Judah: Not according to the covenant that I made with their fathers in the day that I took them by the hand, to bring them out of the land of Egypt; which my covenant they brake, although I was a husband unto them, saith the Lord: But this shall be the covenant that I will make with the house of Israel; After those days, saith the Lord, I will put my law in their inward parts, and write it in their hearts; and will be their God, and they shall be my people. And they shall teach no more every man his neighbour, and every man his brother, saying, Know the Lord: for they shall all know me, from the least of them unto the greatest of them, saith the Lord: for I will forgive their iniquity, and I will remember their sin no more."

Indeed, when the Messiah "took the cup, and gave thanks, [he] gave it to them, saying, Drink ye all of it; For this is my blood of the new testament, which is shed for many for the remission of sins" (Mt 26: 27, 28). And as the apostle Paul said: "Wherefore thou art no more a servant, but a son; and if a son, then an heir of God through Christ. Howbeit then, when ye knew not God, ye did service unto them which by nature are no gods. But now, after that ye have known God, or rather are known of God, how turn ye again to the weak and beggarly elements whereunto ye desire again to be in bondage?" "Beware lest any man spoil you through philosophy and vain deceit, after the tradition of men, after the rudiments of the world".

Here we see that it is not the physical conditions of the person that places them in subjection, but the mental, that is, the psychological reasonings of the person that subjugates them. So whereas historically Reason has proven to be very inward looking and self-interested, giving us the delusion that we can control life and a world that are completely out of control, surrendering to Love and entrusting it with our lives and this world has always proven to be liberating and self-fulfilling in the true and genuine sense. It is by letting go and losing ourselves in love that we become free from the bondage of anxiety and the excessive need to prove ourselves to those outside of ourselves.

Without love we become lost in vanity and oppress self with selfish desires or fears. This is the beginning of our psychological disconnection from the world and from our place in the world. When we become selfish we seek to control and balance the world ourselves. This includes our lives, our friends, our situations, our societies and everything around us, but the reality is that controlling the world and everything in it is not and never was for us to do.

This losing of self in love is and must be first expressed in love of self, but ultimately, and with maturity, we find it includes a letting go of self. Thus we also become in-tuned with Self and stop seeking our own way or the way that best suits our cause or "our people" (the people we most closely identify with) and start seeking the way that is in line with self, our own and those outside of us. This sometimes means doing for people and our environment not what they want, but what is best for them, even at the expense of self. But the suffering of self is the highest manifestation of a self-sacrificing yet unquenchable love, that theodical love that comes only from agape, an agape that can only be respected when the truth of monism is appreciated. In these instances suffering comes from the flesh and a desire to preserve the flesh and not from imperfection or from modern injustices.

Thus for self to truly be free it must first love self then lose self in Self. By losing self in Self one becomes connected to God and interconnected to all things, which is a theocentric monism. And through interconnection to other people we also develop an empathic relation to them. This interlocks us with them and makes them one with us. Empathic and agapic interrelations are called intersubjective, as one identifies with the subjective reality of one outside of their self as though it were of their very own self. The more intersubjective we become the more self dies and Self rises. Here Self is more than just life or consciousness, Self is love, agapic/empathic love, and empathy, when it fully evolves becomes panopathy.

We all have this panopathic potential, even from our infancy, but we find that it is not enough. We get disillusioned with our 'empathic abilities' just before we learn to speak. We then assume the discourse of our parents in the language of our parents; for all, although we feel, we are not yet sensual. The self is only just discovering itself at this point, as an identity cannot be fully developed without an articulate discourse to define it. Interconnection is still apparent to our young mind as the pineal gland's activity reaches its height in infants. It is around about this time that self creates an agapic bubble around itself, which does not become broader until the time of our first memories.

Another thing that is unavoidable is that all children, from the youngest age, seek bodily pleasure. The fact that this pleasure can also come by stimulating their erotogenous zones gives the appearance of infantile sexuality, but as they have no conception of sexuality, being too young to know what sex is, sexuality is transferred onto them by adults. To them it is merely the touching of their own body parts. This kind of category also includes infantile exhibitionism and voyeurism: they are not sexual in nature they are simply exploratory and narcissistic. For adults to transfer onto children a pre-adolescent sexuality is a misconception in itself. A child must be taught the intricacies of sex to develop a mature sex drive.

But Oedipal love still exists between the white son and the white mother, even as Horian love exists between the black son and the black mother. Hence the Horu construct represents the youthful fascination of the black boy with his black mother and the humiliation of his black father. Though not all black fathers are absent from the raising of their sons, the black man is still in a position of humiliation around the world. And even in the cases where they are individually esteemed the black boy's love for his mother is an undeniable reality in the overwhelming majority of black families. Where the Horu son differs from the Oedipal is that his Auset mother connects him to the divine through teaching him spirituality.

The Horu construct of the Kemetic king and the black child is one which should manifest his journey towards divinity. When the Horu child is raised by an Auset he is on the right path. She will give him his rituals and spirituality from early youth. The lessons he learns in early youth he will not forget when he gets older. When he learns to cleanse the body with water and lotions, and when he learns to treasure his body as a holy temple that is a start to him viewing the female body as a holy temple. If, however, he does not learn to treasure his own body he will not learn to treasure any other body.

The living Pharaohs of ancient Kemet were all considered to be Horu in the flesh; thus they were considered the embodiment of black majesty. And as Horu conquered Setek in the story, so the Pharaoh conquered the forces of injustice and oppression in the world. He was the personification of the warrior even as the black man is. However, when the king died he would travel to the stars to be one with Ausar. Thus the dead king became Ausar, the force that helped and protected the living king. Considering these realities, perhaps the best way to explain all the beauties and glories of the black family is to define them from the perspective not of a socializing, but of an organizing and a purifying.

The Hebrew word for purification is the word *tahorah* and is mainly in the ritualistic sense; but as the Messiah said to the Pharisees, "Now do ye Pharisees make clean the outside of the cup and the platter; but your inward part is full of ravening and wickedness. Ye fools, did not he that made that which is without make that which is within also?" So cleanliness is to be a spiritual or pneumatological experience as well as a bodily. Basically, it should include finding and respecting the self and the body. When the self is known and loved as much as the body then the respect of other selves will come naturally. Pneumatological cleanliness is control of sexual, violent and naturalistic energies.

Undoubtedly, the most effective way to attain to the deity is through interiority: embracing love, criticism and intersubjectivity; exteriority: embracing beneficence, mercy and sensuality; and anteriority: practicing petition, gratefulness and meditation. By walking this path you will be sure to acquire the divine nature the apostle Peter spoke about. This path also leads one to a fuller understanding of the Horu construct as it develops in our psychology. Again, teaching these lessons to black boys can more or less give them a fighting chance at avoiding the negative realities of the racial self-consciousness and psychological segregation.

In actual fact, the black boy who is raised as a Horu develops an interconnection to the ancient Pharaohs of Kush and Kemet, seeing self as a divine manifestation. And, as the Messiah himself represented Horu in his own time and the living Pharaohs represented Horu in their own time, even so Ausar represented the Father in the Asarian apocalypse, being the personification of agape and of the dead ancestors of the black family. Where the Messiah reigns in the heart the person must, like the Messiah, fight against all manifestations of injustice and unrighteousness. By struggling for freedom, justice and equality the Messiah proved himself to be a true Horu, but by dying on a cross he proved himself to be a true Ausar.

The elevation of the black person from Horu to Ausar (or Hethor to Auset) must be a process by which the dictatorship of the Messiah (Horu) exorcises all vanities from self to open self up to a place where it will be ready to suffer and suffer long. But while they are still a Horu the individual should be taught to value the right and exact, the pure and clean. Purity should in fact be so important to them that they can see it in all things, as said by the apostle Paul, "Unto the pure all things are pure: but unto them that are defiled and unbelieving is nothing pure; but even their mind and conscience is defiled" (Tit 1:15). Pure and clean living is thus for the interior, exterior and anterior of the purified soul.

The black Horu son and Hethor daughter should be taught this pure and clean lifestyle along with sexuality so as to understand their sexuality from a young age for the purpose of heightening their sensuality and understanding of their erotogenous zones. That is not to say that they should be allowed to do adult things, like start having sex or stop wearing underwear: they should merely be taught about sex to know their bodies more and how to control their baser, more instinctual sensations better. Learning control over their sexual energies from a young age would give them a closer connection to the deity by the time they reach adulthood so that they would be able to become true Ausars and Ausets before death. This black divinity also makes them one with all the dead Pharaohs of history, the dead African kings and queens and all the righteous dead ancestors of the black family, who also see and have seen all that has been going on in the world at the hands of the Western powers.

The psychological realities of Western development show the implacable tenacity of their progressive spirit. They came from Dark Ages to racial supremacy. In competitive terms they were able to gain victory over the inherent obstacles set in the path to their historic rise and set the pace for future development. At this time the world looks designed as if white people were actually superior when their own past is one of intellectual and religious suppression at the hands of the Catholic hierarchy.

To attain to a postmodern system of holism, intersubjectivity and randomness white people had to go through the psychologic of theological upheaval; as Engels also reminds us; historically "the masses of the country people, the peasants...everywhere had to struggle for their very existence with their feudal lords, spiritual and temporal." "The Lutheran Reformation produced a new creed indeed, a religion adapted to absolute monarchy." But, "No sooner were the peasants of North-East Germany converted to Lutheranism than they were from freemen reduced to serfs."

However, "where Luther failed, Calvin won the day. Calvin's creed was one fit for the boldest of the bourgeoisie of his time. His predestination doctrine was the religious expression of the fact that in the commercial world of competition success or failure does not depend upon a man's activity or cleverness, but upon circumstances uncontrollable by him...Calvin's church constitution was thoroughly democratic and republican; and...founded a republic in Holland, and active republican parties in England, and, above all, Scotland." At that time "the English bourgeoisie now had to take a part in keeping down the 'lower orders,' the great producing mass of the nation, and one of the means employed for that purpose was the influence of religion." For which cause to us the existence of God is not based on whether or not he is a Creator or Judge, but as it is written somewhere, "above all things have fervent charity among yourselves: for charity shall cover the multitude of sins." And as the word used here and throughout the New Testament for charity is agape: those who walk in agape are free from sin.

The soteriological implications of this understandings are also hard missed; for the Messiah said to his disciples, "Ye know that the princes of the Gentiles exercise dominion over them, and they that are great exercise authority upon them. But it shall not be so among you: but whosoever will be great among you, let him be your minister; And whosoever will be chief among you, let him be your servant" (Mt 20: 25-27). We can find here the full expression of godhood manifested in practices beyond dogmatic reasonings and the doctrinal proclamations of the Charismatics or their clergy towards personal salvation. Instead there is a steady and mutual flow of respect and sociable caring towards those outside of self that is both merciful and beneficial.

Inasmuch then as the messianic movement was supposed to be beneficial and merciful through agape covering all sins, it matched the old African system of monism and communal association. The accepted notion of primitive aggression and tribal volatility is actually a somewhat fantasist or even racist idea in the light of this reality. Far from being an expression of savagery the tribal system was in fact a form of communal relationship. The old polyamorous families had a more localized subjectivity distinct from the neo-colonial destination affairs and industry currently seem to be at. The land and labour were considered in the pre-modern as communal; and as we head towards a postmodernity communal seems to be making a comeback.

According to Engels, as "The original common ownership of land corresponded, on the one hand, to a level of development of human beings in which their horizon was restricted in general to what lay immediately available, and presupposed, on the other hand, a certain superfluity of land that would allow some latitude for correcting the possible bad results"; "once these barbarians of the middle stage had taken to pastoral life, it would never have occurred to them to leave the grassy watered plains of their own accord and return to the forest regions which had been the home of their ancestors."

For this cause Engels felt that an ideal village economy was one in which, "Either additional land taken from big estates in the neighbourhood is placed at the disposal of the peasant co-operative or the peasants in question are provided with the means and the opportunity to engage in industrial sidelines, primarily and as far as possible for their own use. In either case their economic position [would be] improved and simultaneously the general social directing agency is assured the necessary influence to transform the peasant co-operative to a higher form, and to balance the rights and duties of the co-operative as a whole as well as of its individual members with those of the other departments of the entire community."

Speaking on the same subject Kropotkin explains, using his knowledge of the socio-historical development of human societies, how "A whole series of institutions...developed from that basis of common ownership of land during the long succession of centuries which was required to bring the barbarians under the dominion of States organized upon the Roman or Byzantine pattern. The village community was not only a union for guaranteeing to each one his fair share in the common land, but also a union for common culture, for mutual support in all possible forms, for protection from violence, and for a further development of knowledge, national bonds, and moral conceptions;" so that even to him social relations, in regards to pre-Roman society, was one of village communism and co-operative ownership.

Here we also see "that a long influence of the Roman law and the Christian Church, which soon accepted the Roman principles, were required to accustom the barbarians to the idea of private property in land", even as it was said of the messianic movement: "Neither was there any among them that lacked: for as many as were possessors of lands or houses sold them, and brought the prices of the things that were sold, And laid them down at the apostles' feet: and distribution was made unto every man according as he had need" (Acts 4: 34,35). To which end Marx states, "In the higher phase of communist society, after the enslaving subordination of the individual to the division of labour, and...the antithesis between mental and physical labour, has vanished; after labour has become not only a means of life but life's prime want...only then can the narrow horizon of bourgeois right be crossed in its entirety and society inscribe on its banners: From each according to his abilities, to each according to his needs!"

Engels in exploring this development from village communism to the higher phase of communism reminds us "the great international centre of feudalism was the Roman Catholic Church. It united the whole of feudalised Western Europe, in spite of all internal wars, into one grand political system, opposed as much to the schismatic Greeks as to the Mohammedan countries. It surrounded feudal institutions with the halo of divine consecration. It had organised its own hierarchy on the feudal model, and, lastly, it was itself by far the most powerful feudal lord, holding, as it did, fully one-third of the soil of the Catholic world."

Again, we read from Kropotkin, "The earliest barbarian codes already represent to us societies composed of peaceful agricultural communities...[who] covered the country with villages and farmhouses;...cleared the forests, bridged the torrents, and colonized the formerly quite uninhabited wilderness...[leaving] the uncertain warlike pursuits to brotherhoods, *scholæ*, or 'trusts' of unruly men, gathered round temporary chieftains". These "village communities of the so-called barbarians at a time when they were making a new start of civilization after the fall of the Roman Empire" "continued to till the soil, taking but little notice of their would-be rulers, so long as they did not interfere with the independence of their village communities."

From this premise, to return to Engels for a while, "We of course are decidedly on the side of the small peasant; we shall do everything at all permissible to make his lot more bearable, to facilitate his transition to the co-operative should he decide in favour of it," but, "Our task relative to the small peasant consists, in the first place, in effecting a transition of his private undertaking, private possession to co-operative one, not forcibly but by dint of example and the proffer of social assistance for this purpose. And then of course we shall have ample means of showing to the small peasant prospective advantages that must be obvious to him even today."

He also continues, "Neither now nor at any time in the future can we promise the smallholding peasants to preserve their individual property and individual enterprise against the overwhelming power of capitalist production. We can only promise them that we shall not interfere in their property relations by force, against their will." But our "main point is and will be to make the peasants understand that we can save, preserve their houses and fields for them only by transforming them into co-operative property operated co-operatively."

Engels goes on to say, "The same applies to the big and middle peasant....We are economically certain that the big and middle peasant must likewise inevitably succumb to the competition of capitalist production and the cheap overseas corn, as is proved by the growing indebtedness and the everywhere evident decay of these peasants as well. We can do nothing against this decay except recommend here too the pooling of farms to form co-operative enterprises, in which the exploitation of wage labour will be eliminated more and more, and their gradual transformation into branches of the great national producers' co-operative with each branch enjoying equal rights and duties can be instituted."

Then, to clarify further he explains that with "the big landed estates...we are confronted by rural proletarians in masses and our task is clear...We by no means consider compensation as impermissible" but understand expropriation to be inevitable. "Whether this expropriation is to be compensated for or not will to a great extent depend not upon us but the circumstances under which we obtain power...At any rate the transformation of the capitalist enterprise into a social enterprise is here fully prepared for and can be carried into execution overnight...And the example of these agricultural co-operatives would convince also the last of the still resistant small-holding peasants, and surely also many big peasants, of the advantages of co-operative, large-scale production."

To summarize, small farmers with smallholdings should pool their land together into a farming co-operative. As more small co-operatives consume larger land masses they will become bigger. The more aggregated they become the more funds they will acquire. This will in time allow them to buy out the larger estates from the big landowners and plantation owners. These co-operatives should be linked by a central committee that coordinates allocation with a parliament of workers: one for each workplace, district, region and country. This will allow policies to be based on economic determination and not ruinous bureaucracies. It also means changing our other businesses into co-operative services like those dealing in clothes, oils, ointments, perfumes, incense, cleansers, holistic and martial training courses, etc. Goods, services and information should be distributed fairly (or freely) to everyone within the co-operative as everyone would have contributed something.

But within the current system and situation economic reform based on the old co-operative system is somewhat unlikely. A first step must at least be sought to bring us back to a more natural form of living. Dr. King here provides us with what I consider to be the best first step in the process, "An intelligent approach to the problem of poverty and racism will cause us to see that the words of the Psalmist – 'The earth is the Lord's and the fullness thereof' – are still a judgment upon our use and abuse of wealth and resources with which we have been endowed." This is a very valuable message to remember. The earth is not man's nor does it belong to man; it is the Lord's and he has entrusted it to humanity with the responsibility to cultivate it in due season. Again, as the earth does not belong to us we cannot and should not do just whatever we want with it.

To which Engels also maintains, "at every step we are reminded that we by no means rule over nature like a conqueror over a foreign people, like someone standing outside nature – but that we, with flesh, blood and brain, belong to nature, and exist in its midst, and that all our mastery of it consists in the fact that we have advantage over all other creatures of being able to learn its laws and apply them correctly." And "the more this progresses the more will men not only feel but also know their oneness with nature, and the more impossible will become the senseless and unnatural idea of a contrast between mind and matter, man and nature, soul and body".

THEODICY AND THEOCRACY

The philosophy of the godbody is derived from the history of the black struggle translated through theocentric monism. I can also see that something very important for we Gods to understand, and which interestingly enough has been kept hidden from us, is that under our constitutional right to freedom of assembly, the state has no real right to arrest us simply for practicing our culture. What they can arrest us for is participating in criminal activities or the committing of an illegal action. This is one of the major ways that the state has undermined the representation of our movement and our communities.

Though we godbodies have a duty to bring knowledge of self to those who are uncivilized. We are not tied down to any specific doctrine: what is demanded of us from the godbody elders (the older Gods) is to remember that the God of the Scriptures, whatever holy book it may be, is self and kind. As black men we are very God: and though we blacks as a people happen to currently be going through our psychological Dark Ages – we have not been able to channel our spiritual excellence into psychological empowerment – our destiny is to divinity.

We godbody hope that through a sensual resurrection we can deliver to our people a cultural enrapturement and an appreciation of their interconnection to the righteous dead. It is our hope that through this we can begin to move our people out of this psychological and social slump we seem to be in towards a true divinity. These birthing pangs we are experiencing in our struggles to achieve these ends are merely the norm of most social bodies and movements on their way to self-identity and self-expression.

But with all the corruption and doctrinal squabbling going on within the church today the critical and hypocritical condemnations of the church may fall on their own heads. It was said by the prophet Hosea, "Plead with your mother, plead: for she is not my wife, neither am I her husband: let her therefore put away her whoredoms out of her sight, and her adulteries from between her breasts; Lest I strip her naked, and set her as in the day that she was born, and make her as a wilderness, and set her like a dry land, and slay her with thirst".

Based on these ideas we godbodies should refuse any form of religious or political fornication; completely renouncing the world and their worldly honours, ethics and excesses. This means existing without any religious or governmental backing. If a member of the government or a religious body wants to help our movement that is their right, but we should try to maintain a kind of autonomy along the lines of the co-operative movement. By doing this we will be able to fund ourselves, feed ourselves and govern ourselves. Autonomy is the aim, but it will be difficult to confront this system on our own. By initiating co-operatives we have a legal and unchallengeable method of being more than just a supra-religious community.

Ultimately, the theocracy is just that, it combines the lessons of the godbody with the system of the co-operative. The godbody on their own have a kind of paradise, we just need a working socio-economic programme. However, psychologically and philosophically we have reached into the heavens and made God more real. It was written by the apostle John, "That which was from the beginning, which we have heard, which we have seen with our eyes, which we have looked upon, and our hands have handled, of the Word of life;" for by the Word becoming visible and touchable it allowed we flesh and blood human beings to acquiesce to its guidance.

Consequently, the Messiah represents a manifestation of God for we flesh and blood human beings. But as the apostle John made very clear concerning the schisms of the time "many deceivers are entered into the world, who confess not that Jesus Christ is come in the flesh. This is a deceiver and an antichrist. Look to yourselves, that we lose not those things which we have wrought, but that we receive a full reward. Whosoever transgresseth, and abideth not in the doctrine of Christ, hath not God. He that abideth in the doctrine of Christ, he hath both the Father and the Son." It is doctrine in which Christ provides us with a direct source to our cultural enrapturement: he himself was washed with water, he a preacher to the poor, he himself was sexually ethical, he himself had a solitary Lenten retreat, he a martyr and he a beaten up penitent, and he the founder of both the Agape Feast and the forgiveness of sins. This would also prove to be that example to all we who came after him.

With all this in mind we godbodies intend to inflict the Wrath of God on all those who *oppose* our way of living; acknowledging that a spirit of demonization will be unleashed against our said way of life. Though it is likely that this could reverberate into the classic racial Manichaeism of the black devil/white devil theory, we of the theocracy have expanded our understanding of evil to the causal and mental realms. It is here that we recognize the reality of *Satan* (Hebrew and Arabic for astral, ethical, legal and military adversary, or even for falsehood; though better translated as the great opposition), as the force locked in an epic Armageddon with us godbodies by spreading trick knowledge to the ignorant peoples of the world.

However, we are helped in our Armageddon by four *khajim* (natures) through which we judge the angels and people of this system: *khekmah* (Hebrew for astral, ethical, social and military wisdom, or even sagely; though better translated as the divine composition), which comes through mastering knowledge of self; *qodesh* (Hebrew for incorruptible, sacred and sexual refinement, or even sanctity; though better translated as the divine disposition), which comes through mastering knowledge, wisdom and understanding; *roi* (Hebrew for sensual, precognitive and retrocognitive vision, or even visionary; though better translated as the divine supposition), which comes through mastering the supreme mathematics; and *elohim*

(Hebrew for omnivisional, omnipotent and omnibenevolent deity, or even divinity; though better translated as the divine exposition), which comes through mastering the universal laws of existence.

These are all *khajim* that we gain in the godbody culture. Again, as the godbody culture is a Western counterculture, we should embody these *khajim* of elevation through the rules of our own tradition in our own way. In absorbing these *khajim* you will be better equipped to fight in the Armageddon to come, and better able to challenge attacks from Satan and his body of devils. Therefore the only job of successive leaders should be to administrate, facilitate, protect and enforce the rules, codes and lessons of the godbody culture to the best of their ability. That done, the movement can expand, not only throughout the different classes of the black American community but throughout the different communities of the world.

Again, you are not obliged to follow any of the rules or ideas of the godbody if you are not a member (neither will you be obliged to receive any of its many benefits). And though all this does put us in danger of becoming like our predecessors, at least for this millennium we will have Rapture being what could be called a communion of poor righteous teachers.

The apostle John further reassures us in our ecclesiology, saying "I write unto you, little children, because your sins are forgiven you for his name's sake. I write unto you, fathers, because ye have known him that is from the beginning. I write unto you, young men, because you have overcome the wicked one". And even Antonio Gramsci, an Italian political prisoner during Mussolini's Fascist dictatorship, explains this kind of structure for political parties (though the definition may be extended to include non-political and non-governmental parties too):

1. The principle element, which is the nerve centre. In here you have the mind of the party, body or organization. They themselves are a group of individuals who agree on an outcome and dictate their idea to others. As the nerve centre

this group represents the most important element within the body. Whether by their passion and charisma or their devotion and discipline, these individuals will be the party or organization leaders.

2. The intermediate element, which are those who follow the nerve centre. These take the ideas from the leading members and transmit them to the ordinary, non-organizational members. They are the go-betweens as every big party and organized body needs representatives to go-between the central views of the principle element and the broader masses of the body.

3. The mass element, which are those who follow the intermediaries. The mass element are what could be called the rank-and-file. They give the party or organized body its size and strength as well as its connection to the real world of the non-affiliated mass. Though a group can exist and function without them it will not last too long nor will it remain too powerful. These, again, represent the normal everyday people who routinize the ideas and understandings transmitted to them by the intermediate element and bring them into a social context.

Any revolutionary movement in the truest sense of the word would need a unified and organized leadership committee in order to function in a unified and progressive way. In the case of the godbody the leadership is clearly the captains, the intermediaries would be the lieutenants and the mass element would be the soldiers. But the leaders must also be guided by the goals and principles of the 5 Percent and by a desire to fulfil its ultimate destiny. This also means being guided by our values and ethics until they have become standardized within our hearts. The theocracy is the ideology of the godbody – we have only taken the lessons to the next level. The theocracy itself is a progressive movement from the godbody, to organize our movement into a social programme that incorporates the general ideas and practices of the godbody and makes them applicable to society at large, particularly the black community.

In the current system we of the underclass are marginalized and alienated. To move from marginalization to interconnection and from alienation to emancipation the godbody must form a vanguard within the hood. The riots and damaging of property, burning and looting, that has taken place in the past is not a constructive means of achieving our objective. In order to fulfil our own destiny as the revolutionary section of the underclass we must become more strategic. I recognize that to a lot of people involved in the godbody movement this may seem time consuming and unnecessary but ultimately it does pay off when you begin to see the outcome of your hopes and aims come to fruition. So far all revolutionary actions organized by workers and non-workers have proven futile; this is not due to lack of will, strength or morality, but because they have been unprepared for the forces arrayed against them and the depths to which they would be prepared to sink. As we evolve into a black theocracy, we must take the lead by practicing a revolutionary activism – like our BPP heritage demands – it is necessary for us moreover to return to a more structured and organized form of militancy.

Most people learn from action. Most people in the underclass are illiterate or semi-literate. They all need an example to follow to know what to do and how it is done. Most Muslims nowadays see suicide bombers and kidnappers achieving reasonable success in their fight against immeasurable odds. They are not converted to terrorism by some book or leaflet; they are converted to terrorism by the circumstances of the current system and a desire to change things. The main situation is conditions of the people; any alienated people would desire to be liberated and should be willing to take the necessary actions to attain that liberation. The unfortunate situation is that they just do not know the right course of action to take to achieve their goals. At present the only solution being offered to the people to fight against the obvious corruptions inherent in the system is terrorism.

The young are the main ones that are alienated; they are the ones that are marginalized; as Huey Newton said they will inherit the revolution. They are tired of seeing America politically and militarily bully weaker countries, and they are tired of seeing Europe economically rob and exploit thousands in Africa, Asia and Latin America. They are tired of seeing themselves starve while millionaire bankers and corporate executives have incredible excesses and subsidies granted them by impotent governments. The young people want the power to control their own destiny and not to be forced into the background by systemic mechanisms they do not know or understand. Simply put, the young people of the ghetto, the same ones you ignored, they are the ones coming at you, and they are taking from you everything you ever believed in. As the apostle John said, "I have written to you, young men, because ye are strong, and the word of God abideth in you, and ye have overcome the wicked one".

Notwithstanding, the task they have set before them must be delicately trod: As BPP co-founder Bobby Seale explained, "we will not fight capitalism with black capitalism; we will not fight imperialism with black imperialism; we will not fight racism with black racism", nor will we fight modernism with black modernism. Indeed, black capitalism could in actual fact be more dangerous than white capitalism because it gives the appearance of racial empowerment and equality when the reality is: racial self-denial, self-loathing and materialistic self-gratification.

Ultimately, the black bourgeoisie represent a split personality. On the one hand, there is the side of them that is connected to their beginnings, which in most cases is a poverty based beginning. On the other hand, they seek to maintain respect and credibility within the system they have come to be initiated into. The end result is unfortunately shame, shock and horror when the black man's (or woman's) blackness comes out, as it inevitably will, and they are exposed to the white people they have tried so hard to impress.

We can never win in a war against white supremacy by adopting white lifestyles. That just means we have sold out, wearing a white mask to cover our black face. In the 1960s and 70s black people had the sympathy of the nations, now we are outcasts by all the nations as we are by our own, because we have all sold out. We sold the dream. We gave up on our ideals of a better world and just settled for white acceptance. We bought into capitalism, imperialism and racism and so got complacent. We soon lost ourselves in an effort to prove ourselves to our white patrons and so became the thing we hated the most.

With the persecution and loss of the BPP the next generation became lax, complacent and allowed the power structure to seduce them with talks of reparations and opportunity prospects into sacrificing the revolution for times of prosperity. The children and their now husbandless mothers were now in the position of Horu and Auset without their Ausar, and forced to hold the fort down the Horu son had to become a man way before his time. With lack of guidance and a respectable father figure the black man was unfortunately raised and taught by the white man. And like with even the most intelligent of tigers trying to raise a lion cub, or even a family of mountain lions trying to raise a black lion – even though they belong to the same species – the white man had no idea how to raise or teach black men so they instead corrupted us.

For this cause I have written this book mainly for the black intelligentsia, that they, like Djehuti, may be our spiritual guides and teachers in the struggle to liberate ourselves and our fathers from the bondage of alienation and cultural humiliation. We need them just as much as they need us. We are their past and their future. We are the real them, not the facade they wear to please white society. We are their history, the history of the black struggle. We are their strength, the incarnation of black power. We are Horu, the black man reborn. We just need them to teach us our rights, and means of overcoming the pitfalls of this bourgeois system.

Again, the ghetto most of them came from is crime ridden, crime being the only avenue to survive the harsh realities of the world's uneven social and economic development. This ghetto is in a civil war because their own kind is the only outlet for their frustrations.

They see no end to their poverty and misery in the modern world system and no way out but to resort to crime. That is the ghetto I came from: The ghetto of the antinomian, antipathetic and anti-establishment lifestyle. For which cause also the apostle John said, "Love not the world, neither the things that are in the world. If any man love the world, the love of the Father is not in him. For all that is in the world, the lust of the flesh, and the lust of the eyes, and the pride of life, is not of the Father, but is of the world".

The ghetto culture as it now stands is no culture at all; it is capitalism on a hyper and massive scale. Their clothes are more expensive and so are their cars; their jewellery is bigger and their home accessories are flashier. Pretty much everything they buy has to be great or hyped up. It is an excessive capitalism to the extreme. Therefore, for the sake of theocracy we of the black divinity have come to see that ghetto capitalist culture is not representative of our reality or of our desire. Basically, what we do desire is to replace it with a theocentric culture to resist the modern capitalist annexation. BPP leader Linda Harrison said:

> *"We have no culture but a culture born out of our resistance to oppression. 'No colonial system draws it justification from the fact that the territories [and people] it dominates are culturally nonexistent. You will never make colonialism blush for shame by spreading out little known cultural treasures under its eyes' (quoted from The Wretched of the Earth)."*

So our counterculture is of necessity a messianic-anarchism while popular culture is of necessity a democratic-pluralism. Here we seek not the dictatorship of a politician, party or class of people, but the dictatorship of the Messiah in our hearts until we become like God in the flesh, a living expression of the divine nature. This popular culture, again, poses no real or serious threat to modernism. It is willing to go only so far but falls apart when the system begins to confront it. Sadly, as the system begins its own fight back it causes dissentions among the rank-and-file, which combined with a general lack of patience and perseverance in struggling for their ideals puts an end to any revolutionary self-expression within the culture itself. We godbodies are a counterculture unpopular to the world but made new by regular fellowship. We do not seek pluralism or popularity as ideals to strive for as they both contain disintegrating tendencies.

New controversies arise when one challenges the modern interpretation of society. The modernizing experience did not work for Africa; it only left them lagging behind the post-industrial and the post-communist worlds. To term this slow growth and development process a result of racism is to blind oneself to the fact that Africa is less than seventy years free of colonialism and has been making a start on the post-colonial project. Their lives for over half a century have been defined by another power, a foreign power. There is no way they can compete with the West who have had literally hundreds of years of uninhibited modernism behind them. It is not even for the people of Africa to compete at all. Africa and the post-colonial world now suffer poverty as a result of their former colonization, even as the former communist states are the victims of post-communist poverty. But in both cases it is not real poverty but failure to keep up with the West. It is not that the West is actually better or more developed – most of the countries of the West are in serious debt and poverty – they have just had a longer run at modernity.

The post-colonial world seems to be the victims of a keeping up with the Joneses mentality. This is due to their admiration for modernism. They look to the West to lead them to development as they see the West as having attained a kind of perfection. Modernity has made itself attractive to the post-communist and post-colonial worlds to the destruction of their own cultural realities. All these nations have a history, all have a heritage. Modern society renounces the past because it sees life in the new alone. Not that a postmodern project is successfully eradicating this thirst for the new. The West's attempt to free itself from its own giants and spectres is a bit of a washout. Metanarratives and ideologies still exist today as can be seen by the rise of neoliberal, ecological, post-colonial and religious fundamentalist movements.

Nowadays postmodernists appear naive and backward, looking to a halo of legitimation that can never be reached. They have a desire to capture the rebellious spirit of the post-colonialist and post-communist freedom fighters by endorsing a fight. And indeed there must be a fight with modernism for modernity to be passed. This means more than simply narratives and legitimation this means actual changes in society, in lifestyles and in politics. It is Europe's attempt to capture some of the revolutionary energy that was flowing from the 1950s-80s that created intellectual and cultural postmodernism; but the fact of modernity still remains. To overthrow modernism in truth means to have a movement against democracy.

Africa, having escaped from colonialism, is in a state of trying to build up its life anew. They should not be looking to the West for inspiration on what to be or become but looking to their own history as to what they are supposed to be. Modernism is the West's answer to the global predicament. Postmodernism is the West's answer to the failures of modernism. In all, the West has no answer as to the brokenness of the world. Returns to superstition and to prejudice are the current answers but are devoid of substance as superstition and prejudice are incapable of rectifying the difficulties of a society. The necessity of Africa to see beyond Western solutions to African problems is thus imperative.

In the struggle for existence Africa must redefine itself in languages different from modernity's univocal chorus. They are not underdeveloped, underprivileged or backward. They are ancient, ancestral and traditional. As they exist today they are a recollection of past experience redefined by slavery, colonization, segregation/apartheid and illegitimization. Black people are left with little history that does not involve their subjugation. We have been subject for so long that all our energies have been developed toward liberation from some form of oppression. This time consuming enterprise has left us little space to devote to self-improvement. From institution to institution: from slavery to colonization, from colonization to segregation/apartheid, from segregation/apartheid to illegitimization. It seems as soon as we get free from one form of institutional bondage we find ourselves in another. Yet we have constantly blamed the white man for our oppression. This is not so, we have not taken the time to define ourselves, to learn ourselves, to know ourselves and so we end up subjugated. We seem to have allowed our oppressors and our subjections to define us; if not our liberation movements.

Once we begin to define ourselves as divine and see the genuine divinity in ourselves then we can move from under the heel of history. Once we throw off the chains of our mentally distorted memories we can find memories less humiliating. Once we begin to envisage ourselves as the Gods and Earths we are we stand a chance at creating and co-creating a better future. We no longer need to define ourselves as freedom fighters but as something new, something different, something born of our new struggle for self-definition. The West need no longer be our mentors. We have our own pre-subjugated histories. We have a rich ancestry and we can be proud to call ourselves black.

Modernity is the glorification of the white race over and against all other races. It is the telling of the ethnically different that they need to catch up, keep up, and come up to what is apparently an ethically, intellectually and materially superior position invented and justified by white culture. All non-whites thus must learn from whites how to exploit and subjugate to achieve even as white people had to, and still do, exploit and subjugate in order to achieve. There is no racism without modern legitimation and there is no modernism without white supremacy. Thus what is effectively the overthrow of modernism is also the overthrow of racism. Though, not as freedom fighters, which are just as much a product of modernity as racism, but as Gods and Earths.

We must also understand that for us to be a reasonable rival to the current modernist structure we have to incorporate anti-sexists, anti-capitalists, anti-imperialists, anti-colonialists, anti-racists, anti-fascists and anti-statists of all wings and flavours. And as the apostle John said, "hereby we know that we are of the truth, and shall assure our hearts before him. For if our heart condemn us, God is greater than our heart, and knoweth all things. Beloved, if our heart condemn us not, then have we confidence towards God".

What America has accomplished in its mission to save the world is it has rebuilt the world in its own image. To do this it has had to keep ancient and traditional cultures in a time warp. By doing this it has been able to master them. US neo-colonialism is the basis of the current form of modernism. It paints itself as newer, better and superior to the native and the traditionalist so as to subdue them into its own cultural supremacy. Admittedly, not with evil or ill intent but with the best will in the world it could never add up to what the ancients had despite their so-called superstitions. Colonial and neo-colonial would-be rulers are simply an aggressive guest in someone else's house. They are not a superior ideology or system. In actual fact, while the Christian West was lost in superstition during the Middle Ages the global South was building civilizations. It is not that the global South failed in its historical task, it is that they believed the propaganda of the West. The global South was not lost in superstition like the West was, it was far more educated. In fact, many from among the Western scholars were educated at the university in Timbuktu, Mali – which was the first modern university – or by the Moors of Spain and Portugal, before the West erased that part of their history and started belittling the Africans as savages lost in ignorance and superstition to propagandize for the Reconquest and slave trade.

Demodernization is the project that we now start for the liberation of the global South. This is not one of those inevitable projects, this is a completely new idea based on the failure of modernism to unleash the divine potential within us all and carry us towards a genuine evolution. The psychological stagnation in black people is the basis of their current social subjugation. Thus Marx is in actual fact turned on his head. It is not an economic structure changing an ideological superstructure but a psychological infrastructure changing an ideological structure, which in turn changes a sociological superstructure. When we discover a culture that is complementary to our personal psychology we learn the knowledge of that culture, then, in practicing that knowledge we eventually gain social benefits from it. Ultimately, knowledge is considered and thought out in the psychological dimension, then it is put into practice.

The subject of mental or psychological segregation, though seeming somewhat innocent, is a deceptive conundrum. It is the setting up in your own mind inhibitions that block you from reaching your full potential. The group's consciousness of its own divinity, or its aspirations to attain divinity, are the epitome of self-discovery. Group consciousness for black people thus creates an avenue for us to crawl out of subjugation and into black divinity. By freeing thought to the point of limitless possibility, by not being bound by human frailties, by going beyond the natural boundaries of the body and mind and opening up that centre in the self-same mind that leads to impossibility we manifest that divinity.

Modern humanism cannot unlock these centres as it denies their existence. Bound by a desire to man-please it is caught up in conceptions and phraseologies, terminologies that create inhibition and prevent exhibition. The escaping of the mind from mental segregation is the tearing down of the inhibition placed on it by the system of white domination that has consumed the earth since the Renaissance and Reconquest. Eurocentric modernism is the systemic prohibition of society on black and non-white bodies based on the standards of an Americanized Europe. It is neo-colonial as it is based upon the colonization of the majority by the Washington consensus.

When one begins to question their non-white place in a white society they begin the path of racial awareness. Though race and ethnicity can play a part in how one is treated it would not be to the extent that these individuals see it. This question thus either stems from miseducation or misinformation. Levels and ideas that may have been impossible for our fathers to reach are set right before us.

We are the heirs to their struggle and we need struggle no more. We all represent the same blackness, we all share the same agape and we all acknowledge the same God-collective, we are all brothers and sisters in this collective and must remember our place is within it. God is working everything out towards our concerted and united better. This means, as a black family, we are not held back we are just practicing the wrong system. We currently belong to a universalized white system not an endemically black system.

This is where our blackness takes on a whole new dimension. What system is suited to the collective black soul? What is the black psychology? To be fair, it is not the current church system. Though we do church very well and have mastered the art of praising and testifying, we are not meet for the church rule system, particularly those with regard to sex and violence. I myself am a black man so there is no need to lie: standard within the heart of a black man is a desire for unpacified aggression and deep in the heart of a black woman is a desire for uninhibited promiscuity. These are not faults, flaws or defects as God made us perfect. These are instinctual drives that make us more and more like Ausar and Auset.

Ausar and Auset are again the black expression of the deity. Ausar is the black authentication of God. He is the necessary God, not exclusive to black people but the black way of articulating his existence. He is living agape as he represents the union of the sacred to the sensual. Ausar is that selfhood where heaven touches earth; the closest we can draw to divinity. When we begin to accept our soulishness and sensuality we become more and more divine, as the black soul is only liberated by manifesting its sensuality. Black people for so long have been associated with sex and violence. My personal opinion is that rather than running away from these stereotypes we should just embraced them. The Ashkenazim are commonly stereotyped as greedy and elitist conspirators, but this never stops them from producing millionaires or forming elitist circles. Rather than run from their negative stereotypes they embraced them and so turned them into positives. This is due to their knowledge and love of self, something we black people invented but now lack.

Ra Atum, or the divine self-disclosure, is the start of our dispersal into the areas of our soul that have remained untapped by our consciousness. By self-creation or self-organization we begin the process of re-finding our divinity, of seeing ourselves as divine again. We are also liberated from mental segregation and racial self-consciousness as we become more divine. The union of divine and human is thus complete and we walk as living temples of God. This is not to say we enter a black nirvana or utopia but we find a kind of Eden within ourselves and our Ausar or Auset consciousness. As we become one with Ausar or Auset we suffer, but we gain enrapturement. Our suffering thus becomes a counterbalance to our sensual perfection. We have all suffered: in slavery, colonization, segregation and illegitimization. Here we emulate Ausar and Auset in maintaining a sensual connection despite our persecutions. And like them we become divine through agape.

In all this we must learn to exorcise from ourselves racial self-consciousness and to fill ourselves with Ausar and Auset consciousness. Again, we are already free from the chains of slavery, colonization, segregation and poverty, but all over the world we still suffer from illegitimization to this day and blame white people for it. Our shattered history is no excuse now for our current illegitimization. If we developed our own culture and stuck to it against all the odds we would no longer care about illegitimization because we could take care of each other. This is Tum, self-organization, and Ra Atum, divine self-organization. If we are truly divine, or are truly attaining to that which is divine, then we need no longer blame the white man for our realities. The white man has purged and purified us that we may reach this point of divinity, albeit unwittingly, it is up to us to remain in it.

Here Horu represents to us that enlightened side of our nature just like Ra. The difference is that Horu is power and Ra is knowledge. The Horu construct, based primarily on empowerment, is a part of every black child's natural development. Socialization therefore should consist of bringing the black boy to an understanding of themselves as the resurrection of their father, and of their fathers. Basically, through the development of the Horu construct a black man learns to control their violent and militant nature. Thereby the black boy (and also black girl) learns self-control and no longer needs some outside governmental force to control them.

Police officers, as a manifestation of governmental force, are currently used to protect the communities they are sent to patrol in a respectful manner, thus making them feel safer. But they prove they are not obliged to make black communities feel any safer; if they were really out to make our communities feel safer then they would stop arresting and murdering innocent black lives for such simple things as playing with toys. They are actually making only one group of people safe in society, the bourgeoisie. But who are they saving the bourgeoisie from? From the frustration and disillusionment of the underclass. In order to reach the many with the order of the few, terror, intimidation, brutality and murder are the tactics the police use and have been using. Who suffers? You and I suffer, to them we are the ones that may get out of line; we are the ones that may rage against our exploitation; we are the ones with a revolutionary tendency and nothing to lose by fighting them. In the long run, the police, as pawns in modern bourgeois society will be the main force used to block any movement within our communities by arresting any members of our communities that show any signs of nonconformity.

There are plenty of godbodies who have been to prison and after serving their time came back to the streets. And there are plenty of godbodies who have gone to prisons to share our general message of black divinity. These godbodies, having learned the game from those who were revolutionary, whether in the prison or on the streets, themselves become revolutionary and try to convert others. But even Dr. King, himself, had no problem with calling his own movement a revolutionary movement. He warned the National Cathedral, in 1968 not to sleep through the *great revolution* then taking place in

America. He called it a *human rights revolution*, saying "First, we are challenged to develop a world perspective. No individual can live alone, no nation can live alone, and anyone who feels that he can live alone is sleeping through a revolution."

Now we, the underclass, fill up the jails and prisons of America, whether by bad or good members. Prison, however, is filled with three kinds of prisoners: Those in prison for inherent anti-social incorrigibility, who commit crimes for nothing but the rush; those that Huey Newton called "illegitimate capitalists," who have conformed to the ideas and ideals of the system but see no legitimate means of survival within it but to break its laws; and finally, political prisoners, who have a major problem with the system and its ideals and take actions to change or challenge it, it is this action that landed them in prison.

Illegitimate capitalists and political prisoners can be either apologists or fanatics based on their state of mind. For example, a terrorist in prison may think what they have done was right, they are political prisoners but their thinking is fanatic. However, there are terrorists that seek to explain their actions and justify them to those outside of their circle, these are apologists for themselves and others like them, either way a terrorist is a political prisoner, even though they should be punished for the evil of what they did.

One of the main problems within the black theocracy will always be that in order to practice our counterculture as it is some of us practitioners may have to break some unjust or unreasonable laws; but what does Dr. King say on the subject, "One who breaks an unjust law must do it *openly, lovingly* (not hatefully as the white mothers did in New Orleans when they were seen on television screaming, 'nigger, nigger, nigger'), and with a willingness to accept the penalty. I submit that an individual who breaks a law that conscience tells him is unjust, and willingly accepts the penalty by staying in jail to arouse the conscience of the community over its injustice, is in reality expressing the very highest respect for law."

But prisons are supposed to be for the anti-social, anti-sociality, however, can come in many forms. The most obvious is violating the law, but it can also come in other countercultural practices. If one who is anti-social commits an evil crime they do deserve to be punished even though the state can go overboard. At this point in time most godbodies are illegitimate capitalists. Illegitimate capitalists are those who commit a crime to get money or involving theft; they desire to get possessions or money within a capitalistic system that has marginalized them, and seeing no legitimate way to do so they resort to crime. Again, prisons are supposed to put away the evil and control those deviant from the law; but are there any genuinely evil people, and is the law really as credible at providing justice as we have all been made to accept? This is a question that needs genuine expression.

The apostle Paul said, "Dare any of you, having a matter against another, go to law before the unjust, and not before the saints? Do ye not know that the saints shall judge the world? and if the world shall be judged by you, are ye unworthy to judge the smallest matters? Know ye not that we shall judge angels? how much more things that pertain to this life?" (1Cor 6: 1-3.) The apostle Paul does not beat around the bush, he calls the interpreters of the law unjust. If the interpretation is unjust, then does conviction really make someone genuinely evil? As we godbodies have no intention of obeying the laws of this unjust system it is our current mentality to practice deviance from the law, understanding that a criminal law creates criminal minds. So if one views the law and its interpreters to be unjust and in a countercultural act of defiance breaks their unjust law, to themselves they have committed no crime. Further, these political prisoners show they are true martyrs to their opinions and witnesses against the system, as they are willing to suffer the consequences for holding them.

Suicide bombers could never be true martyrs, they are soldiers at war but not martyrs for God. A soldier for God may die a hero's death but not a martyr's death. Again, soldiers dying and killing for an unjust cause or to preserve an unjust system could never be counted among the soldiers of God. The fact that they *unjustly* kill innocent lives for a warped perception of God kind of defeats the purpose. Terrorists in prison and suicide bombers could never be true martyrs or soldiers of God; however, innocent Muslims suffering at the hands of an oppressive regime, whether it be in the GUSE or the Third World, can be martyrs of God if they hold firm to the cause for which they are suffering.

In the godbody's determination to overcome their sufferings and adversities it is of necessity that they take into consideration the words of Dr. King, "...corrective legislation requires organization to bring it to life. Laws only declare rights; they do not deliver them. The oppressed must take hold of laws and transform them into effective mandates. Hence the absence of powerful organization has limited the degree of application and the extent of practical success." Dr. King is here showing and proving that through practical organization laws can be either changed or enforced. Wherefore we godbodies represent a means of affecting those legislative corrections, for we are not just a counterculture, we are a practical one as well.

Dr. King in seeking to use the law to improve things in America for black people was willing to break what he himself considered to be unjust laws for the main purpose of upholding what he considered just ones. He also condemned the attitude of his ecclesial contemporaries at the time, saying "...the judgment of God is upon the church as never before. If the church of today does not recapture the sacrificial spirit of the early church, it will lose its authentic ring, forfeit the loyalty of millions, and be dismissed as an irrelevant social club with no meaning..." Yet he also took special care to explain his actions to them, saying:

> "You express a great deal of anxiety over our willingness to break laws. This is certainly a legitimate concern. Since we so diligently urge people to obey the Supreme Court's decision of 1954 outlawing segregation in the public schools, it is rather strange and paradoxical to find us consciously breaking laws. One may well ask, 'How can you advocate breaking some laws and obeying others?' The answer is found in the fact that there are two types

of laws: there are just *and there are* unjust *laws. I would agree with Saint Augustine that 'An unjust law is no law at all.'*

Now what is the difference between the two? How does one determine when a law is just or unjust? A just law is a man-made code that squares with the moral law or the law of God. An unjust law is a code that is out of harmony with the moral law. To put it in the terms of Saint Thomas Aquinas, an unjust law is a human law that is not rooted in eternal and natural law. Any law that uplifts human personality is just. Any law that degrades human personality is unjust."

Moreover, the apostle John also helps us, for though he says, "Whosoever committeth sin transgresseth also the law: for sin is the transgression of the law. And ye know that he was manifested to take away our sins; and in him is no sin." He also said, "My little children, these things write I unto you, that ye sin not. And if any man sin, we have an advocate with the Father, Jesus Christ the righteous: And he is the propitiation for our sins: and not for ours only, but also for the sins of the whole world".

This is how the theocracy works: it allows for the committing of undamaging sin and the breaking of unjust laws to bring about the established overthrow of their necessity, internally and externally. However, Dr. King met some obstacles along the way, as will this theocracy. Dr. King explains his obstacles as such: "The persistence of racism in depth and the dawning awareness that Negro demands will necessitate structural changes in society have generated a new phase of white resistance in North and South. Based on the cruel judgment that Negroes have come far enough, there is a strong mood to bring the civil rights movement to a halt or reduce it to a crawl. Negro demands that yesterday evoked admiration and support, today – to many – have become tiresome, unwarranted and a disturbance to the enjoyment of life."

I think at this point I would like to point out another obvious American hypocrisy. It is quite often the sport of many right-wing Americans and foolish Britons, to free their consciences from their own fascist tendencies with regard to the inner cities by calling Muslims the fascists. (Although it must be noted that fascism is in essence a form of racist military government not of religious organization.) How can an Islamist possibly be a fascist or even closely related to the fascists?

I find it rather funny that the American New Right and Alt Right love to call the Islamists a fascist group. The police states of the secret service run Western world are far closer to the Far Right governments of the past, in spite of the so-called 'democratic rights' allowed to their citizens by the various Bills of Rights of their respective national-states. The GUSE for all its bellyaching over Islam, allowed to go completely unchecked the occupying presence in their own ghetto communities; the incessant police patrols of ethnic neighbourhoods like an imperial troop; the torture facilities at Abu Ghraib and Guantanamo Bay; the neo-colonial corporations they built mirroring the huge enterprises of the Nazi system; and the obvious racialism and state organized racial profiling that has gone on within their own land.

However, avoiding the overt Manichaeism of the GUSE in declaring the Other as an irreconcilable evil and self as an incontrovertible good, we godbodies have come to recognize that you cannot seek popularity if you wish to avoid the obvious outcome of the current situation. The theocracy does not tolerate or endorse the tactics used by terrorism but we do understand their reasoning.

While American leaders so foolishly throw it off and say it is all to do with Islam we look for the deeper reality. All the barbaric killings that Christians inflicted over the centuries were not due to their Christianity it was caused by some deeper meaning, whether that be religious misinterpretation, social injustice, 'divine' inspiration, self-defence or some psychological reason. With the Islamists we have the reason: social and religious indignation. They seek a good thing it is just their methods that are so emphatically wrong. The Islamists want righteousness in the world, but what kind of righteousness? Righteousness according to the Quran? Not necessarily. They want a socio-cultural righteousness.

Granted the Muslims may not be as pro-black as most other religious groups are, but I remember back in the late 1990s when the godbodies used to predict that in 2000 there would be a crisis in which black people would be blamed. This crisis would lead to black people getting put into camps and tortured. Interestingly enough, after September 11, 2001 not a single black person batted an eyelash over the treatment of Muslims. The godbodies knew these things would happen, albeit they were mistaken on the target, but as they are not respected within the black community there was no serious outcry against Abu Ghraib or Guantanamo Bay among us blacks.

We hold that the right to promote and practice the traditions and culture of the theocracy as laid out in the preceding chapters must be fought for and maintained in every state and city of the United States where godbodies have access to public organs like magazine or newspaper journalists or sympathetic church, mosque, or community leaders and academics. Whereby we can effectively revolutionize and take care of our own communities and ghettoes without the use of government intervention, whether to punish us, provide for us, protect us or control us. And again, the same should be true in every state and city of the global South.

As Dr. King said, "...unsophisticated though we may be, the poor and despised of [the world] will revolutionize this era. In our 'arrogance, lawlessness and ingratitude', we will fight for human justice, brotherhood, secure peace and abundance for all. When we have won these...then, in luminous splendor, the Christian era will truly begin." In other words, Dr. King understood that the Christian era could not begin without a revolutionary wave sweeping across the establishment and that it was up to us to fight for these things in order to usher them in.

Moreover, Dr. King – understanding the realities suffered by these poor and despised of 1960s America – continued: "Many whites who concede that Negroes should have equal access to public facilities and the untrammelled right to vote cannot understand why a porter or a housemaid would dare dream of a day when his work will be more useful, more remunerative and a pathway to rising opportunity." For him this led to an even deeper understanding: for the world to ever be free from that which blocks, and has blocked, the path to greater brotherhood another kind of revolution would be necessary: "The stability of the large world house which is ours will involve a revolution of values to accompany the scientific and freedom revolutions engulfing the earth...We must rapidly begin the shift from a 'thing'-oriented society to a 'person'-oriented society. When machines and computers, profit motives and property rights are considered more important than people, the giant triplets of racism, materialism and militarism are incapable of being conquered."

Though he would later come to accept militancy into his programme Dr. King does explain how he sees a revolution of values: "A true revolution of values will soon look uneasily on the glaring contrast of poverty and wealth. With righteous indignation, it will look at thousands of working people displaced from their jobs with reduced incomes as a result of automation while the profits of the employer remain intact, and say: 'This is not just.'" Dr. King continues, "This revolution of values must go beyond traditional capitalism and communism."

Again, to show his dislike for capitalism and the results capitalism brought with it, Dr. King said, "The profit motive, when it is the sole basis of an economic system, encourages a cut throat competition and selfish ambition that inspire men to be more I-centered than thou-centered". Dr. King also pointed out that "We must honestly admit that capitalism has often left a gulf between superfluous wealth and abject poverty, has created conditions permitting necessities to be taken from the many to give luxuries to the few, and has encouraged small hearted men to become cold and conscienceless so that, like Dives before Lazarus, they are unmoved by suffering, poverty-stricken humanity."

But Dr. King had a problem with communism too, saying "... communism reduces men to a cog in the wheel of the state. The communist may object, saying that in Marxian theory the state is an 'interim reality' that will 'wither away' when the classless society emerges. True – in theory; but it is also true that, while the state lasts, it is an end in itself. Man is a means to that end. He has no inalienable rights." Dr. King in analyzing both systems found both heavily wanting: "Capitalism fails to see the truth in collectivism. Communism fails to see the truth in individualism. Capitalism fails to realize that life is social. Communism fails to realize that life is personal. The good and just society is neither the thesis of capitalism nor the antithesis of communism, but a socially conscious democracy which reconciles the truth of individualism and collectivism." It is the realization of this dream that blacks around the world have been seeking since the liberation movements of the 1960s.

But to achieve this goal Dr. King also understood we would need to desire such a change. Therefore he presented very patiently his arguments to those in "America, the richest nation in the world – and nothing's wrong with that – this is America's opportunity to help bridge the gulf between the haves and the have-nots...There is nothing new about poverty. What is new is that we have the techniques and the resources to get rid of poverty. The real question is whether we have the will." Here Dr. King agrees with the words of the apostle John, "But whoso hath this world's good, and seeth his brother hath need, and shutteth up his bowels of compassion from him, how dwelleth the love of God in him?"

It was through his desire to right the social wrongs capitalism had inflicted on black people, and all poor people of America, that Dr. King chose to fight for all the poor and despised of America, he also knew from the teachings of the Messiah that God loved the poor and despised, saying

"It seems that I can hear the God of history saying, '...I was hungry and ye fed me not. I was naked and ye clothed me not. I was devoid of a decent sanitary house to live in, and ye provided no shelter for me. And consequently, you cannot enter the kingdom of greatness. If ye do it unto the least of these, my brethren, ye do it unto me.'"

But not only did Dr. King want better for poor people in America, and to be sure, he wanted better for all poor people in America, but he also wanted better for poor people across the world, saying "America has not met its obligations and its responsibilities to the poor." And, "We are challenged to rid our nation and the world of poverty. Like a monstrous octopus poverty spreads its nagging, prehensile tentacles into the hamlets and villages all over our world. They are ill-housed, they are ill-nourished, they are shabbily clad." In all this he showed his solidarity with the poor and oppressed no matter where they stood in society. However, he had also learned from his own difficulties that the demands of the needy usually go unmet, "We know through painful experience that freedom is never voluntarily given by the oppressor; it must be demanded by the oppressed."

True indeed, Dr. King was well aware of the difficulties facing him, "few members of a race that has oppressed another race can understand or appreciate the deep groans and passionate yearnings of those that have been oppressed and still fewer have the vision to see that injustice must be rooted out by strong, persistent and determined action." He knew through his experience that if the poor were to get any changing of their circumstances it would have to come mostly from themselves. That is particularly why he said, "What is most needed is a coalition of Negroes and liberal whites that will work to make both major parties [in America] truly responsive to the needs of the poor." The theocracy just may be the expressed fulfilment of this desire being a coalition of all shades within the ghetto community, struggling for the benefit of those who share in our struggle.

Dr. King also said, "Through our scientific and technological genius, we have made of this world a neighborhood and yet...we have not had the ethical commitment to make of it a brotherhood. But somehow, and in some way, we have got to do this. We must all learn to live together as brothers. Or we will all perish together as fools." Believing that if his own generation did not act the process of racial and economic equality may never get started, Dr. King continued: "I am sorry to say this morning that I am absolutely convinced that the forces of ill will...the extreme rightists...the people on the wrong side – have used time much more effectively than the forces of good will. And it may well be that we will have to repent in this generation. Not merely for the vitriolic words and violent actions of the bad people, but for the appalling silence and indifference of the good people who sit around and say, 'Wait on time.'" And, "Somewhere we must come to see that human progress never rolls in on the wheels of inevitability. It comes through the tireless efforts and the persistent work of dedicated individuals who are willing to be co-workers with God...So we must help time and realize that the time is always ripe to do right."

From an economic standpoint Dr. King also realized, "We have come to the point where we must make the nonproducer a consumer or we will find ourselves drowning in a sea of consumer goods. We have so energetically mastered production that we now must give attention to distribution. Though there have been increases in purchasing power, they have lagged behind increases in production. Those at the lowest economic level, the poor white and Negro, the aged and chronically ill, are traditionally unorganized and therefore...stagnate or become poorer in relation to the larger society." Interestingly enough, black people seem to be the producers, workers and consumers, but never or rarely the owners. When black people do become owners their business usually fails because the rest of we blacks do not support them. And the rest of we blacks do not support them because they have no connection to us. They are entrepreneurs, they are capitalists or petty capitalists, the petty bourgeoisie, or the black bourgeoisie.

The economic organization of black businesses by the black bourgeoisie into co-operatives owned and run co-operatively, that is, owned and run in common, would begin to show the black people in the neighbourhoods of the ghetto that their main motivation is neither money nor profits, but social brotherhood with fellow black people. Workers' parliaments should also be set up in these co-operatives to guarantee that working people have their say about the conditions of their labour and coordinate with consumers on what will be needed and desired from them in a given month.

Consumers' parliaments should therefore also be set up to meet once a month in order to receive all consumption requests from the local, district, regional and national consumers' parliaments and to discuss shopping trends. They should also meet once a year to receive annual consumption requests and to discuss allocation and production analysis. This would be the best way to organize and coordinate all domestic labour and distribution practices within the theocratic co-operatives. With these bodies thus put in place the chaotic malaise existing in the market as a result of laissez faire would be ended.

But the theocracy as a whole includes structures within it that allow it to thrive under any circumstances: the abolition of the monetary system and the constitution of equality through the systematic coordination of labour and distribution; the abolition of the state-apparatus through the arming and training of all citizens in combat and defence of self and neighbourhood, which amounts to the organization of a people's militia; the abolition of the institution of marriage through the formalization of open sexual relationships and the institution of communal child-rearing; the promotion of socially responsible ethics from an interdependence perspective, based on the concept of inevitable reciprocity; and the attaining of divinity through the knowledge that self and all other things are potentially divine, whatever name or label you call God by. This is the best means of removing all the major problems of the modern system; understanding of course that it will not solve every single societal difficulty as human imperfection is unsolvable. But we seek not for pie in the sky, merely to have our actually existing system justified in the world system.

Moreover, we must make sure to have in place workers' and consumers' parliaments to coordinate all local activities in order to guarantee our success. It would be wise for the godbodies of a locality to get together every quarter for ciphers, and get together every month or so for parliaments: consumers' parliaments as organized at the discretion of the cipher, and workers' parliaments as decided within the workplace of a godbody or predominantly black workplace. This is the key to agapic interaction and interchange, that is, interactions and transactions with love at the centre. And as the apostle John also said on this subject, "Beloved, let us love one another: for love is of God; and every one that loveth is born of God, and knoweth God."

With regard to the development of modern society we find that all the societal transformations that have occurred were rooted in some form of philosophical vision; the most obvious parallel being the nineteenth century communists, who visioned a world free from all social injustices. They began their pursuit with fantasy chasing, feeling and believing that by the spreading of propaganda and "model experiments" they would be able to accomplish their dreams. Their ideals, however, for lack of social and economic conditions suitable to their operation and fulfilment remained only such complex fantasies; and though they did allow for the birth of socialistic sensitivities, they entered a competition with the capitalist countries they could never win and so ended up looking inferior. They basically allowed the capitalist countries to make them forget who they were and instead strive to become like them.

Now we godbodies are not utopians painting a picture of paradise or of a better world or system; we already have our paradise, we just seek to have the right to remain in our paradise free from persecution even as the bourgeois have the right to remain in their paradise free from persecution. We will not enter into a battle of the paradises. Many animals in nature are able to peacefully coexist without substantial disturbance; this is merely interdependence: the right to practice our culture our way without bourgeois or governmental interference, and a willingness to use violence to defend this right to the death. We are not being evil here; we are being brave. Brave in that we will not bow down to government coercion or bourgeois trickery, and brave in that we will not hypocritically try to turn our black Gods into a black bourgeoisie.

To us the only reason we are currently at the bottom is because these black bourgeoisies have not been helping us to progress, and not because of our refusal to bow down to the bourgeois system. The laws and rules the bourgeoisie put in place during the process of their own development as a class created a world fit mainly and purely for them that at the same time destroys all other classes and social groups in the process. All human laws, including the current bourgeois laws, are usually the product of idealistic dreamers who believe that by helping their own particular group they can improve things for the world. These laws can also be amended, fulfilled, broken or created by the faith of the lawmakers, and also proven ethical by that same faith.

Universal laws are completely different. They are naturalistic in orientation. Hence, you cannot just break or amend them without some negative consequence occurring. The further you fall from God's universal laws the further you fall from his favour and from its many benefits. And though you will still be in his care and under his grace you will not be as blessed as one who is under and fulfilling his universal laws. Again, the only way to enter the kingdom and rulership of God is to abide by the laws of God. This also means removing from your life those things that prevent you from fulfilling and practicing his law.

The theocracy is an institution for doing just that: practicing his law. It is not the abandoning of law altogether, nor the abandoning of the idea of a living and present God, it is merely the actualizing of God's person without the mystique of spookish protocols and structures. The structure of this theocracy should thus remain simple;

not the rigidity of the early or present Catholic Church rituals and traditions but a more informal and relaxed mechanism. Here the three main ranks or titles would remain captains, lieutenants and soldiers. As for parliaments there should be three kinds: consumers', workers' and students'. These should assist and advise the captains, and at their request organize one of the brotherhoods or neighbourhoods within the territory of that captain; and even individual captains should be commissioned to newer and different areas at the request of the body of captains.

In this our movement should remove every desire to be understood by the environment around us and just simply talk to and listen to, and, at times, when we feel it is most necessary or helpful, explain to them our reality. We should not devote *our lives* to trying to explain or to trying to save or help others, but to communicating self or manifesting self to those outside of our physical self. There is no need for effort in regards to communication, whether we are understood, liked, rejected or misinterpreted should not matter. The point is simply communicating the self and allowing those of impure heart to manifest themselves and those of pure heart to manifest themselves. As iron sharpens iron so real recognizes real. The real will always stay faithful to the real, but fake hypocrites and liars will run for cover at the first sight of real.

It is not ours to hate or condemn the hypocrites and liars but to simply watch them scurry in madness and fear trying desperately to control an uncontrollable world, or hoping for you, me or someone else to control this uncontrollable world. In most forms of this madness the liars will usually call us liars or evil or some other form of negative to maintain or keep hold of the lifestyle and practices they have grown accustomed to and gained benefits from. In their case they will either waste their time trying to convert you or trying to pray against you. Our main objective, however, is not to win them over just to present our truth and allow them to make up their own mind concerning it.

The aim of this theocracy is not to create a utopia, panacea, ideal, nirvana or Shangri-La, it is to give guidance and support to those seeking to find and please God, and to teach them traditions and a counterculture that will ultimately help them find Him within; basically, to see their own divinity despite their social realities. However, we also come into conflict and confrontation with the current standards and views of bourgeois society. These views, based on what socialists call bourgeois rights, are at present contrary to human nature and the reality of human imperfection. These bourgeois rights, in themselves, are the product of historical developments and not genuine justice or ethics in the eternal sense: For the justice of God is found only in his universal laws and his supreme wisdom.

Nevertheless, what is just by one standard is unjust by another. The universal laws (or divine laws) were designed by God to ensure that in all things his principles were not forsaken for vanity. Through knowledge of self one is able to learn and understand their place within the universal setting, thus knowing the laws and structures that govern self. By adhering to these principles one makes self divine or God manifest. We, in essence, define God not as a man, bird, beast or fish, nor as a being that is formed or molded. In fact, we subscribe to the view of the apostle John, "He that loveth not, knoweth not God; for God is love."

At the same time, the English word love is unfortunately a sorry explanation of the reality of God in his actuality; but for lack of a better English equivalent it best conveys his eternal essence and being. A better word would perhaps be the Ethiopic word *täwahedo*, which means unity or communion; but mainly in the sense of, the union of the spiritual with the physical or the divine with the natural, deriving from its miaphysis origins. Another is the Arabic word *tawhid*, which shares the same basic meaning of divine unity, the interconnection of the spiritual with the physical. God, as unconditional love, represents a connection that ties all things together through sentimental and indeed sensual interrelations. By this interconnection we within the *black* theocracy seek to express our reality and maintain our existence.

God as *tawhid* fully conveys his own ubiquity and omnipresence. God is one but God is also all. The reality of this frees us psychologically to love those unworthy of love, and to love even our trials, as they bring us to a place of oneness in God. *Tawhid* is also a bridge that connects the black concept of Horu with the white concept of Oedipus. Both being that based on our sexual and martial – that is, our instinctual – development in its premature estate. The Horu construct, however, is not based on an infatuation with the mother; it is the child's acceptance of their interconnection through desire and aggression to everything in the universe, which also allows we black people to see beyond the tenacity of our collective traumata into the hopeful reality of our collective divinity – leading on to Ausar or Auset consciousness.

God, in his eternal wisdom, foreknew that black suffering to get to this point was inevitable and he still chose to create us, birth us and become us in spite of our faults. God did not create our sufferings nor did he inflict them on us to punish us. We suffer because it is the best way for us to learn new methods of acquiring *tawhid*. With the finitude of our understanding we are unable to perceive our individual trials or collective sufferings but God has a plan in the midst of it. The end result is our divinity. The objective of the theodician is to find the good in the midst of the suffering.

But being black is more than simply a shared suffering, and an even more shared desire for liberation, it is an unswerving belief in self in our respective fields of choice. Do not think, however, that I am blind to the many black people who do not appear to believe in themselves; it is only that the collective traumata we have suffered with slavery, segregation/apartheid, colonization, illegitimization and international poverty – and to be sure, these have affected all black people – have given us the collective psychological impairment of lack of self-knowledge; and how can one develop a stable and proper self-belief if they lack self-knowledge? Not successfully navigating the Horu construct for black boys, just like not successfully navigating the Oedipus process for white boys, is what causes the laziness and disempowerment sometimes manifested in black men. Nevertheless the self-expression of black men from childhood signifies the Horu construct.

The Hethor construct in like manner, manifests the black girl. She is a Goddess from childhood and until she realizes this and learns to control her sexual energy at a young age she will have trouble successfully reaching that Auset phase of a black woman's destiny. The black woman is currently in a position where she is instead forced to adopt male traits to survive in a hostile white world. For this cause both the black boy and the black girl have taken on the Horu construct to generate a militant and aggressive disposition.

Here the current definition of blackness by black adults, male and female, is that of the freedom fighter who saves the world from oppression, subjugation and racism. The definition of blackness by non-blacks, however, is of a volatile, aggressive, violent and sexual animal who is instinctual and motivated purely by nature and emotion not by ethics and reason. We blacks have in our immediate recollection our strengths and strong heroes but we have a tendency to avoid our historical current over against our historical heroes. We are not all Dr. Kings and it is the world's fear of us that causes them to isolate us or crudely define us. We also lack articulate spokesmen and spokeswomen to stand up for us so we come across harsh and over-reactive. Our mind is on fighting social wrongs our appearance is as aggressive, angry nuisances.

The Horu construct pushes the black man to fight against oppression, particularly that of his fathers, until all oppression is overcome. As self-proclaimed freedom fighters, black men have rushed to the rescue of a lot of people trying to avoid punishment in their 'speaking up for the oppressed.' In many ways and in many cases these have not genuinely been oppressed people but troubled people who need to learn. That is not to say all struggle is deserved struggle, but that God teaches us through struggle to draw closer to him, even as the apostle John said, "No man hath seen God at any time. If we love one another, God dwelleth in us, and his love is perfected in us". Obviously, we also understand that God has been seen and heard everywhere and is manifested in the Asiatic black man, but this does not negate the fact that not all black men are Gods, nor that *tawhid* is the standard whereby we identify the truly divine from the ignorant.

The psychological dispositions of the Horu and Hethor constructs are based on the Kemetic apocalypses. Any Egyptologist worth their mettle knows that the Heliopolitan gods and goddesses were never considered mythological fantasies but were psychological states. It was in defining their gods and goddesses as psychological states that the Kemetic people determined what place they were at psychologically, whether they were at a place where their nature was at the predisposition towards negativity, i.e. Setek (or Satan), whether they were at a place where their natural predisposition was towards positivity, i.e. Horu, or whether they transcended both positive and negative and dwelt in the beauty of agape, i.e. Ausar.

Psychological soundness was the hope of all Kemetic traditions in their development towards divinity. That is not to say that the current psychotherapy is the wisdom of the ancestors. It is modern wisdom translated through modern minds. The authentically prophetic, apostolic ministry is missing as it fails to deal with the question of theodicy. What the godbody have done is set in place a means for we black people to enjoy a free and fully unified expression and existence. We can become divine more readily by following the blueprint laid down. We can also reaffirm our status as being our heroes, the Martin Kings and Winnie Mandelas we think we are.

Nevertheless, we must not be so quick to rush out there and save the world. It is imperative that we recognize our place in society is currently bottom rung. We are not viewed as the saviours of the world but as a drain on the world. Those who wish to genuinely save the world must be trained and not rush out there before their time. They must first confirm that it is really their place to save the world, then talk it over with others.

The traces of black subjugation still linger in the air of today's black people. We are to a high degree considered unprofessional, unsophisticated, even childish. The colonial construct has put us in a deskilled, decultured position where we have little-to-no knowledge of self or of our history. And one who does not know their history can never truly know their destiny. This deskilling and deculturing of the black man and black woman has also been applied to other races, though not as effectively. We blacks have lost our relation to ourselves. We have become other than ourselves. Our divinity has been shrouded in flesh; black flesh. We are no longer active but depersonalized and dehumanized. This unfortunate position makes us an easy target for bourgeois criticism.

The modern subjugation of the black person to structures alien to us has caused us to lose touch with that ancient part of ourselves that authenticates us against the colonial carbuncle of bourgeois dehumanization. We are not free we are bourgeofied. Our modern agenda is stolen, inauthentic, unoriginal. We seek to become the white man who colonized and humiliated us. We become the great modern lie. We are the dream of acceptance in the midst of unfaltering rejection. The rejection of our people plagues us even as we become bourgeois. We cannot escape the shackles of the collective traumata. The rejection of one is the rejection of all. The blackness of our skin is inescapable. The humiliation of our race is unavoidable. Though we deny it and run from it by deculturing ourselves we cannot escape the inescapable truth: You are a black person in a world that fears and despises black people. You are black in a bourgeois system that is contrary to the black soul. You are black in a world designed to subjugate your kind.

The unmasking of the bourgeois system, whether by decultured or deskilled black people, never brings in any new solace. The pain instead gets denied, and so internalized, anti-escape fixtures get blocked and avoidance mechanisms get put in place. The dereliction of the now bourgeofied black becomes immediate to behold. They have lost their self completely. The many deep seated mysticisms within any subordination can divorce institutions from all their historical precursors and make them appear eternal constructs.

We black theocrats happen to, and will continue to, face heavy opposition from these bourgeofied blacks and their bourgeois standards; standards, which, being based on bourgeois rights, are the basis of their deculturation to become a part of this system. So it seems that the ones who will be giving us our greatest opposition are the main ones we will be trying to help, that is, the black bourgeoisie. This black bourgeoisie, blinded by bourgeois standards of rights and wrongs (in both spiritual and social senses of the words, considering that it is currently the bourgeoisie who determine what society believes to be spiritually right or wrong), have developed the greatest sympathy for what has been called right by the white bourgeoisie and thus will fight tooth and nail to defend them. And have inherited from the white bourgeoisie a great hostility towards those things called wrong by them and will also fight tooth and nail to oppose and destroy them.

The self-sacrifice exerted by the black bourgeoisie to defend bourgeois standards is the main protector of the bourgeois system among black people, damaged though it is. But this bourgeois system is an amalgamation of various unmixable contradictions: the centralized dictatorship of one class amid highly deregulated democracy; the anarchical competition of various businesses, workers and commodities on the market amid the imperative drive of the market towards monopolization; the vast accumulation of wealth amid the spiralling diminishing of value; the influx of newer and more advanced technologies amid the ever falling rate of utilization; and the high promotion and propagation of sociable morals amid the excesses of anti-social and unsociable behaviours. In these and many other areas the bourgeoisie have failed in their historical task.

Vladimir Lenin explains this story of bourgeois development in the following sequence: "Bourgeois rights, with respect to distribution of articles of *consumption*, inevitably presupposes, of course, the existence of the *bourgeois state*, for rights are nothing without an apparatus capable of *enforcing* the observance of the rights." We must also remember, "The centralized state power peculiar to bourgeois society came into being in the period of the fall of absolutism. Two institutions are especially characteristic of this state machinery: bureaucracy and the standing army."

The white bourgeoisie of America, based on the standard Nation of Islam doctrine, are all devils, which is not too far from the Islamist view that the US Government is the "Great Satan." But the bourgeois mechanisms set in place by white America actually shows that it is not really a thoroughly evil system at all, just an unworkable system. Their neo-colonial methods of globalization have introduced new distortions to the manner of living we all indulge in. But globalization, imperialism's latest form, is a product of forces beyond the realm of visual identification.

Contrary to the Nation of Islam opinion that the devil was created by a eugenics scientist on the island of Patmos, the theocratic view has disputed opinions as to the origin of devils. How I personally see it is that there are embodiments of devils, even as there are embodiments of God, and these embodiment are seen particularly in the children of Japheth. Again, this is not a Manichaean dichotomy of good versus evil, as Satan is seen not as opposed to God *per se*, but as subservient to him. This is an explanation of the social conditions that exist in the world as they are. These conditions allow for adverse circumstances to be realized so as to make the now complacent, yes, now indifferent souls of good minded people so distracted by opposition that they have no time to concern themselves with justice or ethics.

Again, how do we overcome their hypocrisy? The apostle John continues, "This is the victory that has overcome the world, even our faith". And as we said earlier, "it is by faith that we know what we believe in will happen, being completely assured of a reality that is invisible" (Heb 11:1 my rewording). This reality is the realm of the astral; here angelic and human beings interact, along with all other beings that exist, to work together for our concerted deification. These are the forces that have allowed bourgeois right to reign for so long, but its time is up.

CONCLUSION

As the theocracy we seek to bring into existence is neither a utopian nor an idealistic system but an already existing system, our motive is not the ultimate overthrow of the bourgeoisie entirely, it is merely the defending of our already existing culture, traditions and theodical perspectives as they are and to not allow modern standards and opinions to corrupt or contaminate our current system of doing things; regardless of how much persecution we will receive for it. Moreover, we also seek independence from it, while at the same time recognizing our interconnection to it.

The independence we seek works on the obvious and means in a somewhat bourgeois sense, to not need or be dependent on state power or any other entity for our existence, basically to exist in our own right and on our own terms. By interconnection we understand in a more doctrinal, monistic and naturalistic sense our coexistence alongside and in relation to the current system; not to overthrow it but to be of benefit to it, even as it, of necessity, will be of benefit to us. We are presently of benefit to very few. But we seek to allow that grace which has been shown us by Self to be shown to those outside of ourselves. Thus our independence serves as a means to allow us to not simply gain autonomy but also as a means to benefit those we are now given the privilege of helping, basically, interdependency.

The obvious question of those within the status quo at this point would be: so "what's the catch?" The catch is that with full independence we stand a chance of being a rival society or system in the midst of the current one and of in time even overthrowing the current one; but this risk is the reality of any new system. Though well-meaning they all have the very same potential. The reality of an actual overthrow is, however, far more complicated. For this cause the modern state and modern society need not fear too strongly this theodical entity I bring into being as it is merely an informative training to an already existing organization not a political movement to destroy civilization.

Postscript to Third Edition

Though it is true that this book was written for the godbody and has advice on how the movement can go forward it must again be repeated that this is not a godbody book or even a 5 Percent book but a Christian book with godbody leanings. It contains none of the language or lessons of the movement but instead focuses on what the movement can do to become a world class movement. If I have offended any practicing members of the movement I must offer my sincerest apologies and remind them that the majority of the book was written while I was still a new born, its spookish doctrine may be a little hard to digest but it could not be removed without severely damaging the book itself. Having spoken to my Enlightener I have seen how it could be misconstrued that this is a godbody book and therefore offend other members, for this cause I have included this postscript to make clear that its central purpose is to show my personal development as a 5 Percenter: where I came from and what I was before I got deeper into our lessons.

To those who are not 5 Percent who are troubled by some of the lessons I dropped I must say they are all the development of several years of thorough research and of many years of connection to the street life. While I am currently more connected to university students than the streets my years of apprenticeship in the streets and in prison made me quite aware of the realities of what we are. I never lost that mentality. My hope therefore has been to show you, particularly the intellectuals among you, our reality and its value. That we are far more than simply criminals and thugs. We have a philosophical basis that is not only respectable but also credible. In essence, this book was written mainly for you, in the hopes that you would see the value in supporting us and helping us to be for the black community a movement that progresses the people and brings them to a place of genuine divinity and enrapturement.

BIBLIOGRAPHY

The Holy Bible: Authorized King James Version (2004); Authentic Publishing.

The Holy Qur'an; Maulana Muhammad Ali (2002); Ahmadiyya Anjuman Isha'at Islam Lahore Inc., U.S.A.

The Apocrypha Authorized (King James) Version (2011); Cambridge University Press.

Adogame, A (2011); "Introduction." In A. Adogame (Ed), *Who is Afraid of the Holy Ghost: Pentecostalism and Globalization in Africa and Beyond*; Africa World Press.

Afrika, L (2013); Dr Llaila Afrika We Are Different; http://m.youtube.com/watch?v=r6aaP6Ynoj4, accessed in May 2014

Albert, M (2004); *Parecon: Life After Capitalism*; Verso St. Augustine (1958); *City of God*; Bantam Doubleday Dell Publishing Group, Inc.

Avineri, S (1968); *The Social & Political Thoughts of Karl Marx*; Cambridge University Press.

Baudrillard, J (2012); *Simulacra and Simulation*; The University Press.

Blackburn, R (1988); *The Overthrow of Colonial Slavery 1776-1848*; Verso Books.

Brandchaft, B, Doctors, S, Sorter, D (2010); *Toward an Emancipatory Psychoanalysis*; Routledge.

Brown, F, Driver, S and Briggs, C (2014); *The Brown-Driver-Briggs Hebrew and English Lexicon*; Hendrickson Publishers.

Callinicos, A (2003); *An Anti-Capitalist Manifesto*; Blackwells Publishing Ltd.

Chittick, W (1989); *The Sufi Path of Knowledge*; State University of New York Press.

Davis, D (1984); *Slavery and Human Progress*; Oxford University Press.

Diop, A (1991); *Civilization or Barbarism*; Lawrence Hill Books.

Engels, F (1947); *Anti-Dühring Herr Eugen Dühring's Revolution in Science*; Progress Publishers; (1977); *The Origin of the Family, Private Property and the State*; Progress Publishers.

Foner, P (2002); *The Black Panther Speaks*; Da Capo Press.

Fanon, F (1964); *Toward the African Revolution*; Grove Press; (2008); *Black Skin White Masks*; Pluto Press.

Gahlin, L (2007); *Egypt: Gods, Myths and Religion*; Anness Publishing Ltd.

Gordon, L (2011); "Requim on a Life Well Lived: In Memory of Fanon." In N. Gibson (Ed), *Living Fanon: Global Perspectives*; Palgrave Macmillan.

Gramsci, A (1971); *Antonio Gramsci: Selections from the Prison Notebooks*; Lawrence &Wishart Ltd.

Grinker, R, Lubkemann, S, Steiner, C (2010); *Perspectives on Africa: A Reader in Culture, History, and Representation Second Edition*; Blackwell Publishing Ltd.

Harman, C (1999); *Economics of the Madhouse*; Bookmarks Publications Ltd.

Harrison, L (2002); "On Cultural Nationalism." In P. Foner (Ed), *The Black Panther Speaks*; Da Capo Press.

Harvey, D (2006); *Limits to Capital*; Verso Book.

Hawass, Z (2006); *The Royal Tombs of Egypt*; Thames & Hudson Ltd.

Herring, G (2006); *Christianity: From the Early Church to the Enlightenment*; Continuum International Publishing Group.

Jacobs, M (1992); *Key Figures in Counselling and Psychotherapy: Sigmund Freud*; Sage Publications Ltd. Ben-Jochannan, Y (2002); *The Need for a Black Bible*; Black Classic Press.

Josephus, F (2013); *The Works of Josephus: New Updated Edition*; Hendrickson Publishers.

King, M (1986); *A Testament of Hope*; HarperCollins Publishers; (1992); *I Have A Dream; Writings and Speeches That Changed the World*; HarperCollins Publishing.

Koester, C (2014); *Revelation*; Yale University Press.

Koestler, A (1976); *The Thirteenth Tribe*; Random House, Inc.

Kropotkin, P (2002); *Anarchism*; (2006); *Mutual Aid: A Factor of Evolution*; Dover Publications Inc.

Kumar, D (2012); *Islamophobia and the Politics of Empire*; Haymarket Books.

Lenin, V (1968); *V. I. Lenin Selected Works*; Lawrence and Wishart Ltd. Van Loon, H (1960); *The Story of Mankind*; Washington Square Press, Inc.

Luxemburg, R (2004); *The Rosa Luxemburg Reader*; The Monthly Review Press.

Lyotard, J (1986); *The Postmodern Condition: A Report on Knowledge*; Manchester University Press; (1994) *Lessons on the Analytic of the Sublime*; Stanford University Press.

Mackenzie-Grieve, A (1968); *The Last Years of the English Slave Trade Liverpool 1750-1807*; Frank Cass & co. Ltd.

Malcioln, J (1996); *The African Origins of Modern Judaism*; Africa World.

Marx, K (1986); *Capital Volume I*; Lawrence &Wishart Ltd.; (1958); *Selected Works vol 3*; Foreign Languages Publishing House.

Maxwell, M (1998); *Revelation: Doubleday Bible Commentary*; Bantam Doubleday Dell Publication Group, Inc.

Muhammad, E (1965); *Message to the Blackman of America*; Muhammad's Temple of Islam No. 2.

Newton, H (2002); *The Huey P. Newton Reader*; Seven Stories Press.

Roberts, A (2011); *Evolution The Human Story*; Dorling Kindersley Limited.

Sardar, Z, Abrams, I (2012); *Introducing Chaos: A Graphic Guide*; Icon Book Ltd.

Seale, B (2002); "The Ten-Point Platform and Program of the Black Panther Party." In P. Foner (Ed), *The Black Panther Speaks*; Da Capo Press.

Seleem, R (2004); *The Egyptian Book of Life*; Watkins Publishing London.

Snoop Doggy Dogg (1994); *Doggystyle*; Death Row Records.

Stourton, E (2005); *In the Footsteps of Saint Paul*; Hodder Headlin Ltd.

Strong, J (1990); *The New Strong's Exhaustive Concordance of the Bible*; Thomas Nelson Publishers.

Strachey, J (1936); *The Theory and Practice of Socialism*; Victor Gúllancz Ltd.

Turner, L (2011); "Fanon and the Biopolitics of Torture: Contextualizing Psychological Practices as Tools of War." In N. Gibson (Ed), *Living Fanon: Global Perspectives*; Palgrave Macmillan.

Tyldesley, J (2011); *The Penguin Book of Myths & Legends of Ancient Egypt*; Penguin Books.

Watterson, B (2013); *Women in Ancient Egypt*; Amberley Publishing.

Williams, J (1928); *Hebrewisms of West Africa From the Nile to the Niger with the Jews*; Africa Tree Press.

X, M (1968); *The Autobiography of Malcolm X*; Penguin Books; (2004); *Why I am Not an American*; Citizens International.

CPSIA information can be obtained
at www.ICGtesting.com
Printed in the USA
BVHW031036021120
592326BV00001B/147